Spirits of '76

ALSO BY DANIEL W. BAREFOOT

Hark the Sound of Tar Heel Voices: 220 Years of UNC History

Touring North Carolina's Revolutionary War Sites

Touring South Carolina's Revolutionary War Sites

Let Us Die Like Brave Men

General Robert F. Hoke: Lee's Modest Warrior

Haunted Halls of Ivy

North Carolina's Haunted Hundred: Seaside Spectres

North Carolina's Haunted Hundred: Piedmont Phantoms

North Carolina's Haunted Hundred: Haints of the Hills

Touring the Backroads of North Carolina's Upper Coast

Touring the Backroads of North Carolina's Lower Coast

Spirits of '76

Ghost Stories of the American Revolution

DANIEL W. BAREFOOT

JOHN F. BLAIR, PUBLISHER
WINSTON-SALEM, NORTH CAROLINA

JOHN F. BLAIR
PUBLISHER
1406 Plaza Drive
Winston-Salem, North Carolina 27103
www.blairpub.com

Manufactured in the United States of America

COVER IMAGE
"Smoke Obscures the Battlefield" courtesy of David Walbert, LEARN NC

Library of Congress Cataloging-in-Publication Data

Barefoot, Daniel W., 1951–
Spirits of '76 : ghost stories of the American Revolution / Daniel W. Barefoot.
        p.   cm.
Includes index.
ISBN 978-0-89587-362-0 (alk. paper)
1.   Ghosts—East (U.S.)   2. Haunted places—East (U.S.)   3. United States—History—Revolution, 1775–1783—Miscellanea. I. Title.   II. Title: Spirits of seventy-six.
BF1472.U6B366 2009
133.10973'09033—dc22
2009028894

To my dear Kay, one more time

Contents

Preface   xi

Acknowledgments   xv

Introduction   An Angel on His Shoulder:
   The Supernatural and the Father of Our Country   xix

MAINE   1

The Haunted Drumbeat of Liberty—Castine, Maine   3

Still Celebrating Independence—Rockport, Maine   6

Other "Spirited" Revolutionary War Sites in Maine, Briefly Noted   10

VERMONT   11

The Ghost of the Green Mountains—Burlington, Vermont   13

The Retreat of a Revolutionary War Ghost—
   Lake Memphremagog, Vermont   17

Other "Spirited" Revolutionary War Sites in Vermont,
   Briefly Noted   19

NEW HAMPSHIRE   23

Phantom Lovers—Portsmouth, New Hampshire   25

The General, the Devil, and the Ghost—
   Hampton, New Hampshire   28

Other "Spirited" Revolutionary War Sites in New Hampshire,
   Briefly Noted   33

MASSACHUSETTS   35
The Light Burns for John—Gurnet Point (Plymouth Bay),
    Massachusetts   37
Haunted by the Shot Heard Round the World—
    Lexington and Concord, Massachusetts   41
Other "Spirited" Revolutionary War Sites in Massachusetts,
    Briefly Noted   47

CONNECTICUT   53
The Haunts of a Cherished American Hero—
    Coventry, Connecticut   55
Legendary Generals Never Die, They Just Become Ghosts—
    Brooklyn, Connecticut   59
Other "Spirited" Revolutionary War Sites in Connecticut,
    Briefly Noted   64

RHODE ISLAND   71
Ghosts of a Revolutionary Affair—Portsmouth, Rhode Island   73
The March of the Spectral Hessians—Portsmouth, Rhode Island 76
Other "Spirited" Revolutionary War Sites in Rhode Island,
    Briefly Noted   79

NEW YORK   83
Spooky Fort Ti—Fort Ticonderoga, New York   85
A Haunting Tale of Love and Espionage—
    Long Island, New York   89
A Patriotic Welcome—Saratoga Springs, New York   94
Terror in the House of Skene—Whitehall, New York   100
No Peace Here—Staten Island, New York   105
Other "Spirited" Revolutionary War Sites in New York,
    Briefly Noted   111

NEW JERSEY   123
Spooky Ringwood Manor—Ringwood, New Jersey   125
Ghosts from the Heat of the Battle—Monmouth, New Jersey   128
A Traitor, a Spy, and a Martyr: Ghosts All—Navesink Highlands,

New Jersey   132
The Curse and Ghost of Mary Post—Mahwah, New Jersey   138
The Sourlands Spook—East Amwell Township, New Jersey   144
Other "Spirited" Revolutionary War Sites in New Jersey,
  Briefly Noted   148

PENNSYLVANIA   161
Of Ben, Benedict, and Betsy: Haunted Philadelphia
  Freedom—Philadelphia, Pennsylvania   163
Spectres of a Devastating Defeat—Chadds Ford, Pennsylvania   168
Haunted Reminders of Sacrifice and Suffering—Valley Forge,
  Pennsylvania   173
The "Mad" Search for His Bones—U.S. 322 between
  Meadville and Radnor, Pennsylvania   178
Other "Spirited" Revolutionary War Sites in Pennsylvania,
  Briefly Noted   182

DELAWARE   195
Ghost Writer—Dover, Delaware   197
A Ghost Story within a Ghost Story—Newark, Delaware   202
Other "Spirited" Revolutionary War Sites in Delaware,
  Briefly Noted   206

MARYLAND   209
The Patriotic Spirit of Defiance—Annapolis, Maryland   211
The Indefatigable Captain Jones—Annapolis, Maryland   214
Other "Spirited" Revolutionary War Sites in Maryland,
  Briefly Noted   218

VIRGINIA   223
The Ghost of a Mad Housewife—Ashland, Virginia   225
The Ghost of the Brooding Brother-in-Law—Fredericksburg,
  Virginia   229
Here, There, and Everywhere: Mad Anthony, of Course—
  Loudoun County, Virginia   233
The Haunted Twilight of Surrender—Yorktown, Virginia   237
Other "Spirited" Revolutionary War Sites in Virginia,
  Briefly Noted   242

NORTH CAROLINA 253

Patrick, Benjamin, and Other Phantoms—Ronda, North Carolina,
   and Kings Mountain, on the Border of the Carolinas 255
Shadows of a Shady Patriot—Moore County, North Carolina 262
Ghosts of the Pyrrhic Victory—Greensboro, North Carolina 268
Haunted by Love and War—Wilmington, North Carolina 273
Other "Spirited" Revolutionary War Sites in North Carolina,
   Briefly Noted 276

SOUTH CAROLINA 285

The Black Menace at Blackstock's—Cross Anchor,
   South Carolina 287
The Eternal Martyr—Charleston, South Carolina 292
The Endless Summer Siege—Ninety Six, South Carolina 297
When Bloody Bill Called—Roebuck, South Carolina 300
Other "Spirited" Revolutionary War Sites in South Carolina,
   Briefly Noted 304

GEORGIA 315

A Patriot Still at Home—Savannah, Georgia 317
A Vengeful Haunting—Augusta, Georgia 322
Other "Spirited" Revolutionary War Sites in Georgia,
   Briefly Noted 328

Index 331

Preface

Three millions of people, armed in the holy cause of Liberty, and in such a country as that which we possess, are invincible by any force which our enemy can send against us. Besides, sir, we shall not fight our battles alone. There is a just God who presides over the destinies of Nations, and who will raise up friends to fight our battles for us.

PATRICK HENRY

Few periods in the history of the United States are more thrilling, dramatic, fascinating, and haunted than the American Revolution. Thirteen diverse colonies stretching along the Atlantic seaboard from New Hampshire to Georgia triumphed in a long, arduous war that brought freedom and liberty to Americans. The men and women who lived and died during those turbulent times wrote the initial chapter of America's history as an independent nation. Where history abounds, so do ghosts. And thus, the Revolutionary War yielded the first truly "national" ghosts of the United States.

Over the years, tales from the Revolutionary War have appeared sporadically in volumes of historical and traditional American ghost stories. But here for the first time is a book devoted entirely to the supernatural history of the American Revolution. In the pages that follow, you will meet the ghosts of the famous, infamous,

and not-so-famous players in the fight for independence. These accounts will take you to the eighteenth-century battlegrounds, homes,
public buildings, and other sites where the spirits of George Washington, Thomas Jefferson, Benjamin Franklin, Patrick Henry, Betsy Ross,
Molly Pitcher, Mad Anthony Wayne, Nathanael Greene, Lord Cornwallis, Gentleman Johnny Burgoyne, John André, Benedict Arnold,
and others are said to linger.

Arranged geographically from north to south, the forty-four full-
length stories in this volume offer the ghostly lore of the original American colonies, plus Vermont and Maine. In addition, a directory of other
haunted Revolutionary War sites follows the tales for each geographic
area.

Throughout my life, I have dwelled in and around the old "haunts"
of soldiers of the American Revolution. I was born in Charlotte, the
place where Cornwallis began and ended the first British invasion of
North Carolina and where Major General Nathanael Greene assumed
command of the remnants of the beleaguered Army of the South several months later. I grew up in Belmont, a small textile town just across
the Catawba River from Charlotte. There, I lived on the street where
the home of Major William Chronicle once stood. Young Chronicle
was one of the first Patriot officers to fall in the Battle of Kings Mountain. As a child, I was thrilled to relive history on my numerous visits
to that nearby historic battleground. And for the last thirty-three years,
I have lived in Lincoln County (created and named in the midst of the
war for General Benjamin Lincoln), the site of two significant battles—
Ramsour's Mill and Cowan's Ford. In fact, I reside on the very street
where the former battle was fought on June 20, 1780.

As a historian of the Revolutionary War, I have walked many of
the far-flung fields where the great battles for American independence
were waged. Yet I have never encountered a ghost from the conflict.
Nevertheless, I am firmly convinced that seen and unseen spirits of
American soldiers, civilians, and statesmen and British, Hessian, and
French warriors haunt many sites associated with the war.

From the conflict itself come credible tales of hauntings. Even George Washington is said to have seen and been saved by a ghost of an American soldier on the eve of the Battle of Brandywine. And every succeeding generation of Americans has related accounts of incidents involving Revolutionary War ghosts. Regardless of whether you give much credence to these reports of supernatural encounters, everyone seems to enjoy tales of the unusual. And when those narratives have as their basis real people, places, and events, they become more enjoyable because they hint at credibility and believability.

All of the stories in this volume are based in fact. But over the years, some of them have been told and retold to the point that details have become blurred. As with all folklore, whether you choose to believe the accounts on these pages is entirely up to you. A caveat Mark Twain once offered his readers seems appropriate here: "I will set down a tale. . . . It may only be a legend, a tradition. It may have happened, it may not have happened. But it could have happened."

Should you entertain a desire to visit the haunted places described herein, be mindful that some are located on private property. Be sure to obtain permission from the owner before attempting to go upon any site.

As his defeated Redcoats marched to the official surrender ceremonies at Yorktown, Virginia, on Friday, October 19, 1781, Lord Cornwallis ordered his band to play "The World Turned Upside Down." In many ways, his choice of music was fitting. Indeed, thirteen upstart colonies—short on means, manpower, and materiel but long on spirit—had achieved an almost unbelievable victory over the most professional army in the world. That history-making achievement was almost supernatural in nature. Little wonder, then, that the ghosts of the men and women who took part in the Revolutionary War yet dwell among us as tangible proof of the "Spirits of '76."

Acknowledgments

Spirits of '76 was a most enjoyable book to research and write. Over my many years of work on the American Revolution, I have made it a point to collect a large body of materials related to the supernatural elements of the war. But without the kind offices of numerous people, this volume would not have come to print.

An essential element of any book on history—or, in this case, "haunted history"—is research. In the course of my work at libraries, museums, national parks, and other sites, staff members and other knowledgeable individuals have courteously fielded my inquiries and directed me to materials and places related to my study.

Since 1994, it has been my pleasure to work with the outstanding staff at John F. Blair, Publisher, to produce twelve titles representing a wide variety of subjects on American history and folklore.

Carolyn Sakowski, the president of Blair, has always welcomed and encouraged my endeavors.

Throughout my long association with Blair, it has been my good fortune to work with the same editor on each of my projects. Steve Kirk has patiently, skillfully, and professionally helped me turn raw manuscripts into books worthy of the Blair catalog. His constructive criticism, his sharp eye for mistakes and inconsistencies, his command of style and grammar, and his excellent memory have enhanced all my books. Steve has my utmost gratitude and respect.

I am also indebted to Debbie Hampton, Kim Byerly, and the remainder of the Blair staff for their tireless efforts on my behalf.

No author could have a more loving, loyal, and supportive family than I.

From the beginning of my literary career, my sister has strived to bring recognition to my work.

Some of my fondest childhood memories are the nights when my father and I went to the local drive-in theater to watch horror and science fiction movies while my mother attended church circle meetings. From those nights, I developed a lifelong interest in the supernatural. Meanwhile, my parents instilled in me a deep, abiding appreciation for the history of North Carolina and the United States. They took me to battlefields and museums, affording me the opportunity to see the sites and artifacts of epic events; they provided me with books and took me to libraries, encouraging me to read history and biographies; through Santa Claus, they gave me Marx Playsets, thrilling a little boy who loved to re-create history with plastic soldiers; and they sacrificed to ensure that I received a world-class higher education, enabling me to succeed at law, politics, and writing. My late father lived to see five of my books in print, and my mother continues to extend the love, support, and encouragement I have been blessed with every day of my life.

My daughter, Kristie, is an only child. Many of our family trips were history vacations in my quest to gather information for future books. Kristie was an excellent traveler. To be sure, she enjoyed visits to the beach and amusement parks, but to this day her favorite family vacation was spent on the battlefield at Gettysburg, Pennsylvania. Now a teacher of honors English at one of the largest high schools in North Carolina, Kristie has grown from a tiny traveler to a teenager who typed her father's handwritten manuscripts to a beautiful, extremely talented young lady. Her love and steadfast support are among my greatest treasures.

Neither this book nor any of my others would have been possible without the love, encouragement, enthusiasm, assistance, and patience of the most wonderful wife and soul mate a man could have. It was Kay who suggested that I combine my loves of history and the supernatural to write ghost tales from America's haunted past.

Kay is the epitome of forbearance. My writing a dozen books in fourteen years while serving a five-year stint in the state legislature and a ten-year term as city attorney has required countless sacrifices by my wife—sacrifices that few other ladies would have been willing to make. She has endured many lonely days and nights while I was on the road or in Raleigh; she has lived the life of an author's "widow" as I toiled over manuscripts at odd hours; and she has accompanied me on innumerable trips to libraries, on family vacations that invariably included quirky spots in my search for history, and on countless speaking engagements.

Through it all, never has she complained. Whether at my side in our home or in the audience at my speaking events, her wonderful, radiant, one-of-a-kind smile always says it all.

Kay and I came to be on Saturday, September 4, 1971, when we met on the campus of the University of North Carolina at Chapel Hill, the renowned institution established in the aftermath of the American Revolution by some of the heroes of the war. Less than three years later, our "spirited" romance became a lifelong union. Then, on July 4, 1976, the bicentennial of the Declaration of Independence, Kay and I celebrated my graduation from law school under a sky ablaze with fireworks. And now, thirty-three years later, our "revolutionary" love affair is a thing of beauty. How lucky can one guy be?

Introduction
An Angel on His Shoulder:
The Supernatural and the Father of Our Country

The hour is fast approaching, on which the Honor and Success of this army, and the safety of our bleeding Country depend. Remember Officers and Soldiers, that you are free men, fighting for the blessings of Liberty—that slavery will be your portion, and that of your posterity, if you do not acquit yourselves like men.

GEORGE WASHINGTON, 1776

No volume about the ghosts of the American Revolution would be complete without the story of the supernatural world of the father of the republic. Throughout George Washington's life, the intrepid soldier and officer had numerous brushes with death on the battlefield. He repeatedly cheated the Grim Reaper, often in miraculous fashion. In some instances, it was as if Washington were protected by a higher power.

Credible evidence suggests that America's first president yet abides with his nation in spirit form. Over more than two centuries, in historical settings related to both peace and war, countless Americans have encountered the ghost of George Washington.

Washington has been experienced as a ghost in civilian form at several places in his native Virginia. At his magnificent Mount Vernon on the Potomac River, employees and visitors have reported a variety of eerie occurrences. Disembodied footsteps, cold spots, doorknobs turned by phantom hands, furniture moved by an invisible force, and strange tapping sounds have all been attributed to Washington's ghost.

The accounts of visitors who observed the first president's spirit in his pine-paneled study at Mount Vernon gained credibility after a female employee caught a glimpse of Washington at his desk, quill in hand. According to the woman, she was preparing to close the room for the evening when she saw the spectre. As she stared in shock, Washington's apparition looked directly at her and motioned for her to approach. Though frightened, she felt obliged to follow its directions. As she neared the translucent figure, it faded away.

Washington built Woodlawn Plantation adjacent to Mount Vernon as a wedding gift for Eleanor Parke Custis, his foster daughter. On moonlit nights, his ghostly image has been observed galloping the Woodlawn grounds.

Likewise, Washington's spirit is in residence at the site of an old gristmill he operated at Dogue Run on the Potomac. Unexplained occurrences inside the mill—lamp cords unplugged by invisible hands, light bulbs unscrewed in locked closets—have been blamed on Washington. For years, the ghost of his horse was spotted tied to a tree near the mill. And to this day, local folks swear that during storms the voice of George Washington can be heard over the rain and thunder, calming his spectral steed.

Twenty years before the first military action of the Revolutionary War, Lieutenant Colonel George Washington is said to have avoided sure death through divine intervention. In the late spring of 1755, the twenty-three-year-old Washington left Williamsburg with an army of a thousand British regulars and three hundred Virginia militiamen under the command of General Edward Braddock. This expeditionary force had as its target Fort Duquesne, a French outpost near what is now Pittsburgh.

Washington, acting as aide-de-camp to Braddock, rejected his mother's plea to forgo the dangerous mission with these words: "The God to whom you commended me, Madam, when I set out upon a more perilous errand, defended me from all harm, and I trust He will do so now."

Despite those words, the young officer understood that the expedition was fraught with hazards. Based upon his experience, Washington warned General Braddock of the threat posed by the Indian allies of the French. Braddock, satisfied that his army was up to the challenge, refused to heed Washington's advice.

Ten miles from Fort Duquesne, the combined force of British and Americans rode into a trap laid by the Indians. For nearly two hours, Braddock attempted to salvage his army by using standard European military tactics in a ferocious melee with Indians fighting from behind trees. Braddock and his officers, including Washington, were particularly prized targets for the Indians.

Hundreds of Braddock's soldiers fell. Five horses were shot from under him. When the general mounted yet another animal, an Indian sharpshooter mortally wounded him. At that moment, Lieutenant Colonel Washington was the only staff officer yet able to fight. To relay the orders of his dying commander to the rapidly thinning ranks, Washington rode about the battleground under a hail of fire. One observer noted, "I expected every moment to see [Washington] fall. Nothing but the superintending care of Providence could have saved him."

Washington, later writing to his brother on his narrow escape, agreed with the soldier's observations: "By the all-powerful dispensations of Providence I have been protected beyond all probability of expectations, for I had four bullets through my coat and two horses shot under me, yet escaped unhurt, although death was leveling my companions on every side of me!"

In 1770, Washington gained a greater appreciation of the special intercession on his behalf. While traveling with a friend on the western frontier of the thirteen British colonies, he treated with an elderly Indian chief around a council fire. Speaking through an interpreter, Red Hawk, known far and wide as a marksman, spoke about the confrontation near Fort Duquesne fifteen years earlier. The chief said, "I have traveled a long and weary path that I might see the young warrior of the great battle. It was on the day when the white man's blood mixed with the streams of our forest that I first beheld this chief [Washington]. I called to my young men and said, 'Mark you the tall and daring warrior. Quick let your aim be certain, and he dies.' Our rifles were leveled, rifles, which, but for you, knew not how to miss—'twas all in vain, a power mightier than we shielded you. Seeing you were under the special guardianship of the Great Spirit, we immediately ceased fire."

Chief Red Hawk said he had fired his weapon eleven times at Washington, who stood six-foot-three and weighed two hundred pounds, a rather large target.

At the Battle of Brandywine in September 1777, General Washington was in the sights of a rifle aimed by Major Patrick Ferguson, widely considered the best marksman in the British army. His finger ready to squeeze the trigger, the Scot suddenly changed his mind and lowered his gun. As Ferguson later explained, "It was not pleasant to fire at the back of an unoffending individual who was acquitting himself very coolly of his duty, so I let him alone."

When informed the following day that he had spared the life of none other than General George Washington, Ferguson remarked that he did not regret his chivalrous act. Ironically, the sharpshooter sustained a severe wound at Brandywine. His right elbow was shattered, leaving his arm permanently crippled and rendering it impossible for him to use the famous breechloading rifle he had invented. (For further supernatural events at Brandywine involving Washington, see 168-72; for those involving Ferguson at Kings Mountain, see 255-62.)

These two flirtations with death seem to indicate that Washington had an angel on his shoulder. The story of a Revolutionary War veteran strengthens that possibility. Anthony Sherman, an old Continental soldier and a close friend of Washington, provided the details to Wesley Bradshaw, the publisher of the *National Tribune*, a forerunner to *Stars and Stripes*, in Philadelphia on July 4, 1859.

Bradshaw recalled the circumstances surrounding the interview: "The last time I saw Anthony Sherman was on the fourth of July 1859 in Independence Square. He was ninety-nine years old, and becoming very feeble. But though so old, his dimming eyes rekindled as he gazed upon Independence Hall, which he had come to visit once more."

Sherman related a fascinating story: "I want to tell you of an incident of Washington's life, one of which no one knows of except myself; and if you live long, [you will] see it verified. . . . From the opening of the Revolution we experienced all phases of fortune, now good and now ill, one time victorious and another conquered. The darkest period we had, I think, was when Washington, after several reverses, retreated to Valley Forge, where he resolved to pass the winter of 1777."

Sherman continued, "One day, I remember well, the chilly winds whistled through the leafless trees, though the sky was cloudless and the sun shone brightly. He [Washington] remained in his quarters nearly all afternoon, alone. When he came out, I noticed that his face was a shade paler than usual, and there seemed to be something on his mind of more than ordinary importance. Returning just after dark, he dispatched an orderly to the quarters of an officer."

Alone with Sherman, Washington told of a strange experience: "I do not know whether it is going to the anxiety of mind, or what, but this afternoon, as I was sitting at this table engaged in preparing a dispatch, something in the apartment seemed to disturb me. Looking up, I beheld standing opposite me a singularly beautiful being. So astonished was I, for I had given strict orders not to be disturbed that it was some moments before I found language to inquire the cause of a visit. A second, a third, and even a fourth time did I repeat the question, but received no answer from my mysterious visitor except a slight raising of the eyes. By this time I felt a strange sensation spreading over me. I would have risen but the riveted gaze of the being before me rendered volition impossible. I assayed once more to speak, but my tongue had become useless, as if paralyzed. A new influence, mysterious, potent, irresistible, took possession of me. All I could do was to gaze steadily, vacantly at my unknown visitor. Gradually the surrounding atmosphere seemed to fill with sensation and grew more luminous. Everything about me seemed to rarefy, the mysterious visitor also becoming more airy and yet more distinct to my eyes than before. I began to feel as one dying, or rather to experience the sensations, which I have sometimes imagined accompanied death. I did not think, I did not reason, I did not move. All were alike impossible. I was only conscious of gazing fixedly, vacantly, at my companion."

Washington continued, "Presently I head a voice saying, 'Son of the Republic, look and learn,' while at the same time my visitor extended an arm eastward. I now beheld a heavy white vapor at some distance rising fold upon fold. This gradually dissipated, and I looked upon a strange scene. Before me lay, spread out in one vast plain, all the countries of the world, Europe, Asia, Africa, and America. . . . 'Son of the Republic,' said the same mysterious voice as before, 'look and learn.' At that moment I beheld a dark, shadowy being, like an angel, standing or rather floating in mid-air, between Europe and America. Dipping water out of the ocean, in the hollow of each hand, he sprinkled some upon America with his right hand, while with his left he cast some over Europe. Immediately, a cloud rose from these countries, and joined in mid-ocean. For awhile it moved slowly westward, until it enveloped America in its murky folds. Sharp flashes of lightning gleamed through it at intervals, and I heard groans and cries of the American people. This may have been interpreted to have been the Revolutionary War then in progress. A second time, the angel dipped from the ocean and sprinkled it out as before. The dark cloud was then drawn to the ocean in whose billows it sank from view."

The angel was not yet finished with Washington. It appeared to warn of a great civil war that would cause a division of the American republic: "A third time I heard the mysterious visitor saying, 'Son of the Republic, look and learn.' I cast my eyes upon America and beheld villages and towns and cities springing up one after another until the whole land from the Atlantic to the Pacific was dotted with them. Again, I heard the mysterious voice say, 'Son of the Republic, the end of the century cometh, look and learn.' And this time the dark shadowy angel turned his face southward. From Africa I saw an ill-omen spectre approach over our land. It flitted slowly and heavily over every town and city. . . . The inhabitants presently set themselves in battle array against each other. As I continued looking, I saw a bright angel on whose brow rested a crown of light, on which traced the word, 'Union.' He was bearing the American flag. He placed the flag between the divided nation and said, 'Remember, ye are brethren.'"

Less than eighty-five years later, the American nation was engulfed in the great maelstrom foretold by the angel. At the Battle at Gettysburg on the afternoon of July 2, 1863, the fate of the republic nurtured by George Washington hung in the balance. On Little Round Top, a crucial Union defensive position, Colonel Joshua Chamberlain commanded the Twentieth Maine, a regiment of fewer than four hundred soldiers. Time after time, waves of Confederates from Alabama and Texas stormed the slopes, only to be beaten back by the Maine warriors.

Finally, the defenders expended their ammunition. Colonel Chamberlain, a soft-spoken professor of rhetoric and oratory at Bowdoin College, reasoned that he had but one option. He promptly ordered his surviving soldiers to affix their bayonets in preparation for a charge down the hill. Sword in hand, Chamberlain had stepped to the front of his regiment to lead the attack when suddenly a strange apparition on horseback appeared from the gun smoke swirling about the hill.

Attired in the uniform of a Revolutionary War officer, the tall horseman galloped up the hill, sword raised. The ghost exclaimed, "Fix bayonets! Charge!" With Chamberlain out front, the Yankees poured down Little Round Top in one of the most famous and successful bayonet charges in military history.

In the twilight of his life, Chamberlain, a four-term governor of Maine, was asked about the legend that the ghost of George Washington had rallied his weary, outnumbered forces on Little Round Top. For several minutes, the respected scholar, soldier, and statesman pondered the question as he gazed from the window of his study. Then he responded, "Yes, that report was circulated through our lines, and I have no doubt that it had a tremendous psychological effect in inspiring the men. Doubtless it was a superstition, but who among us can say that such a thing was impossible? We know not what mystic power may be possessed by those who are now bivouacking with the dead. I only know the effect, but I dare not explain or deny the cause. I do believe that we were enveloped by the power of the other world that day[,] and who shall say that Washington was not among the number of those who aided the country that he founded[?]"

To this day, the ghost of George Washington, wearing a tricorn hat, is said to gallop about the preserved battlefield at Gettysburg atop a splendid white charger on hot summer nights.

There is little doubt that George Washington was favored by destiny. Some call it divine providence; Presbyterians refer to it as predestination; the more secular-minded term it serendipity. In 1770, Chief Red Hawk attributed it to the benevolence of the Great Spirit when he proclaimed, "I am old and soon shall be gathered to the great council fire of my fathers in the land of shades, but, ere I go, there is something bids me speak in the voice of prophecy. Listen! The Great Spirit protects that man [Washington], and guides his destinies—he will become the chief of nations, and a people yet unborn will hail him as the founder of a mighty empire. I am come to pay homage to the man who is the particular favorite of Heaven, and who can never die in battle."

Now, centuries removed from the man who spoke those words, who among us dares argue?

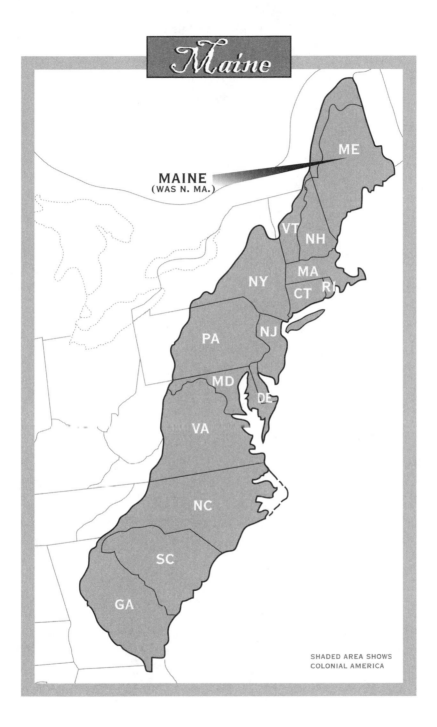

Maine

MAINE
(WAS N. MA.)

ME

VT
NH
NY
MA
CT RI
NJ
PA
MD
DE
VA
NC
SC
GA

SHADED AREA SHOWS
COLONIAL AMERICA

The Haunted Drumbeat of Liberty
CASTINE, MAINE

*Is life so dear or peace so sweet as to be purchased at the price
of chains and slavery? Forbid it, Almighty God. I know not
what course others may take, but as for me, give me liberty or
give me death.*

PATRICK HENRY

During the American Revolution, the area encompassed by the
present state of Maine was annexed to the colony of Massachusetts as
a wilderness territory. Because of its strategic location along the border
with Canada, Maine was the site of several significant land and sea battles. One of the most important occurred in the late summer of 1779,
when a substantial expeditionary force from Massachusetts failed in
an amphibious assault on Fort George, a three-acre rectangular British
compound overlooking Penobscot Bay on the central coast of Maine
at Castine. Today, a reconstructed fort serves as the centerpiece of Fort
George State Memorial. Its oldest resident is the ghost of a nameless
Patriot drummer boy. Since his death on that August night so long ago,

the *rat-a-tat-tat* of his drum has filled the air at this historic site.

In early July 1779, British forces under General Francis McLean sailed into the harbor at Castine and promptly commenced construction of Fort George on one of the highest points overlooking the bay. The fortification would serve as an outer defense for Nova Scotia and provide a strategic base from which attacks could be dispatched against Patriot forces to the south.

In Boston, concerned authorities, forgoing consultation with either the Continental Congress or the Continental Army, assembled a large assault force comprised of an armada of nineteen heavily armed warships and twenty-four troop transports carrying a landing party of twelve hundred marines and militiamen from some of the finest families in Massachusetts. In command of the ground troops was General Peleg Wadsworth. Colonel Paul Revere served as the commander of the American artillery. Henry Wadsworth Longfellow, General Wadsworth's grandson, would years later pen "The Midnight Ride of Paul Revere," bringing immortal fame to his grandfather's comrade in arms.

On July 21, 1779, the forty-three-ship strike force set sail from Boston Harbor for the attack on Fort George. Some historians have deemed it the largest amphibious operation of the entire war. For almost three weeks, the Massachusetts warriors confronted the British compound from land and sea. Despite their numerical superiority, the American ground forces could not overcome the stalwart Seventy-fourth Regiment of Foot (Argyle Highlanders). In mid-August, the Americans put an end to the disastrous mission and retreated from Penobscot Bay. On the return trip to Massachusetts, many ships were scuttled to avoid capture by the Royal Navy.

A court-martial was subsequently convened in Boston. Paul Revere was acquitted, but Captain Dudley Saltonstall, the naval commander of the expedition, was convicted. In financial terms, the failed expedition cost more than seven million dollars. Among the numerous human casualties was the young American drummer who haunts Fort George.

Two divergent stories tell how the Patriot musician died.

William Hutchins, a fourteen-year-old who lived several miles from the battle site, offered an eyewitness account of the fighting: "One night the Americans undertook to surprise the English but they fell in with the British guard at Bank's battery and had a sharp fight. Quite a number were killed on both sides. I afterwards saw up by the [Bagaduce River] narrows some bloody uniforms tied up in a blanket that had been stripped from English soldiers who were killed that night. A drummer was killed that night of the skirmish at the battery near Bank's house, and for a good many years after people used to say they could hear his ghost drumming there at night."

Another account maintains that the drummer boy was taken prisoner during the Battle of Castine and incarcerated in the dungeon at Fort George, where he subsequently died of starvation.

Regardless of the cause of the young Patriot's death, his spirit has abided at the fort ever since. Not only are the sounds of a phantom drum heard in the reconstructed fort and underground dungeon, but the misty form of a teenage drummer has been encountered as it floats about the site.

Perhaps because the American colonies ultimately prevailed in their bitter fight for independence, the debacle at Castine—considered by some the greatest American naval defeat before Pearl Harbor—has been relegated to a historical footnote. But if you happen to be strolling the grounds of old Fort George in the dark of night, particularly in mid-August, maintain a keen eye and a close ear for the spectral form of the drummer boy who continues to beat the call for liberty.

The address for **Fort George State Memorial** is Battle Ave. and Wadsworth Cove Rd., Castine, Maine 04421.

Still Celebrating Independence
ROCKPORT, MAINE

*In defense of the freedom that is our birthright . . . we have
taken up arms. We shall lay them down when the hostilities shall
cease on the part of the aggressors, and all danger of their being
renewed shall be removed, and not before.*

                                        JOHN HANCOCK

Less than thirty years after the American colonies achieved independence, the patriotic folks of Goose River (now Rockport), Maine, supplied three hundred casks of lime to the federal government for repairs to the Capitol Building, which had been badly damaged by British raiders during the War of 1812.

Back during the Revolutionary War, British forces regularly menaced the citizens of Goose River, then as now a small village on the central coast of Maine. Never willing to allow the invaders to have their way without stiff resistance, the spirited locals did all they could to annoy the aggressors. William "Bill" Richardson, a fisherman from Goose River, emerged from the war as a local hero because of his derring-do in the struggle against the Brits. Murdered by unrepentant Tories amid the revelry attending the war's conclusion, Richardson continues to make merry by offering celebratory toasts to passersby on the bridge over the Goose River.

Throughout the long fight for independence, Goose River had no organized defense and no fortifications. Most of the able-bodied menfolk were fighting on distant battlefields. Consequently, British naval vessels found the village an enticing target as they prowled the waters of the North Atlantic. Landing parties frequently came ashore for pillage and plunder. Villagers—primarily the elderly, housewives, and children—were sent scurrying into the wilderness as the torch was set to their homes and farms.

Anger over the wanton acts mounted. Daring ladies began taking to the woods when they saw British landing parties approaching the village. From their hiding spots, they fired deadly volleys at the unsuspecting raiders. On occasion, the old men of Goose River attempted to scare off the invaders with an "army of two." One of the elders pounded roll call on his drum, while his compatriot yelled military commands to a nonexistent force of American troops.

In 1779, the villagers took great pride in William Richardson when he exacted revenge against the enemy. One day, Commodore Samuel Tucker, licensed by the Americans as a privateer, caught sight of a British ship heavily laden with tea sailing in the open waters off Maine. Tucker managed to capture the prize and make off with its valuable cargo. When a British warship gave chase, he sought refuge along the irregular coastline. Unfamiliar with the local navigational hazards, he drew his ship alongside a fishing boat manned by Richardson. Commodore Tucker enlisted Richardson to pilot the privateer to safe harbor near Harpswell, sixty miles south of Goose River. There, Richardson anchored Tucker's ship along the rocky ledges in water too shallow for the heavy, deep-draft pursuer.

The captain of the British ship blockaded Harpswell and awaited additional warships. As the blockade wore on, Tucker grew fearful that all was lost, but Richardson urged him to stay put until the next storm at sea. As soon as the weather worsened, the privateer, with Richardson once again serving as navigator, stole away into the stormy night. By the time the blockaders realized their prey had escaped, the American ship was en route to Boston, where less than six years earlier British tea had been dumped in the harbor during the Boston Tea Party.

When news of the Treaty of Paris reached Goose River in 1783, no citizen was more exhilarated than Bill Richardson. He decided to host the grandest bash ever held in the area. Residents of nearby communities were invited to the extravaganza, which opened with cannon fire resounding down the Penobscot range. Soldiers still attired in their blue and buff uniforms and militiamen who had survived the long war marched proudly through the streets of Goose River to the cheers of appreciative citizens. Richardson opened his home as the party headquarters. Musicians played as hundreds of celebrants danced, feasted on roasted beef, pork, and lamb, and consumed copious quantities of ale provided by their gracious host.

At length, Richardson decided to make merry in the village streets after downing several mugs of his brew. He wandered about Goose River with a pitcher of ale in his hand, offering salutations to all he encountered. He made his way down to the river. As he ambled over the bridge, three horsemen galloped toward him. Before Richardson could recognize them as belligerent Tories, he offered them his pitcher. One of the riders slammed his rifle butt into the head of the Patriot. The Tory trio sped away into the darkness, leaving their helpless victim to die.

But his apparition never left the bridge or its subsequent replacements. For as long as anyone can remember, the ghost of William Richardson, pitcher in hand, has been observed on the Goose River Bridge.

In modern times, the area near the approaches to the bridge has been used as a lovers' lane. Two memorable encounters with the ghost of the Revolutionary War hero took place there in the middle of the twentieth century.

During a romantic walk on a summer evening in 1953, a teenage couple was making its way toward the bridge when the girl suddenly stopped in fear. She directed her boyfriend's attention to a man dressed in clothes from a bygone era who was approaching them. Mustering his courage, the young fellow assumed a position to defend his gal against the potential threat. But in the blink of an eye, the phantom was gone.

A dozen or so years later, two infatuated couples parked their vehicle at the "passion pit" near the bridge. When the glass steamed up, the fellow in the backseat rolled down a window for some fresh air, only to find himself peering into the spectral face of a man who offered him a pitcher of drink. The terrified young man quickly rolled up the window and screamed for the driver to speed away.

Signs near the historic river crossing give fair warning: "No trespassing between sunset and sunrise." But visitors really have no need to fear the friendly ghost of the Goose River Bridge. After all, old Bill wants only to share his excitement about an independent America with all who pass his way.

The **Goose River Bridge** is located on Pascals Avenue just blocks from historic U.S. 1 in Rockport, Maine.

Other "Spirited" Revolutionary War Sites in Maine, Briefly Noted

BUCKSPORT—BUCKSPORT CEMETERY

Colonel Jonathan Buck, a stalwart Revolutionary War officer, founded the town on the central coast of Maine that now bears his name.

Legend has it that, as a jurist, Buck convicted a local woman of witchcraft and sentenced her to death by hanging. Just before her execution, the "witch" pronounced a curse: "Over your grave they will erect a stone that all may know where your bones are crumbling into dust. . . . Upon that stone the imprint of my feet will appear and for all time . . . will the people from far and near know that you murdered a woman. Remember well, Jonathan Buck, remember well."

Buck died on March 18, 1795. Nearly a half-century later, members of his family erected the fifteen-foot granite obelisk that still stands atop his grave. Soon thereafter, a curious imprint of a human leg and foot appeared on the monument just below the name *BUCK*. All attempts to remove the strange marking have failed. No rational explanation has been put forward. It is said that the witch danced on Buck's grave, carrying out her death curse.

The cemetery is located just outside Bucksport on U.S. 1.

OGUNQUIT—OGUNQUIT PLAYHOUSE

This long-established playhouse on the coast of Maine bills itself as "America's Foremost Summer Theatre." For unknown reasons, several Revolutionary War soldiers haunt the site.

The address for the Ogunquit Playhouse is 6 Main St., Ogunquit, Maine 03907; the telephone number is 207-646-5511.

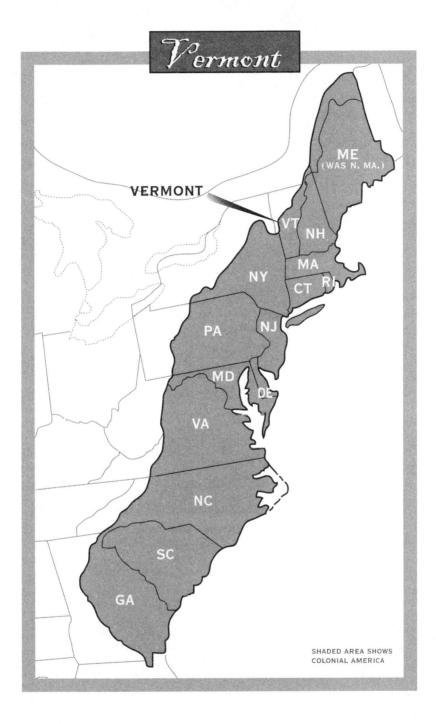

Vermont

VERMONT

ME
(WAS N. MA.)

VT
NH
MA
NY
CT RI
NJ
PA
MD
DE
VA
NC
SC
GA

SHADED AREA SHOWS
COLONIAL AMERICA

The Ghost of the Green Mountains
BURLINGTON, VERMONT

*Ever since I arrived to a state of manhood, I have felt a
sincere passion for liberty.*

ETHAN ALLEN

Snaking its way through Vermont's famed Green Mountains for
ninety miles from Montpelier in the north to Burlington in the south
to its confluence with Lake Champlain, the picturesque Winooski River
was home to beloved Revolutionary War hero Ethan Allen (1738–89).
Allen's spirit, in the form of a famous white horse, yet roams the banks
of the waterway in the vicinity of Burlington.

At the time of the American Revolution, the territory now con-
stituting Vermont was not a colony. Conflicting claims to the area by
neighboring New York and New Hampshire were the source of an intense squabble. Even before the war of words between Great Britain
and the American colonies grew into a war of bullets, residents were
so bold as to declare Vermont an independent republic. Widely recognized as "the father of Vermont," Ethan Allen achieved immortal
fame as a fighter for the independence of Vermont and the American

colonies. Though he died before Vermont was admitted as the four-teenth state, Allen stood head and shoulders above all other Vermonters as a champion of liberty.

In physical appearance, Allen was striking. He stood well over six feet tall and had bright red hair. His engaging personality and the military experience he gained during the French and Indian War enabled him to emerge as a crafty guerrilla leader of Vermonters who opposed New York's efforts to make good on land claims in the early 1770s. Because of the tactics of Allen's band of warriors, the Green Mountain Boys, the government of New York offered a substantial reward for the capture and arrest of the red-headed commander.

Despite having a bounty of one hundred pounds on his head, Allen participated in the American cause at the onset of the Revolutionary War. On May 10, 1775, he and Benedict Arnold led a bold expedition across Lake Champlain to the British stronghold of Fort Ticondero-ga, strategically situated on the southwestern lakeshore in New York. While the Green Mountain Boys encircled the fortress, Allen shouted, "Come out of there, you sons of British whores, or I'll smoke you out!" Receiving no response, he made his way into the fort and called at the headquarters of Captain William Delaplace, the British commander. Eschewing formalities, Allen demanded, "Deliver this place!" Delaplace offered a curt retort: "By whose authority?" Without blinking, Allen raised his sword and proclaimed, "In the name of the great Jehovah and the Continental Congress!" Delaplace, quickly assessing his position, acquiesced, turning the fort over to the Americans without the loss of a single life. Some historians consider the capture of Fort Ticonderoga the first American victory of the Revolutionary War.

In the wake of their success, Allen and Arnold led the effort to at-tack British outposts and towns on the Canadian border. The spoils of war taken during the raids enabled American forces to bring an end to the British siege at Boston less than a year later.

A failed effort to take Montreal in September 1775 led to Allen's capture by British forces. Identified as the commanding officer who invested Fort Ticonderoga, he was shipped to an English prison at Pendennis Castle in Cornwall. Fearful of repercussions in the colonies, the British government ultimately returned the prisoner to America, where he was paroled in New York City in October 1776. Anxious to fight again, he hurried to the side of General George Washington at Valley Forge, Pennsylvania.

On May 14, 1778, Allen was appointed colonel in the Continental Army in recognition of "his fortitude, firmness and zeal in the cause of his country, manifested during his long and cruel captivity, as well as on former occasions." Not only was he a fierce competitor on the battlefield, he was an influential political advocate for the citizens of Vermont. In 1778, he offered an impassioned plea to the Continental Congress to recognize Vermont as a state. Concerns about the claims of New York and New Hampshire made Congress reluctant to act. But the groundwork laid by Allen led to the subsequent acceptance of Vermont as the first state to follow the original colonies.

George Washington once noted "an original something in [Allen] that commands attention." In both his professional and private life, Allen was known as an independent thinker. A deist, he believed in the Almighty, but he disdained organized religion, choosing instead to order his life in accordance with his own written statement of faith, *Reason: The Only Oracle of Man*. Witchcraft, long practiced in New England, terrified him.

Allen settled in a home he constructed in the delta of the Winooski River in an area that is now part of Burlington. His restored cabin still rests on a ridge overlooking the river meadows.

On February 12, 1789, the hard-charging, hard-drinking proponent of a free Vermont died of a stroke in Burlington at age fifty-one. He was buried in the public graveyard, appropriately named Green Mount Cemetery. Atop his grave was erected a forty-two-foot granite shaft resting on a massive eight-foot base. Surmounting the shaft was an eight-foot statue of the hero crafted from Carrera marble.

Some years after Allen's death, archaeologists were astonished to find none of the soldier's remains after opening his grave. Even the coffin was gone. Perhaps, as some said, the burial actually took place in a different plot to thwart graverobbers, in accordance with the dead man's wishes. However, others believe that Allen's body was stolen for use in the practice of witchcraft, realizing his worst fears.

Yet another explanation for the missing body touches on the supernatural. Allen firmly believed in reincarnation. On more than one occasion, he told friends that when he died, he would return to the world as a magnificent white horse. His listeners took his claim lightly because Allen was known as a storyteller.

Nonetheless, a phantom white stallion gallops about the river meadows and the forests near the Allen homestead. Numerous eyewitnesses have observed the stallion, its head held high, on the very land Allen called his own. All attempts to capture the steed have met with failure. Once approached, it dissolves into the river mist. The graceful, pure white ghost horse represents independence, adventure, and freedom—the qualities most admired in Ethan Allen.

The **Ethan Allen Homestead** is in Winooski Valley Park. The address is 1 Ethan Allen Homestead, Burlington, Vt. 05408; the telephone numbers are 802-865-4556 and 802-863-5744.

The Retreat of a Revolutionary War Ghost
LAKE MEMPHREMAGOG, VERMONT

*For my own part, I am such an enthusiast for independence
that I would hesitate to enter heaven thro' the means of a second-
ary cause unless I had made the utmost exertions to merit it.*
                                    GENERAL ANTHONY WAYNE

Of the many important personages of the Revolutionary War, one
seems to manifest himself in ghostly form more than all the others—
Major General Anthony Wayne (1745–96), known to posterity as "Mad
Anthony." Born in Pennsylvania, the highly respected military genius
etched his name into the history books as one of America's greatest soldiers by virtue of his leadership at places like Stony Point, New York.

In 1775, Wayne, then a colonel, was dispatched to Canada to follow up on the victories achieved by Ethan Allen and Benedict Arnold
at Fort Ticonderoga and points along the border with New York and
Vermont. As a result of Wayne's sojourn in the area, his ghost lingers
not only at old Fort Ticonderoga but also at his favorite place in all of
Vermont—Lake Memphremagog.

Located on the boundary between Newport, Vermont, and Magog, Quebec, the freshwater lake stretches twenty-seven miles. Wayne came to know its magnificent beauty while he and his scouting party were making their way through Vermont en route to Canada. As they neared Lake Memphremagog, one of the colonel's guides informed him of a nest of four or five bald eagles along the lakeshore. Colonel Wayne had always wanted a pair of the birds, knowing that young eagles could be trained as hunting companions, like falcons.

With great dispatch, the party made its way to the nest. While the adult eagles were away in search of food, Wayne robbed the nest of two young birds, but not before their claws carved into his cheeks and nose, leaving permanent scars. Unperturbed by the painful injury, he personally trained the two eagles, treasuring them for as long as they lived.

Charmed by the lake and the abundant wildlife on its shores, Wayne constructed a log fort along the waterfront and used it for brief respites from his military duties.

Not long after his death, his ghost began making appearances near the site of his crude fortification on Lake Memphremagog. For more than two hundred years now, area residents and visitors to the lake have encountered the phantom officer dressed in his leather wilderness outfit. Often, the arms of the apparition are extended, a bald eagle perched on each wrist. On nights of a full moon, the spectre of Mad Anthony Wayne has been sighted as it gazes toward the opposite side of the lake. Many a startled witness has watched as the ghost floats across the water and vanishes on the other side.

As revealed later in this volume, Wayne did not rest after his death. But his ghost has apparently found a measure of peace at the general's Lake Memphremagog retreat.

The southern tip of **Lake Memphremagog** is located near the junction of U.S. 5 and Vt. 105 in Newport, Vermont.

Other "Spirited" Revolutionary War Sites in Vermont, Briefly Noted

BENNINGTON—BENNINGTON BATTLE MONUMENT

Towering 306 feet above the Bennington landscape, the granite obelisk was the tallest battle monument in the world when it was constructed in the twilight of the nineteenth century. Still the tallest man-made structure in Vermont, the Bennington Battle Monument commemorates the Patriot triumph here in August 1777 over a detachment of General John Burgoyne's army. Anxious to gain badly needed supplies in Bennington, Hessians, in advance of British regulars, moved on the town and came face to face with General John Stark and the waiting rifles of his American soldiers. Stark inspired his men to victory with these words: "There are the Red Coats; they will be ours, or tonight Molly Stark will be a widow." Stark's warriors, in ghostly form, continue to watch for the enemy from the monument to this day.

Visitors once reached the top of the tower by way of 412 steps winding their way past almost three dozen landings. Although the staircase is now closed to the public, an elevator whisks visitors to the 200-foot observatory level, where windows provide a breathtaking panoramic view of the old battlefield.

Once the monument is closed for the night, supernatural forces go to work on the inside. Security staff often report the sounds of steps on the abandoned stairs. From the lookout windows, phantom Revolutionary War–era lanterns cast an eerie glow, a haunting reminder that the spirits of the freedom fighters of old are yet on watch.

The address for the monument is 15 Monument Circle, Bennington, Vt. 05201; the telephone number is 802-447-0550.

BENNINGTON—OLD BURYING GROUND

At the ancient graveyard in Bennington, the battle fought in the town in 1777 continues to rage among ghosts. After the sun goes down, whispering can be heard from the graves of American, British, and Hessian soldiers buried following the clash. Faint voices, some speaking German, argue. Living persons who have heard the otherworldly war of words report that the ghosts often use profanity, causing the faces of the stone angels atop markers throughout the cemetery to frown. As the sun rises each new day, the strange commotion ends.

The Old Burying Ground is located adjacent to First Congregational Church on Monument Avenue in Bennington.

LAKE CHAMPLAIN—MOUNT INDEPENDENCE

Located directly across Lake Champlain from Fort Ticonderoga, Mount Independence served as a landmark during the Revolutionary War and played a prominent role in the military events surrounding the great fort, which was controlled by both armies. From the heights of the mountain and the waters of the lake, the ghost of a brave Patriot courier is often observed swimming Champlain.

During the successful American effort to recapture Mount Independence in mid-October 1777, two intrepid Vermonters, Ephraim Webster and Richard Wallace, volunteered to swim the bitterly cold lake to deliver crucial military information. Enclosing the dispatches in waterproof packets tied to their foreheads, the Patriots shed their clothes, reckoning they could swim faster in the nude. Against unbelievable odds, they avoided numerous British patrol boats on their two-mile swim to the other shore.

Richard Wallace never recovered from the harsh elements, dying as a result. Perhaps that is why his naked spectre has been observed in the lake. Some boaters have even heard the chattering teeth of the ghost as it plies the frigid waters.

The address for this landmark is Mount Independence State Historic Site, Orwell, Vt. 05760; the telephone number is 802-948-2000.

ROYALTON/TURNBRIDGE—
ROUTE OF THE ROYALTON RAID

Each autumn, the trees along the six-mile route of Vt. 110 between the villages of Royalton and Turnbridge are ablaze in colorful glory.

As the leaf season was coming to a close in October 1780, local residents were savagely attacked by three hundred Indian raiders supplied, organized, and commanded by John Horton, a British lieutenant. Anxious to demoralize local Patriots, Horton led the men on a rampage as they pillaged farm after farm, killing men, capturing women and children for slaves, and laying waste to homes and barns.

On October nights, the horrifying cries of the ghosts of the helpless victims of the Royalton Raid fill the air along the historic route. One of the most famous ghosts is that of Hannah Handy, who was pulled from her house and assaulted as her nine children were taken into custody. She fought back fiercely, so impressing the attackers that they did no further harm to her and released her children.

Vt. 110 connects Royalton and Turnbridge in central Vermont.

WESTMINSTER—GRAVE OF WILLIAM FRENCH

Located on the border with New Hampshire, tiny Westminster is the oldest town in Vermont. It was the site of the Westminster Massacre, a skirmish that produced the first American martyr of the Revolutionary War. His ghost lingers about his grave and the nearby monument erected in his memory.

On the night of March 13, 1775, Patriots held control of the local courthouse and refused to allow supporters of the British Crown to enter the building. Amid the controversy, gunshots were fired into the courthouse. William French, one of the Patriots, was hit five times. His death was instant.

The grave of the man who was the first to spill his blood for the American cause lies in the ancient cemetery on the north side of Westminster. It is marked by a headstone etched with the details of his death. Just across the road stands an enormous white granite chair erected in honor of French. Around sunrise and sunset, his ghost is said to lounge in his stone chair. Legend has it that anytime an American flag passes the old graveyard, William French's apparition stands at attention to honor the country for which he made the first ultimate sacrifice.

Less than two years after the Westminster Massacre, on January 15, 1777, the town hosted the convention that proclaimed Vermont to be free and independent.

Westminster is located off U.S. 5 in southeastern Vermont.

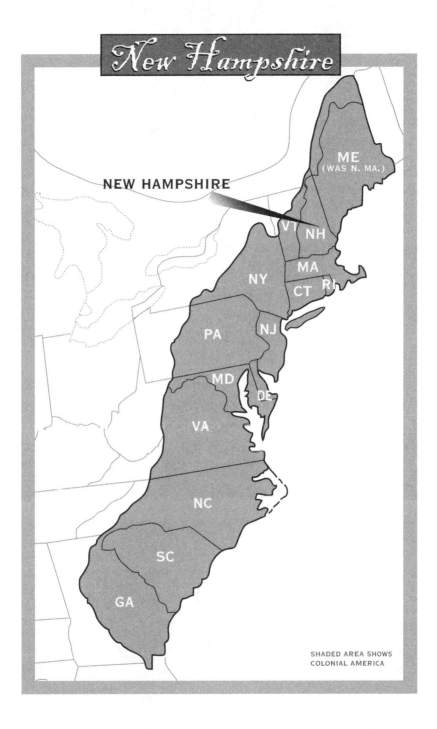

New Hampshire

NEW HAMPSHIRE

ME
(WAS N. MA.)

VT NH

MA

NY
CT RI

PA NJ

MD

DE

VA

NC

SC

GA

SHADED AREA SHOWS
COLONIAL AMERICA

Phantom Lovers
PORTSMOUTH, NEW HAMPSHIRE

It seems to be a law of nature, inflexible and inexorable,
that those who will not risk cannot win.

JOHN PAUL JONES

Most Americans, when asked to name the most famous naval hero of the Revolutionary War, will respond with John Paul Jones. Born on the southern coast of Scotland, Jones (1747–92) settled in America under the name John Paul in the years leading up to the war. By the time hostilities began, he adopted Jones as his last name. An early volunteer for the American cause, he became on December 22, 1775, the first man assigned the rank of first lieutenant in the fledgling Continental Navy. During the war that followed, he emerged as a genuine American hero for his daring exploits on the high seas.

Ironically, Jones spent many months of wartime service in shore duty at Portsmouth, New Hampshire, where he superintended the construction of American warships at the Portsmouth Naval Shipyard, which survives today as the oldest such facility in the United States.

If eyewitness accounts are to be believed, Jones's spirit never departed Portsmouth. Two buildings in the historic city on the northern coast of New Hampshire are thought to be haunted by the ghosts of Jones and a special lady friend.

Jones was assigned to Portsmouth in 1777 to oversee construction of the *Ranger*, the first man-of-war to bear the American flag. Once the frigate was completed, its command was given to Jones. While the vessel was under construction, the young officer boarded at a handsome yellow three-story gambrel-roofed house erected in 1758 by Captain Gregory Purcell for his bride, Sarah Wentworth. Mrs. Purcell was a widow by the time Jones boarded at her home, the likeness of which has appeared in national television commercials for Sears Weatherbeater paint.

In 1781, Jones arrived in Portsmouth for his second extended stay. This time, he was assigned by the Continental Navy to supervise the construction and outfitting of the USS *America*, designed to be the largest ship in the fleet. That same year, a fire ravaged a number of fine homes in the city, including the estate of Woodbury Langdon, located adjacent to the Purcell house. Langdon moved his wife and family into the Purcell dwelling while his new palatial home, now the Rockingham Hotel, was being erected. Two years later, Langdon purchased the Purcell house. The Langdon family was prominent in the business and governmental affairs of New Hampshire. Woodbury's brother, John, served as governor and was an important shipbuilder. John Paul Jones and John Langdon were often at odds.

During Jones's tours of duty in Portsmouth, rumors of a love affair between the swashbuckling naval hero and Mrs. Woodbury Langdon circulated. And perhaps their trysts continue in supernatural form, if the ghosts in the side-by-side historic buildings are who they are thought to be.

At the old Purcell house—now restored and maintained as the John Paul Jones House Museum—numerous witnesses have been startled to see a spectral lady with a pure ivory face staring out the ancient windows at times when the museum is locked tight. Folks about town maintain that the apparition is that of Lady Langdon pining for John Paul Jones.

The phantom lovers have also been experienced during regular hours. On more than one occasion, museum guides have encountered the ghosts in the shawl room. The doors of the cabinet used for storing shawls have suddenly opened before the amazed eyes of docents. A spirit believed to be that of Jones often opens and closes the back door to the museum when no humans other than staff are present. Paranormal investigators who spent time in the venerable structure detected Jones's ghost in his former dressing room and bedchamber.

Next door to the museum stands the Rockingham Hotel, once the lavish home of Lady Langdon. In modern times, the structure has been converted into a condominium complex. According to various accounts, the ghost of Jones's alleged lover continues to inhabit the building. Esther Buffin, the first poet laureate of Portsmouth, penned "The White Lady of Rockingham" after she encountered the ghost in her apartment in the five-story building. She and other witnesses have described the apparition as a misty figure in a white dress. An encounter with the ghost is always preceded by the pungent scent of brine.

The old haunts of the Scottish sailor turned American naval hero yet stand on the New Hampshire coast. And maybe, just maybe, the illicit romance of the man known as "the father of the American navy" and his wealthy next-door neighbor continues beyond the grave.

The **John Paul Jones House Museum** is located at the corner of Middle and State streets in downtown Portsmouth, New Hampshire. The telephone number is 643-436-8420. The **Rockingham Hotel** stands adjacent to the museum on State Street.

The General, the Devil, and the Ghost
HAMPTON, NEW HAMPSHIRE

*Every citizen should be a soldier. This was the case with the
Greeks and Romans, and must be that of every free state.*

THOMAS JEFFERSON

In the world of the supernatural, a fine line stands between fact and
fiction. Over time, that line often disappears, and the two blend. And
so it is with the story of Jonathan Moulton, a hero of King George's
War, the French and Indian War, and the Revolutionary War. His life
in the coastal town of Hampton, New Hampshire, is said to have been
haunted by the devil and the ghost of his first wife.

Moulton (1726–87) was born into a modest family. Apprenticed to
a cabinetmaker as a youngster, he joined the military at age nineteen.
First as a captain in the New Hampshire militia and then as an officer
of the Crown, he quickly achieved fame by slaying countless Indian
warriors during King George's War.

In 1749, Captain Moulton came home to Hampton to begin what

he hoped would be a life of peace and prosperity. Not long afterward, Abigail Smith agreed to marry him. Over the course of their twenty-seven-year marriage, Abigail would bear eleven children.

The newlyweds struggled financially for a time as Jonathan labored to build an import business. But suddenly, townspeople began to speak of the unusual conversation that reportedly took place one morning at the breakfast table in the Moulton kitchen. Jonathan pounded the table with his fist and exclaimed to Abigail, "We need more money—lots more! I've got to get hold of some money! More wealth!" And then he rose from his chair and made a statement that terrified his wife: "Abby, I'd sell my soul to the devil to gain all the gold on the face of the earth!"

Soon, neighbors began to notice an unusual stranger who paid visits to the Moulton home on the first of each month. As Jonathan grew rich almost overnight, word spread throughout Hampton that he had made a pact with the devil. Rumors had it that, in exchange for Jonathan's soul, the devil would fill the mortal's boot with gold coins on each visit.

Jonathan quickly amassed a fortune in gold without any earthly explanation. Jealous folks were bewildered and amazed at his ever-increasing affluence. And no matter what he had, he never seemed satisfied. He always wanted more.

One day, Jonathan purchased a pair of the tallest riding boots in all of Hampton. But even when one of the new boots was filled with gold guineas, he demanded more. So, as the legend of Jonathan Moulton goes, he attempted to trick the devil.

After removing the sole, Jonathan placed a boot over a hole in an upstairs room. On his next monthly visit, the devil discovered that no amount of gold would fill the boot. After several ensuing visits brought the same result, the devil discovered the ruse. In the room under the soleless boot, the Prince of Darkness found gold coins piled to the ceiling. The year was 1769.

Not long thereafter, the stranger was seen for the last time about the Moulton property. A short time later, the house caught fire, forcing the family to flee for their lives. On the site of the ruins, Jonathan subsequently erected a grander house that stands to this day.

Despite the suspicion surrounding the wealthiest man in Hampton, Jonathan's fellow citizens selected him for several important positions—moderator of town meetings, member of the local Committee of Safety, and delegate to the Patriot assembly at Exeter—on the eve of the American Revolution. Because of his military experience, he was appointed colonel of the Third New Hampshire Regiment of militia.

On September 21, 1775, while Colonel Moulton was away commanding his regiment in defense of New Hampshire's eighteen-mile coastline, Abigail died of smallpox. Hampton residents disputed the cause of death, maintaining she passed away under "very suspicious circumstances." To add fire to the speculation, Colonel Moulton stripped all the jewelry, including the wedding ring, from Abigail's corpse at the funeral.

Less than a year later, Jonathan, then fifty years old, married Sarah Henry, Abigail's best friend and a woman fourteen years his junior. On their wedding day, Jonathan lavished jewelry upon her, including the fine pieces that had once belonged to his first wife.

On their wedding night, the couple retired to the master chamber in the Moulton House. Sarah went to bed wearing some of her new gems. Adorning her finger was Abigail's wedding ring. In the wee hours of the morning, a terrified Sarah shrieked in agony. Jonathan, awakened by his wife's cries, attempted to calm her. In an almost hysterical voice, Sarah managed to tell him that a spectral lady in white had taken her hand in a deathlike grip and violently removed the rings from her fingers. Sarah was certain the ghost was Abigail, come to reclaim her jewels.

But Jonathan would have none of it. To his way of thinking, there must be a rational explanation. Wearing only his nightshirt, he jumped from the bed, lit a candle, and made his way through every room. Nothing was amiss, and no one else was in the place. All doors and windows were securely bolted from the inside. Grabbing a cloak, Jonathan made his way out into the darkness in search of the culprit. Finding no foot-prints in the yard, he ambled back toward the house. En route, he en-countered an eerie cold spot.

Day after day, night after night, Sarah Moulton was haunted by the ghost of her best friend, whose husband and bed she had taken. She heard the disconcerting swish of a lady's skirt and witnessed the morti-fying sight of a wraithlike figure floating from room to room.

Whether due to the exigencies of war or the ghost of his former wife, Colonel Moulton returned to active military duty. He and his reg-iment performed admirably in New York when the Americans bested the British commanded by General John Burgoyne in the fall of 1777. During his absence, Sarah continued to encounter Abigail's ghost.

Two years after the war, Jonathan was named brigadier general of the Fifth New Hampshire. Rarely did his duties take him away from home. The hauntings continued unabated.

In 1789, two years after Jonathan's death, George Washington stopped at the Moulton residence to pay his respects to Sarah, who was yet tormented by the spirit of the first Mrs. Moulton. Slaves about the estate likewise reported seeing the apparition.

After Sarah died, the house went through a succession of owners, all of whom claimed it to be haunted. One owner, the Whipple family, attempted an exorcism, which worked for a brief time. According to one family member, the household staff was terrified by ghosts: "My grandfather Whipple being absent, the servants insisted that General Moulton and his wife disturbed the house so much at night, he thump-ing his cane, and her dress a-rustling down the stairs, that nothing could allay their terror." The family's housekeeper noted that the apparition of Jonathan Moulton always appeared in a "snuff-colored suit and enor-mous wig, holding a gold-headed cane."

So widespread were the stories about the haunted house that the famed John Greenleaf Whittier composed a poem entitled "The New Wife and the Old." In part, it reads,

God have mercy!—icy cold
Spectral hands her own enfold,
Drawing silently from them
Love's fair gifts of gold and gem.

Long known in the Hampton area as "the haunted house," the old Moulton place remains a private residence. By all accounts, Abigail Moulton, in spirit form, continues to claim the place for herself to this day.

Still another tantalizing piece adds to this eerie tale. Just after Jonathan's death, his neighbors and fellow citizens—the very people who had gossiped about him for much of his adult life—demanded that his coffin be unearthed and opened. When the lid was removed, the casket was empty! Some argued that the body had been taken by graverobbers aware of Moulton's enormous wealth. But was there another explanation? Did old Lucifer claim the remains of the mortal with whom he had made a pact in life and death? You decide!

The **Moulton House** is located on the corner of U.S. 1/Lafayette Road/Drakeford Road in Hampton. It is private property not open to the public.

Other "Spirited" Revolutionary War Sites in New Hampshire, Briefly Noted

CHARLESTOWN—
FORT NUMBER FOUR RECONSTRUCTION

This colonial fort was the mustering site of Patriot soldiers who fought at the Battle of Bennington and other area Revolutionary War skirmishes. Visitors and reenactors have experienced the spirits of soldiers. Phantom footsteps, eerie cold spots, and the touch of invisible hands have been reported.

Fort Number Four Reconstruction is open to the public. Its address is 267 Springfield Rd. (N.H. 11), Charlestown, N.H. 03603; the telephone number is 603-826-5700.

MERRIMACK—COMMON MAN RESTAURANT

Owners and patrons of this restaurant, housed in a structure dating from colonial times, have seen a shadowy figure thought to be the ghost of one of the two men who lived here during the Revolutionary War. Edward Goldstone Lutwyche owned the dwelling at the onset of the war, but his loyalty to the British Crown resulted in the confiscation of the property by the Continental Congress. When Matthew Thornton moved to Merrimack in 1780, the house was "sold" to him by the grateful American government. Colonel Thornton, a talented physician, was one of New Hampshire's three signers of the Declaration of Independence. His grave is located just across the street in the cemetery that bears his name.

The resident ghost wears eighteenth-century clothing.

The address for Common Man Restaurant is Daniel Webster Hwy. and Greeley Rd., Merrimack, N.H. 03054; the telephone number is 603-429-3463.

NEW LONDON—NEW LONDON INN

This popular New England hostelry, housed in a beautiful, rambling eighteenth-century building, is home to a convivial ghost dressed in an ill-fitting Revolutionary War uniform. The resident spook is thought to be a veteran who was fond of drink. Eyewitnesses have described the unidentified Patriot ghost as a merrymaker who raises his tankard in a toast just before he vanishes. Sometimes, only the shiny metal buttons of his uniform can be seen. When the gleeful spirit is invisible, the distinct sounds of someone gulping a drink can be heard at the ghost's favorite spot near the fireplace.

The inn's address is 353 Main St., New London, N.H. 03257; the telephone number is 800-526-2791.

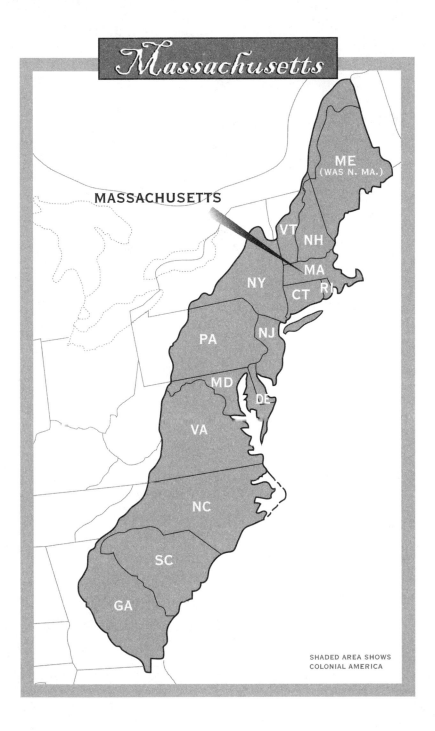

Massachusetts

MASSACHUSETTS

ME
(WAS N. MA.)

VT
NH
NY
MA
CT
RI
PA
NJ
MD
DE
VA

NC

SC

GA

SHADED AREA SHOWS
COLONIAL AMERICA

The Light Burns for John
GURNET POINT (PLYMOUTH BAY), MASSACHUSETTS

When you reach the end of your rope, tie a knot in it, and hang on.

THOMAS JEFFERSON

Serving as a navigational aid to maritime interests in and around Plymouth Bay, the Gurnet Point Lighthouse is a thirty-four-foot white octagonal wooden tower, the successor to the light constructed here in 1768. John Thomas, descended from a distinguished Massachusetts family, was appointed the first keeper of the light, which was constructed on land provided by him and his wife, Hannah. When the Revolutionary War forced John to bid farewell to his family in 1775, Hannah assumed her husband's duties, thus becoming the first female lighthouse keeper in American history. If modern accounts are true, Hannah has never abandoned her post. Her ghost maintains a lonely vigil at the light, apparently waiting for her husband, who never returned from the war fought so long ago.

Cognizant that Plymouth was one of the primary ports in New England, the Massachusetts legislature in 1768 appropriated funds to construct a light at Gurnet Point at the northern corner of the mouth of Plymouth Bay. The eighth lighthouse built in the colonies, it was America's first twin lighthouse, lanterns being affixed to each end of the thirty-foot-long keeper's house.

John Thomas was an experienced soldier, having served as a physician during the French and Indian War. Once political difficulties arose with Great Britain, he assumed a prominent role in the Sons of Liberty. Early in 1775, he raised a regiment of Massachusetts volunteers and prepared for the coming maelstrom.

Less than six weeks after the battles at Lexington and Concord, authorities notified John of his appointment as brigadier general of Massachusetts troops. Upon receiving orders to report to active duty, the six-foot-tall, fifty-one-year-old officer broke the news to Hannah. She reportedly responded, "But what about the lighthouse?" John countered, "I know you can handle it, Hannah. And the fee for keeping the lights will be very useful to you while I am gone."

For the first year following John's departure, Hannah saw to it that the lamps burned every night. A small military garrison was stationed at Gurnet Point, where Fort Andrew, a crude six-cannon battery, was constructed in a desperate attempt to protect the light. A gun battle with a British warship, the HMS *Niger*, resulted in damage to the walls of the lighthouse and the destruction of one of the lights. The Gurnet Point facility thereby gained the distinction of being the only American lighthouse pierced by artillery fire during the war.

In 1776, Hannah decided to extinguish the light because its signal had become beneficial to ships of the Royal Navy regularly attacking unarmed American merchant vessels in the waters off Massachusetts.

About the same time, Hannah's soldier husband attracted the attention of General George Washington, thanks to his leadership at the siege of Boston. John Thomas was promoted to major general and dispatched to participate in American incursions against British positions in Canada. He would not return alive. Exposed to smallpox near Montreal, he died on June 2, 1776.

Following John's death, Hannah remained at the darkened lighthouse, where she did all she could to aid the cause of independence. On Christmas night in 1778, the *General Arnold*, an American privateer, ran aground near Gurnet Point during a blizzard. Hannah's valiant effort to make her way to aid the stranded vessel was unsuccessful because of ice floes in the harbor.

At the conclusion of the war, Hannah resumed operation of the light as its keeper.

In 1789, the ninth law enacted by the new federal Congress provided for the establishment of a series of lighthouses along the coast. A year later, the United States government assumed operation of all lighthouses on the Atlantic seaboard. By that time, Hannah's son, John Jr., had reached sufficient age to assume the keeper's duties from his aging mother. Accordingly, General Benjamin Lincoln, then serving as superintendent of lighthouses, wrote to Alexander Hamilton, the secretary of the treasury, "I have now with me Mr. Thomas, son of the late General Thomas, whose mother has the care of the lighthouse at Plymouth. When she was first appointed to that trust, he was a minor; otherwise he probably would have had the appointment himself. He is a young gentleman of good character and I think is a fair candidate for the appointment under the United States."

In the years since her death, Hannah's spirit has remained at the lighthouse and its replacement, erected in 1843. Even the automation of the light in 1986 did not lead her to abandon her post. When the structure was moved 140 feet inland in 1999 to protect it from toppling over a 45-foot cliff, Hannah's spirit made the move. Apparently, she is duty bound to the place.

Visitors and maintenance staff have witnessed the misty figure of Hannah Thomas on the lighthouse grounds. But the most haunting of all recent encounters occurred when a husband-and-wife photography team spent the night in the keeper's house. Describing their eerie experience, the wife said, "At some point, something woke Bob. He raised up on his elbow and watched the light come around, illuminating the windows for five seconds each time. Then he looked over toward [where I] was sleeping soundly. Above me, he saw the head and shoulders of a woman. He described her as being a green electric spark color. He said she had an old time hairdo, sunken cheeks, and the saddest face he ever saw. Bob told me that she wasn't wrinkled and he didn't think she was an old woman. He said he felt no threat from her, but only her sadness. As he watched her, out of the corner of his eye he could see the rays of the lighthouse come around several times, brightening the room. He looked toward the light, then looked back to where she had been and she was gone."

Throughout the Revolutionary War, countless American women kept the home fires burning for their men who were away in military service. Some of those soldiers returned. Others like General John Thomas did not. Through the centuries, the ghost of his beloved wife has kept their special light burning, hoping and waiting for his return—in spirit, at least.

The **Gurnet Point Lighthouse** is open to the public one day each year—the Saturday of Memorial Day weekend. However, the keeper's quarters are available for nightly or weekly rental. For information, contact the Massachusetts Chapter of the U.S. Lighthouse Society, 314 Spring St., Hanson, Mass. 02341.

Haunted by the Shot Heard Round the World
LEXINGTON AND CONCORD, MASSACHUSETTS

By the rude bridge that arched the flood,
Their flag to April's breeze unfurled,
Here once the embattled farmers stood,
And fired the shot heard round the world.

RALPH WALDO EMERSON

April 19, 1775, is recognized as one of the red-letter days in the history of the American republic. On that date, the political feud between the thirteen colonies and the British government erupted into a clash of arms. American freedom fighters—comprised of Minutemen, militia troops, and armed farmers—intercepted British troops as they marched the eighteen miles from Boston to Concord to arrest Sam Adams and John Hancock and destroy the military supplies of the colonists. Today, this famous route is known as Battle Road. Numerous markers and structures related to what Ralph Waldo Emerson called "the shot heard round the world" are in the area. Two buildings, one in

Lexington and one in Concord, stand much as they did on that spring day in 1775. The ghosts dwelling in them represent the very people who were eyewitnesses to the blood spilled in the fighting that opened the curtain on the Revolutionary War.

General Thomas Gage, the British commander in chief in America and the military governor of Massachusetts, set the stage for Lexington and Concord just after he landed in Boston in April 1775. He ordered a sizable military force, including eight hundred elite red-coated soldiers, to make ready for action. Lieutenant Colonel Francis Smith, a rather portly fifty-two-year-old officer, was given command of the troops.

Although the purpose and destination of the mission were highly guarded secrets, word of its planning leaked to a prominent Boston Patriot leader, Dr. Joseph Warren (who would subsequently die at the Battle of Bunker Hill). Warren hastily directed Paul Revere and William Dawes, two of Boston's most energetic Patriots, to prepare to sound the alarm to Hancock, Adams, and the citizens of the neighboring villages. By the evening of April 18, word was about the streets of Boston that a British troop movement was likely. At ten o'clock, Paul Revere made arrangements with friends in nearby Charlestown for the famous "One if by land, two if by sea" signal to be flashed by lantern from the belfry of the Old North Church. And then he was off on the road to Lexington. En route, he reportedly shouted his famous cry: "The British are coming! The British are coming!"

Just after midnight, Revere and Dawes met up in Lexington. Less than two hours later, they were spreading the warning along the road to Concord when Revere was captured by a British patrol. Dawes escaped and galloped back to Lexington, where he persuaded Dr. Samuel Prescott to join him in the call to arms.

As the sun rose on Wednesday, April 19, the vanguard of the British army, commanded by Major John Pitcairn, marched toward the town green in Lexington, where it came face to face with four dozen armed Minutemen commanded by Captain John Parker. Immediately, the British regulars assumed a battle formation. As the tension mounted,

Captain Parker attempted to steady his nervous charges. Legend has it that Parker shouted, "Don't fire unless fired upon! But if they want a war, let it begin right here!"

As the minutes passed, Parker surmised that the standoff would end without gunfire and ordered his men to stand down. As the Americans began to disassemble, a single shot from an unknown British triggerman broke the stillness. Then came another and another. A British officer screamed, "Fire!" and two platoons of Redcoats emptied their weapons into the disbanding Patriots. Only a half-dozen or so of Parker's men were able to return fire, and the Battle of Lexington came to a swift end. Eight Americans were killed and ten wounded.

Among those who witnessed the terrible events that morning were the residents of the Jacob Whittemore House. Now used as a dwelling place by rangers at Minuteman National Historical Park, the structure is also home to the ghosts of former residents who had a ringside seat to the bloodshed at Lexington.

Children of a park ranger have reported seeing the ghost of a little boy in colonial dress playing with and taking their toys. Rangers and their families have heard strange noises throughout the house. Phantom footsteps are common. Doorknobs turn without a human hand touching them.

Before the National Park Service acquired the Whittemore place, previous owners claimed that the house was haunted by spectres from the American Revolution. Some witnessed the shadowy figure of an unidentified man in the clothing of olden times, while others were terrified by a misty white female ghost without feet roaming the ancient corridors.

In the aftermath of the attack at Lexington, the British squadron marched on Concord, six miles distant. By seven that morning, Colonel Smith's advance units reached the outskirts of the town. But thanks to the overnight ride of Samuel Prescott, the townspeople had almost six hours' notice. During that time, most of the military stores Smith was under orders to destroy had been hidden. Additionally, more than 150 citizens from surrounding villages had rushed to Concord to join the three companies of Minutemen assembled to rudely greet the invaders.

When the Redcoats entered town, they crossed the Old North Bridge over the Concord River without resistance. They marched to the Barrett farm, where they were dismayed to find that the military stockpile had disappeared.

The Redcoats then turned their attention to Concord Town Hall, in the center of the village. As they searched it, a fire, most likely accidental, began to ravage the building.

Minutemen, some three hundred to four hundred strong, watched the enemy from a position on the high ground above the Old North Bridge. Observing the smoke billowing from the town hall and assuming the raiders were burning their public buildings and homes, they sprang into action. Upon crossing the bridge, they encountered nearly one hundred Redcoats awaiting orders. The British regulars fired warning shots into the water. Undeterred, Joseph Hosmer, one of the American officers, yelled to his men, "Will you let them burn the town down?" In unison, the Minutemen screamed, "No!" Then came the order from another Patriot officer, Major John Butterick: "Fire, for God's sake, fire!" Within five minutes, the British soldiers at the bridge were in full retreat.

Unlike the affair at Lexington, the Redcoats suffered significant losses at Concord. Nineteen of their officers and 250 men were killed or wounded. American casualties were estimated at 90.

Many of the Minutemen were carried to the nearby home of Dr. Timothy Minot, which was hastily converted into a makeshift hospital. There, Dr. Minot waged a desperate struggle to save as many Patriot lives as possible.

His home, expanded many times since the battle, is now the centerpiece of Concord's historic Colonial Inn, located in the center of town. The inn seems to have one permanent resident—the ghost of the Revolutionary War surgeon. Many supernatural occurrences have taken place over the years. Room 24 has been the site of most of them.

Dr. Minot's spirit remains at work in that room, tending the ill.

Not many years ago, a guest in the room awoke at 2:45 one morning with an excruciating stomachache, which she attributed to overeating the previous evening. Familiar with stories about Dr. Minot's ghost, the lady, a flutist with the Wellesley Symphony Orchestra, called out for the phantom physician. She explained what happened next: "I was flat on my back, arms at my sides, when I suddenly felt a tingling sensation in the back of my head, hairs standing straight on end like goose bumps. The tingling sensation quickly traveled through my body. I felt as if electricity were going through me; I was slightly vibrating and my body was rigid. My eyelids were fluttering as my body vibrated, but I could not move. I was paralyzed. The total experience lasted only 3–5 seconds, then disappeared. There may have been four episodes like this. I seemed to be more relaxed after each episode and was finally able to sleep. . . . I can't help but wonder if Dr. Minot not only made his presence known to me but also eased my stomachache."

Another incident involving the spirit of the good doctor took place in Room 24 one evening in 1966. "I have always prided myself on being a sane individual, but on the night of June 14, I began to have my doubts," a guest recounted. "On that night I saw a ghost. . . . I was awakened in the middle of the night by a presence in the room. . . . As I opened my eyes, I saw a grayish figure at the side of the bed, to the left, about four feet away. It was not a distinct person but a shadowy figure that remained still for a moment and then floated to the foot of the bed, in front of the fireplace. After pausing for a few seconds, the apparition slowly melted away."

Other guests have also been spooked in the room. On one occasion, just after a woman had repeatedly failed in her attempts to lock the room door, the fire alarm sounded, forcing an evacuation of the building. When she returned to her room, the guest found that the lock worked perfectly.

Some guests have complained that the air conditioning in Room 24 was much too cold during their stay. Upon inspection, inn employees have discovered that the unit was not even turned on. Others have reported a ghostlike figure ruffling their bed coverings.

Dr. Minot's spirit has made its presence known in other portions of the inn as well. One evening, a bartender commented that she did not believe in ghosts. No sooner had the words left her mouth than the glass in her hand shattered, causing a deep laceration that required medical attention. On yet another night, employees in the reception area were discussing the inn's haunted past when books flew off the shelves with great force.

Perhaps Dr. Minot and the Jacob Whittemore family witnessed "the shot heard round the world" on April 19, 1775. No doubt, they saw the carnage on that memorable day in American history. And now it seems they have never been able to let go of those sights and sounds.

The address for **Minuteman National Historical Park** is 174 Liberty St., Concord, Mass. 01742; the telephone number is 978-369-6993. The address for the **Colonial Inn** is 48 Monument Sq., Concord, Mass. 01743; the telephone number is 800-370-9200.

Other "Spirited" Revolutionary War Sites in Massachusetts, Briefly Noted

BOSTON—THE FREEDOM TRAIL

Boston was the site of many of the events and the home of many of the people who played prominent roles in the war for independence. Today, the Freedom Trail, a two-and-a-half-mile red-brick walking trail, provides a fascinating look at more than a dozen historic structures and places—including the Bunker Hill Monument, the site of the Boston Massacre, the Paul Revere House, and the burial ground of famous Patriots—related to the American Revolution.

Along the route, visitors commonly report ghostly sightings and other supernatural events. In summer, cold spots are experienced on the trail. Phantomlike figures in colonial attire often turn up in pictures taken at landmarks. Apparitions from the Revolutionary War sometimes approach pedestrians in a pleasant manner, only to fade into the mist.

The address for contacting the Freedom Trail is 99 Chauncey St., #401, Boston, Mass. 02111; the telephone number is 617-357-8300.

BOSTON—GRANARY BURYING GROUND

This historic cemetery adjoining Boston Common holds the graves of many people whose names are etched in the history of the American

Revolution—John Hancock, Samuel Adams, and Robert Treat Paine (all signers of the Declaration of Independence), the victims of the Boston Massacre, and Paul Revere.

On occasion, a ghostly image has been seen and photographed directly in front of Revere's tombstone. The strange, misty form is said to represent the spirit of the famed Patriot who made the midnight ride to warn neighboring towns that the British were on the march.

The graveyard, included on the Freedom Trail, is on Tremont Street at its junction with Bromfield Street in Boston.

BOSTON—SITE OF THE BOSTON MASSACRE

One of the most famous events precipitating the American Revolution took place in Boston on March 5, 1770, when a rather insignificant quarrel between a British soldier and an apprentice wigmaker resulted in the confrontation acclaimed by Samuel Adams as the Boston Massacre. Five Bostonians died that day after British soldiers opened fire on a crowd of club-wielding, rock-throwing civilians. Of the American casualties, the name of only one is generally recognized today—Crispus Attucks. According to legend, his ghost haunts the spot where he fell.

A circle of cobblestones near the Old State House marks the site of the red-letter event. On the anniversary of the massacre, the apparition of Attucks has been seen here. When his ghost is approached, it suddenly collapses, as if reenacting the fateful moment in 1770.

The Old State House is located at the intersection of State and Congress streets in Boston.

CAMBRIDGE—APTHORP HOUSE

Constructed in 1760, this exquisite frame structure was one of the finest and largest houses in Cambridge in Revolutionary War times. The ghost of a British general remains in residence at the historic structure, which has been incorporated into Adams House, the most historic home on the Harvard University campus.

In 1775, General Israel Putnam sequestered Apthorp as his temporary headquarters as he planned the Battle of Bunker Hill. Two years later, British general John Burgoyne was held as a prisoner of war in the mansion after his surrender to General Horatio Gates at the Battle of Saratoga. Tradition has it that Burgoyne voiced his disgust about the furnishings, or lack thereof, at Apthorp. Apparently, his discontent lingers, because his ghost continues to roam the venerable structure.

The address for Adams House (which includes Apthorp House) is 26 Plympton St., Cambridge, Mass. 02138.

CHARLEMONT—THE CHARLEMONT INN

Located in the Berkshires in western Massachusetts, this eighteenth-century inn is haunted by at least a half-dozen very active ghosts. One of them is an unidentified Revolutionary War soldier. Among the supernatural activities reported have been slamming doors, flying objects (such as potato chips and coffee) thrown by an invisible hand, and disembodied footsteps.

The address for the inn is Route 2, Mohawk Trail, Charlemont, Mass. 01339; the telephone number is 413-339-5796.

CHARLESTOWN—BUNKER HILL MONUMENT

Located atop Breed's Hill on the outskirts of Boston, the Bunker Hill Monument towers 221 feet to honor the gallant Americans who took part in the first major battle of the Revolutionary War, fought here on June 17, 1775. Construction of the granite obelisk began in 1824, when the Marquis de Lafayette assisted in the laying of the cornerstone.

Patriot ghosts thought to represent victims of the battle are said to inhabit the shaft. Apparently, they are unaware that the great battle concluded long ago. On occasion, a spectre is said to climb the 294 steps to the top of the monument and shout, "Those bloody Brits!" Some visitors have reported hearing the faint sound of gunfire around the monument. Perhaps the resident ghosts are continuing to wage the first battle on the road to American independence.

The address for the Bunker Hill Monument is 42 Monument Sq., Charlestown, Mass. 02129; the telephone number is 617-242-5641.

NORTHAMPTON—SESSIONS HOUSE

In 1710, Captain Jonathan Hunt erected the grand dwelling that survives as the oldest house on the campus of Smith College. The ghosts of Hunt's granddaughter and her paramour, British general John Burgoyne, are said to reside here. While "Gentleman Johnny" was being held as a prisoner of war at Sessions House, he and Lucy began a secretive affair. Although the real-life Burgoyne never legitimized his relationship with Lucy, their spirits have often been seen renewing their romance on the staircase in the house.

Sessions House is located on Elm Street in Northampton. The telephone number at Smith College is 413-584-2700.

SUDBURY—LONGFELLOW'S WAYSIDE INN

Dating from 1716, this bed-and-breakfast takes its name from Henry Wadsworth Longfellow, who penned his *Tales of a Wayside Inn* while staying here in 1862. During the Revolutionary War, the hostelry was known as Howe's Tavern. Its owner was Ezekiel Howe, who also served as colonel of the Sudbury militia. A stalwart Patriot, Howe marched his men to Concord Common on that fateful April 19, 1775. To this day, visitors to the ten-room inn report the distinct sounds of cannon fire and fifes. Howe and his men, in supernatural form, seem to be duty bound.

The address for this landmark is 72 Wayside Inn Rd., Sudbury, Mass. 01776; the telephone number is 800-399-1776.

UXBRIDGE—OLD TAFT TAVERN

Built in 1770 by Samuel Taft as both a tavern and a home for his twenty-two children, this large gambrel-roofed building served as an inviting place for independence-minded Americans during the Revolutionary War. Taft's personal friend George Washington enjoyed the hospitality here.

After serving the American cause during the war, Taft resumed his duties as owner of the tavern until his death. His spirit has never left. Over the years, guests have been awakened by the spectre of a man standing at the foot of their bed. The ghost, dressed in colonial clothing, reportedly bears a striking resemblance to Taft.

Located on Sutton Street, the building now serves as a private residence and is not open to the public.

WEST STOCKBRIDGE—TOM BALL MOUNTAIN

Franz Wagner, a Hessian soldier in the command of General John Burgoyne, was wounded at the Battle of Saratoga in 1777. He managed to escape capture when the British surrendered. During his flight, Wagner stumbled across the New York border into western Massachusetts, where he died in the village of North Egremont. He was buried there. Soon, his ghost began making appearances throughout the area. Frightened citizens were afraid to leave their homes after the sun set.

Neighborhood men, anxious to rid the place of the supernatural force, reasoned that if they dug up Wagner's coffin and reinterred it in another locale, the Hessian warrior might rest in peace. They loaded the coffin onto a wagon under the cloak of darkness and proceeded some miles north to Tom Ball Mountain, a prominent landmark. Suddenly, the stillness of the night was disturbed by horrible screams. Looking behind them, they witnessed the misty apparition of Franz Wagner sitting atop his coffin. The ghost attempted to talk before fading into the night. The frightened men promptly dug a hole, threw the coffin in, covered the grave, and fled the scene without marking it.

Although Wagner's ghost has never again been seen in North Egremont, it has been spotted in the forested areas of the mountain and around the town of West Stockbridge, north of Tom Ball.

West Stockbridge is located on Mass. 41 near the New York border.

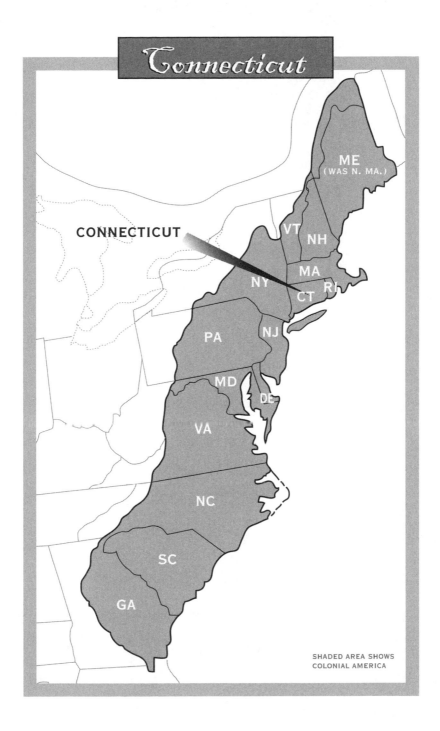

Connecticut

CONNECTICUT

ME
(WAS N. MA.)

VT
NH
MA
NY
RI
CT
NJ
PA
MD
DE
VA
NC
SC
GA

SHADED AREA SHOWS
COLONIAL AMERICA

The Haunts of a Cherished American Hero
COVENTRY, CONNECTICUT

Every kind of service, necessary to the public good, becomes honorable by being necessary.

NATHAN HALE

At 2299 South Street in Coventry, Connecticut, stands the Hale Homestead, an expansive multistory dwelling that dates from 1746, when Deacon Richard Hale settled here. He and other members of his family continue at the place in spirit form. Deacon Hale's sixth child, whose wartime sacrifice made him a legendary American hero, may be one of the supernatural entities at the house, now operated as a museum.

The little lad born at the Hale Homestead on June 6, 1755, was so frail that even his father, a highly respected man about Coventry, did not believe he would survive. But the infant lived, thrived, and grew to manhood. In 1773, on the eve of the American Revolution, Nathan Hale graduated from Yale University with honors at the age of eighteen.

Nathan was a young schoolteacher and a licensed minister when news of the Battle of Lexington reached New London, Connecticut. There, at a subsequent town meeting, he took the floor and proclaimed an exhortation to action: "Let us march immediately, and never lay down our arms until we have obtained independence."

Putting his defiant words into action, Nathan promptly volunteered for service in the Continental Army. Despite his youth, his natural skills as a soldier and his ardent commitment to American liberty led to his rapid promotion.

By early 1776, matters were bleak for the independence-minded colonies. Little or no money was available to pay the Continental Army. Nathan Hale reached into his own savings for the men in his command so they could continue waging the fight against Great Britain.

Several months later, General George Washington summoned his high-ranking officers to a meeting, at which he explained his desperate need for a trustworthy spy to provide detailed information about the plans of the British army. The assembled officers knew well that, if captured, an American spy would be executed. Captain Nathan Hale, who had just returned to active duty from illness, broke the hush at the council of war by saying to General Washington, "I will undertake it, Sir."

After securing invaluable intelligence behind enemy lines, Nathan, dressed as a Dutch schoolmaster, had set out to report to Washington when he was taken prisoner by British soldiers on Long Island. Soon thereafter, he was condemned by General William Howe to die as a spy.

In the early-morning hours of Sunday, September 22, 1776, just two and a half months after the signing of the Declaration of Independence in Philadelphia, Nathan was taken to the gallows at First Avenue and Fifty-first Street in New York City. As the young man prayed, the British provost called out, "Make your dying speech." Legend has it that Nathan lifted his eyes and said in a loud, clear voice, "I regret I have but one life to lose for my country." Outraged by such defiance, the Brit screamed, "Swing the Rebel off!" His order was promptly obeyed, and Nathan Hale became a martyr for the cause of American liberty.

Nathan's bereaved father lived in the family homestead until his death in 1802. The house and surrounding farm remained in the family for many years thereafter.

By the dawn of the twentieth century, the Hale place was abandoned and hastening to ruin. In 1914, George Dudley Seymour, a local patent attorney, purchased it. An admirer of Nathan Hale, Seymour went about restoring the house and grounds to their former glory. Meanwhile, he conducted extensive research about the legends surrounding the Hale family. In the course of his investigation, he learned that the house had been haunted for many years. Countless eyewitnesses have since verified his findings.

The ghost of Deacon Richard Hale inhabits the premises. Not long after Seymour acquired the house, he was anxious to show it to a friend. Upon their arrival by buggy, the excited friend jumped out and made haste to the old Hale family schoolroom. As he peered through the window, he was startled to see the apparition of Deacon Hale staring at him, as if trying to determine who was about to enter.

A female ghost thought to be that of Lydia Carpenter, a housekeeper for the Hale family, has made appearances in the restored main house. In life, Lydia was known as a nosy individual, always sneaking around to pick up family gossip. Likewise, her apparition has been observed eavesdropping about the house. Her broom is often heard sweeping the floors.

Six of Deacon Hale's sons rendered service in the Continental Army. One of Nathan's brothers, Lieutenant Joseph Hale, was wounded and captured by the British at Fort Washington, New York, in mid-November 1776. Incarcerated as a prisoner of war, he was subsequently exchanged. Lieutenant Hale survived the war and returned to his father's homestead in Coventry. However, he could never erase the horrors of war from his mind. Since his death in 1784, the sounds of rattling prison chains have emanated from the cellar of the Hale house.

One of Nathan's older brothers, Lieutenant John Hale, is also said to abide at the homestead in spirit form. He and his wife, Sarah, died in the house just months after the passing of Deacon Hale. The ghosts of the couple have been heard walking down the interior steps.

When George Seymour died in 1945, "the Birthplace," as the home had long been known in homage to Nathan, devolved to the Antiquarian and Landmarks Society, which has since maintained the property as a museum. From time to time, Revolutionary War reenactors camp at the homestead and parade about the grounds to entertain and educate visitors. But when the reenactors are not in residence, some patrons have noticed apparitional Revolutionary War soldiers on the grounds. Could those ghosts be Joseph and John Hale, or even Nathan?

No one has ever specifically identified Nathan's ghost at his birthplace, but some have sensed his presence in one of the bedrooms. As an adult, Rebecca Hale, one of Joseph's three daughters, recalled that during her childhood, a "shadow portrait" of her famous uncle had appeared on the back of her chamber door. On a visit to her former home many years later, Rebecca was dismayed to find that the image had been painted over.

When George Seymour learned of Rebecca's story, he had the paint stripped from the door. Once again, the silhouette of Nathan Hale appeared, drawn on the wood with a pencil. Perhaps Nathan's spirit is at rest in the home where he developed the undying love of the country for which he so willingly gave his life.

The **Nathan Hale Homestead** is open to the public. Its address is 2299 South St., Coventry, Conn. 06238; the telephone number is 860-742-6917.

Legendary Generals Never Die, They Just Become Ghosts
BROOKLYN, CONNECTICUT

Men, you are all marksmen—don't one of you fire until you see the whites of the eyes.

GENERAL ISRAEL PUTNAM

Located in northeastern Connecticut, Brooklyn is the burial place of one of the most legendary generals in American history. Near the town green, a magnificent bronze statue rests atop the sarcophagus of General Israel Putnam (1718–90). At the outbreak of the Revolutionary War, Putnam was already an American folk hero. His subsequent heroics at the Battle of Bunker (or Breed's) Hill served only to increase his reputation. Now, his ghost continues to perpetuate the fame of "Old Put" more than two centuries later.

Born in Salem, Massachusetts, Putnam learned at an early age what it was like to live in the public spotlight. His father, Joseph, was an outspoken opponent of the witchcraft trials famous in the town. When fellow citizens began to look upon Joseph as a warlock, the Putnam family faced threats to their lives. Consequently, the gun was always loaded and the horses saddled at Israel's childhood home.

In 1739, twenty-one-year-old Israel Putnam settled with his wife on a farm in the Mortlake district of northeastern Connecticut. Less than four years later, he emerged as a local hero when he killed a wolf that had attacked some six dozen goats and sheep on area farms. Local farmers resolved to lure the she-wolf from its rocky den. An effort to smoke the animal out proved futile. When a hound was sent into the den, it quickly scurried away yelping, its body deeply lacerated. A slave who witnessed the dog's wounds refused to enter the cave. Determined to put an end to the menace, the diminutive Putnam, standing only five-foot-six, crawled into the darkness with a torch. Fellow farmers tied a rope to his ankles, agreeing to pull him to safety if he encountered trouble. After making his way twenty-five feet into the cave, Putnam caught sight of the wolf's glaring eyes and deadly teeth. When he signaled his friends to pull him out so he could get his gun, they dragged him with such haste that he sustained painful bruises and cuts. Undeterred, he reentered the cave with his weapon. One squeeze of the trigger produced a deafening blast, a cloud of smoke, and a dead wolf. Today, wolf heads adorn the monument at Putnam's grave, and the nearby cave is preserved as part of a state park.

From 1755 to 1765, Putnam proved himself an intrepid Indian fighter as an officer in the French and Indian War. His miraculous escapes from death won the acclaim of soldiers and citizens. Once, he came close to being burned alive by his Indian captors. At the close of the hostilities, Putnam returned home as a lieutenant colonel. His body bore scars from fifteen serious combat wounds.

A ten-year respite from active military duty allowed him to recuperate and prosper on his Connecticut farm. Meanwhile, he was an ardent member of the Sons of Liberty.

Putnam and a team of oxen were laboring in his fields on the morning of Thursday, April 20, 1775, when a courier galloped up to deliver the news of the clash at Lexington, Massachusetts. Because he was a colonel in the Connecticut militia, Putnam immediately turned the reins over to his son, Daniel. He mounted his horse, blew a kiss to his wife, and sped away to assemble his warriors. Then, over an eighteen-hour period, he rode a hundred miles to reach Cambridge, Massachusetts.

Upon arriving at the scene of the action, Colonel Putnam was included in the councils of war leading up to the Battle of Bunker Hill on June 20. In that battle, he was the officer around whom the Americans rallied. Amid the fierce fighting, Putnam steadied his charges by delivering one of the most memorable lines in American history: "Don't one of you fire until you see the whites of the eyes."

Just two days after the American victory at Bunker Hill, the Continental Congress appointed Putnam as a major general in the Continental Army.

During the siege of Boston, which lasted almost a year, he commanded the center of the American line. At the conclusion of the siege in the spring of 1776, Putnam and the bulk of the Continental Army were transferred to New York. Always daring, the major general displayed his disdain for the British while serving as American commander in the Hudson Highlands in 1777. William Tryon, the Royal governor of New York, dispatched a communiqué demanding the release of Nathan Palmer, a Tory in Putnam's custody. The fiery American general promptly offered a response:

> Sir:
>
> Nathan Palmer, a lieutenant in your service was taken in my camp as a spy; he was tried as a spy; he was condemned as a spy; and you must rest assured, sir, he shall be hanged as a spy.
>
> Israel Putnam
>
> To His Excellency Governor Tryon
>
> P.S. Afternoon. He is hanged.

By 1779, the many years of fighting and farming had taken a toll on the once-agile Putnam. Noted historian Douglas Southall Freeman observed, "A great name had lost its resonance. . . . The frail nag, reputation, could no longer carry an obese rider." That December, a stroke forced General Putnam to retire from active duty. Before he set out for home, Old Put reviewed his troops one last time. Tears streamed down the cheeks of the war-hardened soldiers as their commander bade them farewell and Godspeed. Israel Putnam spent the last few years of his life in what is now the town of Brooklyn, located near his old farm.

At least four locations in and around Brooklyn appear to be haunted by the general.

Pomfret, approximately seven miles from Brooklyn, is home to Mashamoquet Brook State Park, the site of the cave where young Israel tangled with the wolf. Some years back in Pomfret, the folks at the Abington Social Library, a public facility that dates to 1793, decided to honor Putnam by commissioning a wolf statue. Mysterious things began to happen almost as soon as construction commenced. The first two statues, crafted of wood, were destroyed by fires of unexplained origin. A third statue was delivered on an unusually warm winter day. Inside the library, however, every person experienced a distinct chill. And then they heard the unmistakable howl of a wolf. That night, the weather changed and snow blanketed the ground. The next morning, the prints of wolf paws were found about the library grounds.

Located in Brooklyn proper, Mortlake Manor is an expansive two-and-a-half-story frame building that served as the longtime residence of the Reverend Joseph Whitney, a close friend of Putnam. When the general died, his wake was held at the house. In the room where his lifeless body lay, a soldier in Revolutionary War garb has since been observed pacing the floor, only to disappear before the eyes of witnesses. Extensively modified in the twentieth century, Mortlake Manor has housed a post office, a rest home, and a bank. Bank employees have encountered numerous power outages and alarm problems for which no explanations have been forthcoming. Without being adjusted by human hands, radios in the bank suddenly blare music. Frequently, the apparition of a praying clergyman has been observed immediately before and after the radio disturbances.

When darkness envelops Brooklyn, eerie things occur on the grounds of the building now known as Mortlake Commons. A spectral Revolutionary War officer sits atop a phantom horse. Both disappear as soon as a light is directed toward them.

Next door stand the impressive statue and tomb of Israel Putnam, erected in 1888 on the town green. His earthly remains were reinterred here after being moved from the general's original grave site. Witnesses have reported seeing Putnam's ghost at the tomb and monument. His apparition usually materializes from ground fog. The ghostly Revolutionary War officer bears a striking likeness to the man honored by the statue.

Apparently, Old Put was not satisfied to leave this world as Connecticut's greatest folk hero. Instead, he has chosen to remind subsequent generations of the energy, zeal, patriotism, craftiness, and duty that were Israel Putnam.

The address for the **Israel Putnam Monument** is Conn. 169 (Canterbury Rd.) and U.S. 6, Brooklyn, Conn. 06234. The address for **Mashamoquet Brook State Park** is 147 Wolf Den Dr., Pomfret Center, Conn. 06259; the telephone number is 860-928-6121.

Other "Spirited" Revolutionary War Sites in Connecticut, Briefly Noted

CANTON—OLD ALBANY TURNPIKE

Canton, located in north-central Connecticut, is a small, sleepy town that was home to the Hosford Tavern, or Dudley Case's Tavern, during the Revolutionary War. One evening in 1781, a paymaster of the French army enjoyed the comforts of the inn as he prepared to set out early the next morning to deliver saddlebags heavily laden with gold and silver to his comrades in New York, who were anxiously awaiting their military pay. Locals in the tavern took special note of the officer's resplendent uniform and the weighted bags he carefully guarded while he took his meal.

Several months later, a group of French and American officers stopped at the tavern to inquire about the paymaster, who had never reached his destination. Indeed, no one had seen him on his intended route beyond Canton. The "cooperative" innkeeper told the officers that he had roused the Frenchman from slumber, provided him breakfast, and sent him on his way. Nonetheless, suspicion grew when several boys found the skeletal remains of a horse and the remnants of a fine saddle while fishing in a nearby pond. Horseshoes of a special design were still attached to the hooves. To make matters worse, the innkeeper seemed affluent despite a downturn in his business.

Over time, locals began to report the shocking sight of a headless horseman in a European cape galloping along the Albany Turnpike on dark nights. The sightings were still common in the early twentieth century when the old Hosford Tavern was ravaged by fire. During the cleanup, workmen discovered a male skeleton in the cellar. Some distance away, they found a human skull.

Even today, some area residents remain reluctant to travel the roads leading north from Canton on dark, cloudy nights for fear of coming upon the headless French officer, who still rides his ghost steed, intent upon completing the mission assigned to him so many years ago.

Canton is on U.S. 44.

EAST GRANBY—OLD NEW-GATE PRISON

Located north of Canton, the New-Gate Prison was established in 1773 at the site of an old copper mine. During the Revolutionary War, the facility was considered escape-proof. Consequently, it was used to house notorious Tories and other enemies of the American cause. General George Washington chose to incarcerate certain individuals he termed "atrocious villains" at New-Gate because of its reputation for security.

Wartime conditions at the prison were inhumane. Desperate prisoners attempted to escape through myriad tunnels. One guard was bayoneted to death during an escape attempt on May 18, 1781.

Now operated as a state historic site and museum, the remains of the old prison are haunted by ghosts of the American Revolution. Strange mists, apparitions, and ectoplasms have been sighted and photographed in and about the tunnels and subterranean holding cells.

The address for the Old New-Gate Museum is 115 Newgate Rd., East Granby, Conn. 06026; the telephone number is 860-653-3563.

NEW HAVEN—FORT NATHAN HALE

To protect the harbor at New Haven from British attacks, Connecticut authorities constructed a military outpost on a point southeast of the city. Named Fort Black Rock, the outpost, manned by just nineteen soldiers, surrendered to the British in 1779 during the Battle of New Haven. The invaders subsequently burned wooden barracks at the site.

In 1809, as America prepared to go to war again with Great Britain, the fortification was rebuilt and renamed Fort Nathan Hale in honor of Connecticut's Revolutionary War hero.

Today, the restored fort serves as a twenty-acre public park and museum. Phantom soldiers of old have been witnessed roaming the historic landscape. Green orbs have been photographed around a Revolutionary War cannon at the complex.

The address for Fort Nathan Hale/Fort Black Rock is Woodward Ave., New Haven, Conn. 06512; the telephone number is 203-946-8790.

NORTH STONINGTON—JOHN YORK HOUSE

John York built his namesake structure as a private residence in 1741. When the Revolutionary War began, it became an inn. For most of the years since, it has served as such.

As the fight for American independence raged, two friends in the Continental Army stopped here for rest and refreshment. As they relaxed with drink in the Great West Room, they enjoyed an engaging conversation until the talk turned to a certain lady. When the soldiers realized they were both in love with the same girl, their heated words led to a brawl. In the course of the fight, one of the men stabbed his friend to death and fled the scene. Days later, the despondent killer took his own life. The ghosts of the two soldiers have haunted the John York House for years.

Now operated as a bed-and-breakfast, the ancient structure has two supernatural residents from the eighteenth century who make their presence known in a variety of ways: furniture mysteriously moves; wall hangings change position without the aid of human hands; phantom footsteps pound the steps; clothes and shoes are piled in the middle of the floor; unusual noises sounding like cannon fire echo through the building; and pipe smoke is in evidence when no one is partaking. Psychic investigators have sensed the guilt and sadness of a spirit attired in a Revolutionary War uniform.

The address for the John York House is 1 Clark Falls Rd., North Stonington, Conn. 06359; the telephone number is 860-599-3075.

NORWICH—OLD NORWICHTOWN CEMETERY

No American officer of the Revolutionary War ranks higher on the roll of infamy than Benedict Arnold. Born in 1741 in Norwich, Connecticut, as Benedict Arnold V, he emerged as one of the most talented generals in George Washington's inner circle until he betrayed his country. Following his military service to Great Britain in the final years of the war, Arnold spent the remainder of his life in England. However, legend has it that his ghost returns to the town of his birth each Halloween for a special purpose.

On the night of October 31, a strange character in a cape covering a Continental Army uniform can be found standing at a marker in the Old Norwichtown Cemetery. After pausing at the grave of Hannah Waterman King Arnold, the mysterious figure wearing a tricorn limps away and disappears into the darkness. Hannah Arnold was the mother of General Benedict Arnold, who was twice wounded in the same leg during the war.

Old Norwichtown Cemetery, also known as Colonial Cemetery, is located off Town Street on Cemetery Lane in Norwich, Connecticut.

REDDING RIDGE—THE SPINNING WHEEL INN

Constructed in classic New England salt-box style in 1742, the Spinning Wheel was already a popular wayside inn by the time Connecticut joined the other colonies in the fight for independence. In 1777, Governor William Tryon of New York hastily marched his Loyalist forces past the inn en route to Danbury, where they would burn supplies intended for the American cause. Little did Tryon know that contraband was stored in secret rooms in the Spinning Wheel. Today, the ghost of the Patriot who built and stocked the special storage areas remains in residence at the inn.

The address for the Spinning Wheel Inn is Conn. 58, Redding Ridge, Conn. 06876; the telephone number is 203-938-2511.

TERRYVILLE—TORY DEN

In north-central Connecticut, a legendary cave formed by one huge rock leaning against another served as a hiding place for area Tories during the Revolutionary War. Known as Tory Den, the rocky enclosure had a sizable front entrance and a smaller opening at the rear. Local British sympathizers such as Chauncey Jerome, Steven Graves, Ebenezer Johnson, Joel Tuttle, and Moses Dunbar came and went as they attempted to avoid Patriots on the prowl for them.

Conditions in the cave were miserable, particularly during winter. Some Tories escaped capture by hiding here, while others like Tuttle and Dunbar met their fate at the end of a rope. The spirits of these unfortunate men are said to haunt Tory Den. At night, strange, inexplicable lights are seen in and around the cave. Moans and heavy breathing can be heard within the empty chamber.

To reach Tory Den, turn off U.S. 6 onto Hill Street in Terryville. Hill Street becomes West Chippers Hill Road. A hiking path leads to the site.

TOLLAND—DANIEL BENTON HOMESTEAD

Daniel Benton built this home of wood and brick in 1720. It is one of the most haunted places in Connecticut.

Daniel died in 1776. Little did he know of the tragedies that were to befall his three grandsons, who had already left the homestead to serve in the Continental Army. Two of the grandsons perished in battle. The third, Elisha, contracted smallpox while a prisoner of war. The twenty-four-year-old was exchanged in order that he might die at home. Back at the Benton place, Elisha's fiancée, Jemina Barrows, ministered to him. In a short time, she, too, came down with the dread disease. They died before they could marry. Elisha and Jemina were interred on the west lawn of the old house, but neither of their spirits could rest. Visitors to the historic site regularly see the ghost of Jemina attired in the dress she was to wear at her wedding. Elisha's apparition has been encountered on the grounds and in the house, apparently looking for his intended. Phantom sounds of weeping echo throughout the dwelling.

Other Revolutionary War ghosts are also in residence here. In 1777, two dozen Hessian soldiers were confined in the cellar. At least one of them is believed to have died at the Benton place. Unearthly noises frequently come from the cellar. The spectre of a German soldier sometimes appears on the steps leading up to the house.

The Daniel Benton Homestead is operated as a museum by the Tolland Historical Society. The homestead's address is 160 Metcalf Rd., Tolland, Conn. 06084; the telephone number is 860-974-1875.

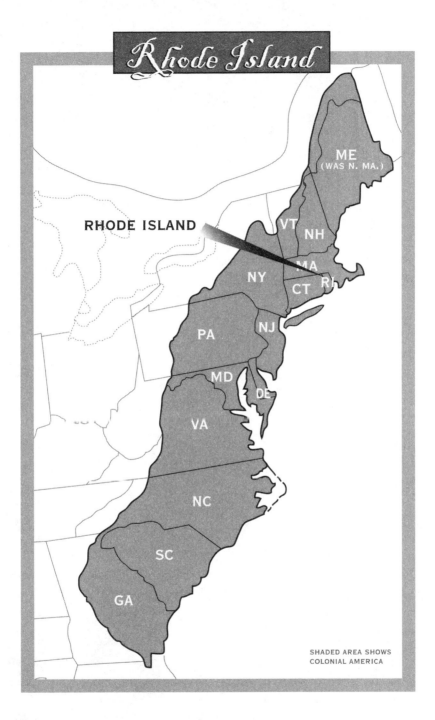

Rhode Island

RHODE ISLAND

ME
(WAS N. MA.)

VT
NH
NY
MA
CT
RI
NJ
PA
MD
DE
VA
NC
SC
GA

SHADED AREA SHOWS
COLONIAL AMERICA

Ghosts of a Revolutionary Affair
PORTSMOUTH, RHODE ISLAND

I am perfectly tranquil in mind and prepared for any fate which an honest zeal for my King's service may have devoted me.

JOHN ANDRÉ

On maps prepared by the United States Geological Survey, historic Aquidneck Island is listed by its formal geographic name, Rhode Island. In contrast, the official name of the political entity of which Rhode Island is a part is "the State of Rhode Island and Providence Plantations."

Throughout the Revolutionary War, Aquidneck Island was prized as a naval base, thanks to its proximity to ever-vulnerable New York. From the fall of 1776 until 1779, British army and navy forces controlled the island and its outstanding harbor. During the occupation, one of the most important officers on Aquidneck was Major General Richard Prescott. Although Prescott died in England in 1788, his ghost and that of his lover dwell at the Prescott Farm, located on R.I. 114 (West Main Street) near its junction with Union Street in Portsmouth.

When Richard Prescott arrived on Aquidneck Island in December

1776 to assume command of the British occupation forces there, he was already a marked man in the eyes of freedom-seeking Americans. Friend and foe alike considered Prescott haughty, arrogant, insolent, and splenetic. His harsh treatment of Ethan Allen after the Vermonter was taken prisoner in November 1775 had made him one of the most disliked men in America.

Prescott resided in two places on Aquidneck Island. His town house was the dwelling of John Bannister at 56 Pelham Street in Newport. In the countryside, the general used the Henry Overing House, a red two-and-a-half-story gambrel-roofed wooden structure now preserved as a part of the Prescott Farm restoration.

Anxious to exact revenge against Prescott for his mistreatment of Ethan Allen, Major William Barton of the Continental Army planned a daring raid to capture the general. Acting on intelligence that Prescott was spending time at the Overing residence with light security, Barton launched an expedition designed to nab him. On the night of July 4, 1777, Barton's well-trained commandos entered Mount Hope Bay in boats from the American fort at Tiverton. After spending several days recruiting volunteers, the Patriot raiders left their assembly area on the night of July 9 and reached their destination without detection early the following morning. Under the cloak of darkness, they stormed the Overing House and captured Prescott in his bedroom literally with his pants down. They pried the shocked officer from the arms of his lover and took him as a prisoner of war.

When news of the shameful incident made its way to London, Prescott was widely ridiculed by the British press. In the colonies, Major Barton was acclaimed a hero.

For nearly a year, Prescott languished in an American prison. On May 6, 1778, he was exchanged for General Charles Lee, the officer regarded by many as second only to George Washington in the American chain of command.

Ample evidence exists that the lovers surprised in flagrante delicto at the Overing House that summer night in 1777 remain in residence in supernatural form. The most notable encounters with the phantom lovers occurred in the second decade of the twentieth century. At the time, the historic dwelling was owned by Kittymouse Cook. One afternoon while Mrs. Cook's father was busy installing plumbing and electrifying the house, he commented to his daughter, "There's the prettiest girl in your house, over in the corner near the closet." No other human was about at the time. A year or so later, the female apparition was spotted by Mrs. Cook, who described the ghost of Prescott's paramour thusly: "She was in the prettiest water-silk taffeta dress with a small, tight bodice and little velvet buttons. She had black hair, parted in the middle. Gradually she just faded away."

Reports have also circulated of the "spirited" presence of General Prescott at the site of his romantic escapades and great humiliation. On one occasion, Benjamin Cook, Kittymouse's husband, heard what sounded to be a heavy boot drop in an upstairs bedroom. He laid aside his newspaper and inquired of his wife as to the identity of the person on the second floor. When she responded that no one else was in the house, Benjamin noted, "Oh, Kittymouse, you and your ghosts." He scrambled up the steps and made a thorough inspection of the upper stories but found nothing. No sooner had he returned to the first-floor library and resumed his reading than loud footsteps bounded down the stairs and out of the house.

Now open to the public as a historic landmark, the house is an integral part of the Prescott Farm restoration. Visitors to Richard Prescott's former boudoir might want to knock before they enter. Otherwise, they might surprise the resident ghosts, just as Major Barton did their human counterparts so many, many years ago.

For more information on the **Prescott Farm**, contact the Newport Restoration Foundation, 51 Touro St., Newport, R.I. 02840; the telephone number is 401-849-7300.

The March of the Spectral Hessians
PORTSMOUTH, RHODE ISLAND

*Bodily decay is gloomy in prospect, but of all human
contemplations, the most abhorrent is body without mind.*

THOMAS JEFFERSON

Aquidneck Island, the largest landmass in Narragansett Bay, was
the site of the largest Revolutionary War battle in Rhode Island. Three
towns—Portsmouth, Middletown, and Newport—share the island that
hosted the ferocious but rather indecisive Battle of Rhode Island on
August 29, 1778.

A number of historical markers call attention to the sites of the
fighting, in which the Continental Army and the French fleet failed in
a coordinated attempt to wrest the island from British control. Consequently, visitors enjoying a pleasant afternoon drive to the many resorts
on the modern island should not be surprised when they encounter
Revolutionary War reenactors walking the historic byways. But on
nights when thick fog drifts over the landscape and masks the route
of R.I. 114, motorists often strain their eyes to avoid smashing into the

phantom legion of five dozen Hessian troops marching on the roadside. Over the years, numerous encounters with this band of ruffian soldier ghosts have been recorded.

Nearly thirty thousand German mercenaries—commonly known as Hessians because the majority came from the Hesse-Kassel region of their homeland—fought as part of the British military effort during the Revolutionary War. In the early stages, Patriot forces feared Hessian warriors because they reputedly had a cruel nature. By contrast, British military leaders admired their fighting skills. However, as the war dragged on, Ambrose Serle, the secretary to British general William Howe, noted, "Hessians are more infamous and cruel than any. It is a misfortune we ever had such a dirty, cowardly set of contemptible miscreants."

More than a fourth of the Hessians who came to America to participate in the war perished. At the Battle of Rhode Island, Hessian casualties were extremely heavy because their seven regiments constituted nearly half of the British military units in the clash. British general Robert Pigot and a small Royal Navy fleet were able to hold back the combined Franco-American effort, which included land forces under Generals John Sullivan and Nathanael Greene and the French armada of Admiral d'Estaing.

Most of the paranormal encounters with the band of German ghosts have occurred along R.I. 114 in the vicinity of Hessian Hole, a mass grave site where a large number of mortally wounded mercenaries were dumped after the battle. A willow tree stood there at the time of their burial, but it vanished long ago. The exact location of Hessian Hole is currently unknown. Some locals believe that the ancient depression in the earth probably lies near the Carnegie Abbey Golf Club, located just west of R.I. 114. Baker's Bloody Brook, so named when its waters ran blood-red for several days after the fighting in and around Portsmouth in late August 1778, flows nearby.

Those who have witnessed the spectral group of mustached German soldiers have reported that the ghosts appear in full dress uniforms as they march in a westerly direction. Maybe they are seeking their final place of rest in the hours after sunset. But maybe they are intent on continuing their fight against the Continental Army of 1778.

Regardless of their purpose, if you happen to be driving late at night along the stretch of **R.I. 114 in Portsmouth,** you will do well to maintain a keen watch for the spirits of the bloodthirsty soldiers who often gave no quarter to Americans. Perhaps their ghosts act in a similar manner. But who is willing to test them?

Other "Spirited" Revolutionary War Sites in Rhode Island, Briefly Noted

COVENTRY—GENERAL NATHANAEL GREENE HOMESTEAD

Perhaps no general besides George Washington deserves more credit for masterminding the American victory in the Revolutionary War than Major General Nathanael Greene. At the beginning of the conflict, he left his two-and-a-half-story frame home in Coventry with the lowest military rank of all—militia private. His fighting and leadership skills quickly became apparent. "The Fighting Quaker," as he soon became known, was credited by Washington with winning the war in the South. Washington considered Greene his most talented subordinate and even selected Greene to succeed him as commander in chief of the Continental Army in the event of tragedy.

After the war, General Greene was forced to sell his Rhode Island property to pay creditors for the money he had borrowed to feed his troops. He died of sunstroke in 1786 on his estate on Cumberland Island, Georgia, given to him by grateful citizens of that state. Sometime thereafter, his spirit returned to his old dwelling in Rhode Island, where it lingers to this day. Visitors to the grand home, which now serves as a museum, may hear slamming doors, disembodied footsteps, screams, and cannon fire. Eerie cold spots abound in the structure.

Surrounded by well-landscaped gardens, the General Nathanael

Greene Homestead overlooks the Pawtuxet River. Its address is 50 Taft St., Coventry, R.I. 02816; the telephone number is 401-821-8630.

JAMESTOWN—FORT WETHERILL

To protect Newport during the Revolutionary War, American forces constructed a crude earthwork fort on Dumpling Rock near Jamestown on Conanicut Island. So strategic was its location that the fortification was enlarged and improved for use in subsequent conflicts, including World War I and World War II. Now the center of Fort Wetherill State Park, the old military installation has but one permanent resident, a phantom black dog that has menaced the place since the fight for independence.

British invaders captured Fort Wetherill without firing a shot when General Henry Clinton's forces took New Haven in December 1776. Soon, the garrison of Redcoats began to complain about a terrifying, enormous black dog prowling the fort. In British folklore, a black dog symbolizes death.

When the French navy captured the harbors around New Haven in late July 1778, the British garrison was only too happy to abandon the fort and its black canine. But just a month later, the Redcoats were back, and the monster dog with glowing red eyes resumed frightening them. On October 25, 1779, the garrison made a hasty evacuation without explanation. Legend has it that the soldiers could no longer keep their sanity in the presence of the dreaded animal.

Visitors to the fifty-one-acre state park have heard, felt, and seen the phantom black dog that continues to call the fort home. Barking and howling are heard within the compound when no animals are present. More than one person has been terrified to see the black menace, its eyes glaring and fangs showing, pass directly through the walls.

Fort Wetherill State Park is located on hundred-foot granite cliffs overlooking Newport. Its address is Fort Wetherill Rd., Jamestown, R.I. 02818; the telephone number is 401-423-1771.

NEWPORT—ADMIRAL FARRAGUT INN

Constructed around 1702, this historic inn was used to quarter soldiers when the French occupied Newport during the Revolutionary War. The ghost of one French soldier yet abides here. Visitors and workmen have been frightened by its supernatural activities.

The inn's address is 31 Clarke St., Newport, R.I. 02840; the telephone number is 800-524-1386.

NEWPORT—OLD CITY STREETS

Newport, blessed with outstanding natural harbors, was prized by the navies of the warring parties during the American Revolution. While the British controlled the area from 1776 until 1779, they had the run of the city. After consuming copious quantities of stolen alcohol, they partied long and hard. Night after night, inebriated Redcoats strolled the avenues in a shameful display of wanton conduct. They appropriated furniture from stores and homes and used it to build roaring fires. No local lady was able to pass the raucous assembly without receiving unwelcome advances.

Phantom fires and boisterous noises are still experienced on the ancient streets of Newport. On warm summer nights in the old port town, visitors sometimes encounter the Redcoats' spectral parties. Numerous people have reported hearing loud British voices and seeing the light of glowing fires from adjacent streets, only to find everything dark and quiet when they turn the corner.

NEWPORT—VERNON HOUSE

The Comte de Rochambeau selected this two-story late-Georgian frame house, built around 1760, as his headquarters during the French occupation of Newport. Here, he entertained the likes of his countryman the Marquis de Lafayette and General George Washington. At the time, William Vernon, an important shipbuilder for the American government, owned the home. Vernon's ghost is thought to haunt it still.

At a dinner party held in the grand dwelling in the late twentieth century, the hostess noticed an elderly man dressed in a blue uniform of the Revolutionary War walk in the door and up the stairs to the second floor, acting as if he owned the place. The strange man was not on the guest list, nor was he ever found during a subsequent search.

Cold spots are often encountered on the magnificent staircase. When politics are discussed in the house, those present experience cold drafts.

The Vernon House, a private residence, is located at 46 Clarke Street in Newport.

New York

ME
(WAS N. MA.)

VT   NH

NEW YORK

NY   MA   RI

CT

PA   NJ

MD

DE

VA

NC

SC

GA

SHADED AREA SHOWS
COLONIAL AMERICA

Spooky Fort Ti
FORT TICONDEROGA, NEW YORK

*General [George Washington], if you only plan it, I will
storm hell.*

GENERAL ANTHONY WAYNE

When Ethan Allen wrested control of Fort Ticonderoga from
the British in May 1775 (see 85-89), the place was already haunted by
soldiers from its prior service during the colonial wars between Great
Britain and France. Allen, unwilling to rest on his laurels, left the fort
within a week to take part in American operations in Canada. In the
wake of Allen's departure, General Anthony Wayne was dispatched to
command the garrison assigned to Fort Ticonderoga by the Continental
Congress. Though his tenure at Ticonderoga was short, Wayne, whose
ghost may be found in more places than that of any other Revolutionary War figure, left his supernatural imprint.

The fort occupies a spectacular setting on Lake Champlain at the
north end of Lake George. French military forces constructed the massive stone fortification from 1755 to 1759. Though it was known as Fort
Ticonderoga by the time of the American Revolution, the installation

was originally named Fort Carillon because water from Lake George sounded like the chiming of bells. Its location on a water highway connecting New York with Vermont and Canada was of immeasurable importance to the French in protecting their interests to the north.

In 1759, a British expedition led by General Jeffrey Amherst captured the fort. It remained in British hands until Ethan Allen delivered it to the Americans on May 10, 1775. It traded hands again in July 1777 when British general John Burgoyne mounted guns across Lake Champlain atop Vermont's Mount Independence and forced General Arthur St. Clair, the American commander, to evacuate the compound. Less than six months later, in the aftermath of the British debacle at Saratoga, Fort Ticonderoga was abandoned. It saw no further significant action for the duration of the war.

Now maintained as Fort Ticonderoga National Historic Landmark, the heavily reconstructed fort is open to the public. From the entrance, a picturesque road lined with historical markers leads to the site of the ancient fort. On the short drive, motorists are awed by the spectacular scenery and can sometimes sense the presence of the men who lived and died here in the eighteenth century.

Inside the fortress, visitors occasionally come face to face with ghosts of the past. In the general mess hall, guests have encountered the grayish mist of a soldier wearing a French uniform with its traditional blue cuffs. A phantom soldier also makes appearances in the officers' dining room. On the upper floor of the barracks building, staff members have reported hearing the sound of someone pacing the floor before the facility opens. A mysterious blue light has been seen on the same floor.

On the grounds of the fort, the staccato beat of an invisible drummer breaks the morning stillness. A ghost horse bearing a spectral soldier has also been seen and heard.

Several of the revenants at Fort Ticonderoga have been identified. Duncan Campbell and his cousin are two of them. Their story was romanticized by Robert Louis Stevenson in *The Master of Ballantrae*.

In his native Scotland, Duncan Campbell gave sanctuary to the man who killed his cousin. In a subsequent nightmare, Duncan heard his cousin say, " 'Til we meet again, Duncan, at Ticonderoga." At the time, the name Ticonderoga meant nothing to Duncan. Years later, Major Duncan Campbell was shipped to America as a member of the king's Black Watch Brigade. He saw his first combat in the British attack on Fort Carillon. To his dismay, he learned that the alternate name of the fortification was Ticonderoga. Memories of the nightmare flooded over him, causing him to scream, "This is Ticonderoga! I shall die to-day!"

In the course of the fighting, Duncan was slightly wounded in the arm. However, the limb was amputated after infection set in, and he died nine days later. His body was buried at the fort and subsequently reinterred at Fort Edward in eastern New York. But Duncan's spirit remained at Ticonderoga, where it was joined by the spirit of the cousin. Their spectres have been observed about the grounds, particularly at night when the weather is stormy.

Unquestionably, the most prominent ghost in residence at Ticonderoga and its environs is that of Mad Anthony Wayne. Over the years, numerous reports of supernatural encounters with the general's ghost have come from people camping in the lake wilderness near the fort. The incidents begin with the sound of a galloping horse approaching the campsite. This phantom sound is always followed by the appearance of General Wayne's ghost atop his favorite horse, Nab. These occurrences most often take place in the springtime.

Inside Fort Ticonderoga, the general's ghost is sometimes observed sitting at a table in his former quarters. Even more frequently, it is seen along the ramparts, where it appears to be scouring the horizon for the enemy.

On a December morning some years ago, a mason was busy repairing the stonework of the fort when he noticed a shadowy figure walking back and forth atop the bulwark facing Mount Independence. For a moment, the mason resumed his labors, deeming the man on the ramparts to be a park ranger. But when the figure approached, the mason was shocked to see that it was a ghost in a blue cape covering a blue and white uniform similar to those worn by the Continental Army. Suddenly, the spectral officer pointed to Fort Defiance on a nearby New York mountain and muttered, "I told them to guard the top of that mountain but St. Clair gave up my fort without a fight."

In the blink of an eye, the blue-clad spook made its way down the steps of the bulwark and leaped onto a phantom horse. Its departing words, delivered by the December winds to the astonished laborer, were, "On to Stony Point." With that, the phantoms disappeared into thin air, perhaps on their way to a supernatural appearance at the site of General Wayne's victory over British forces commanded by General Burgoyne in July 1779.

During his sojourn at Ticonderoga, Mad Anthony Wayne maintained his reputation as a lothario. Nancy Coates, one of his female companions, became unstable when the general began lavishing his affections on another lady. Overcome with despondency, Nancy plunged into the waters at the fort's edge and drowned.

From Nancy Coates's death to the present day, her ghost has abided at the fort. It has been observed floating about the numerous chambers and passageways. Her doleful laments echo about the place. On walking trails around the fort, hikers have unwittingly come face to face with the mournful spectre. Others have seen her apparition in Lake George.

During the first dozen years of its existence, Fort Ticonderoga was the scene of an almost ceaseless battle for its control. Over the succeeding centuries, spirits of the armies that occupied the place in its early history, as well as the ghost of an American officer's lover, all seem reluctant to surrender the fort.

Fort Ticonderoga is open to the public from May 10 to October 20. For more information, contact Fort Ticonderoga National Historic Landmark, Box 390, Ticonderoga, N.Y. 12883; the telephone number is 518-585-2821.

A Haunting Tale of Love and Espionage
LONG ISLAND, NEW YORK

*I suffer in the defence of my country; I must consider this
hour as the most glorious of my life.—Remember that I die as
becomes a British officer, while the manner of my death must
reflect disgrace on your Commander.*

JOHN ANDRÉ

In London's Westminster Abbey stands a monument to the brave
officer who has been called "the British Nathan Hale." John André, a
soldier of exceptional talent, was hanged by Americans in 1780 as a result of his collaboration with General Benedict Arnold in a plot to surrender the strategic American position at West Point on the Hudson.
Ghosts from this Revolutionary War drama of espionage, treason, and
romance are found at Raynham Hall, an eighteenth-century mansion
at Oyster Bay on Long Island.

Promoted from captain to major at the age of twenty-seven in 1778,
André was the darling of the social scene during the British occupation
of Philadelphia and New York. While stationed in the Pennsylvania
city, he resided in the former home of Benjamin Franklin and renewed

a relationship with Peggy Shippen Arnold, the wife of Benedict Arnold
(see 163-64). André had romanced Mrs. Arnold, an avowed Loyalist,
prior to her marriage.

In April 1779, the British high command placed André, then its
adjutant general, in charge of secret intelligence in the colonies. A year
later, he and Arnold, the highly esteemed Continental Army general in
command of West Point, conspired to deliver that fortification to the
British. In return, Arnold was to receive a reward of twenty thousand
pounds. Though Arnold was well aware that West Point was necessary
to prevent the British from separating all of New England from the
other colonies, he was in severe financial distress. As it turned out, he
valued his personal well-being over that of his country.

Early negotiations between the two conspirators had taken place
through intermediaries and communiqués. During the latter part of
September 1780, they met face to face for the first time in a wooded area near Haverstraw, located down the Hudson from West Point.
General Arnold presented six papers written in his own hand to André.
Those missives provided detailed instructions to the British authorities
as to the manner in which West Point could be taken.

André secreted the documents in his stocking. Because he was behind enemy lines, he dressed in nonmilitary clothes and assumed the
name of John Anderson. During his attempt to return to his superiors,
he encountered three men—John Paulding, Isaac Van Wart, and David
Williams—at nine o'clock on the morning of September 23 near Tarrytown on the east bank of the Hudson. Mistaking them for Tories,
André exclaimed, "Gentlemen, I hope you belong to our party." One
of the trio responded, "What party?" André replied, "The lower party,"
meaning the British. With that, he was taken prisoner by the three
Patriot partisans.

Six days later, General Washington handpicked a tribunal of senior
officers including the Marquis de Lafayette to hear the case against
Major André. At the conclusion of the trial, the tribunal decreed, "Major André, Adjutant General of the British army, ought to be considered

as a Spy from the enemy, and that agreeable to the law and usage of the nations, it is their opinion he ought to suffer death."

As André's date with the gallows loomed, he wrote an impassioned plea to George Washington to spare his life. Although Washington refused to commute the sentence, he authorized attempts to exchange André for Benedict Arnold. Sir Henry Clinton, then the British commander of New York, refused the exchange even though André was one of his favorite officers.

On October 2, 1780, André, attired in his Royal regimentals and boots, stood erect as the noose was slipped over his neck at Tappan, a village on the west bank of the Hudson near the New Jersey line. The American officer assigned the dubious duty at the gallows offered the condemned man an opportunity to speak his last words. Without emotion, Major André lifted the handkerchief from his eyes, looked at the assembled multitude, and proclaimed, "I pray you bear me witness that I met my fate like a brave man."

Friend and foe alike admired John André for his courage and gallantry. Lamenting his death, Alexander Hamilton wrote, "Never perhaps did anyone suffer death with more justice, or deserve it less."

André's corpse was unceremoniously buried in a makeshift grave at the gallows. A grateful British nation recovered his remains in 1821 and reinterred them at Westminster Abbey. But it seems that the spirits of John André and the people associated with his plan to steal West Point are alive and well in New York.

At Oyster Bay on Long Island stands Raynham Hall, a twenty-room museum that served as the home of the Samuel Townsend family during the Revolutionary War. While the British occupied New York City, the Townsends were forced to quarter Redcoats. Among the regular visitors to the house was Major John André.

André often consulted with Lieutenant Colonel John Graves Simcoe, one of the British officers headquartered at Raynham Hall. Sally Townsend, Samuel's pretty young daughter, seems to have been infatuated with the handsome Simcoe, commander of the vaunted Queen's

Rangers. She also had an eye for the personable Major André. But André had done little to engender goodwill in the neighborhood. During a curfew imposed by the British army, an elderly man in Oyster Bay was arrested as a violator. Major André ordered that he be tied to a tree and flogged.

Sally wrestled with her loyalties, knowing full well that her family was dedicated to the cause of American independence. One night, she fell asleep on the parlor sofa while fretting over her quandary. When she awoke, she came across a letter addressed to Colonel Simcoe. It detailed the secret plan between André and Arnold. After reading the startling news, Sally returned the letter to the place where she had found it. Later, she told her father. As legend has it, the information, promptly dispatched to General Washington, proved instrumental in the capture of Major André. As for Simcoe, he was captured and released just before Yorktown. After the conflict, he settled in Canada, where he was instrumental in the founding of Toronto.

Deprived by war of the two men she loved, Sally Townsend never married and died a spinster at the age of eighty-two. Nevertheless, the spirits of Major André, Sally, and Colonel Simcoe are yet in residence at old Raynham Hall.

In 1938, Julia Weeks Cole, then the owner of the venerable house, peered out a window and saw the spectre of John André atop his horse.

Sally's mournful ghost has been observed in her second-floor bedroom. Even in the warmest part of summer, the room is ice cold. Museum curators find it necessary to wear wool vests when working in the haunted bedroom.

Annual encounters with a legless phantom attired in a dark wool coat with brass buttons have also been recorded at Raynham Hall. The ghost is said to be that of John Simcoe. Although Simcoe was wounded several times in the war, it is uncertain whether he lost his legs or whether his spirit simply fails to fully materialize.

The Arnold-André affair, one of the most tragic dramas played out during the Revolutionary War, continues to haunt many Americans. So do its lingering spirits.

Raynham Hall is open to the public. Its address is 20 West Main St., Oyster Bay, Long Island, N.Y. 11771; the telephone number is 516-922-6808.

A Patriotic Welcome
SARATOGA SPRINGS, NEW YORK

*An unpaid patriot who, alone and in great peril, gave
the first and only information of Burgoyne's intended advance . . . which led to timely preparations for the Battle of
September 19th.*

EPITAPH ON THE GRAVE MARKER
OF ALEXANDER BRYAN

Historians have termed the American victories at Saratoga in the
autumn of 1777 the turning point of the Revolutionary War in the
North. Had it not been for vital intelligence provided to General Horatio Gates by a modest local innkeeper turned spy, it is quite possible
that the outcome would have been different. Alexander Bryan, the unassuming man who provided the espionage, returned to his vocation
following the war. His former hostelry, the Olde Bryan Inn, now houses
a well-known restaurant. Its former proprietor's ghost still drops by to
offer eighteenth-century hospitality.

Born in Connecticut in 1733, Bryan settled in New York in his youth. On the eve of the Revolutionary War, he was the proprietor of an inn located near the west bank of the Hudson River approximately twenty miles north of Albany and two miles south of Stillwater, the actual site of the Battles of Saratoga.

A contemporary description of Bryan at the onset of the war indicates he was "a person endowed with great powers of endurance; well-acquainted with the country; shrewd, discreet, and reticent; gifted with a fine address and presence; and considering the meager educational advantages of the time, possessed of much more than ordinary intelligence." Because his inn was situated on a primary route used by partisans from both armies, he welcomed guests with divergent viewpoints and varying quantities of information. His winning personality allowed Bryan to earn the confidence of both warring factions. Each side believed him to be in its camp.

On August 19, 1777, General Horatio Gates, the newly appointed commander of the American army in the North, arrived in Stillwater in desperate need of information concerning the plans of the ten-thousand-man British army under Gentleman Johnny Burgoyne. Gates prevailed upon the Committee of Safety at Stillwater to provide him the name of an intrepid, trustworthy local who could serve as a scout and undercover agent for the American cause. Members of the committee were unanimous in their response: Alexander Bryan.

At his initial meeting with Gates, Bryan was asked to make his way inside British lines and bring back detailed reports about enemy troop strength and intended deployments. The agile forty-four-year-old accepted the dangerous assignment. Hoping not to arouse suspicion, Bryan rode north on a circuitous route of more than thirty miles to a large enemy encampment near Fort Edward. There, he renewed friendships with former patrons who, in the course of conversation, provided the information Bryan sought. Convinced that an attack on Gates's army was imminent, he had no time to waste in relaying the crucial intelligence.

At first light on the gray morning of Monday, September 15, 1777,

Bryan, an outstanding horseman, mounted his speedy steed. As he set out south, he had no idea that British agents, suspicious of his motives in the camp, were trailing him. Following a hot chase, Bryan eluded his pursuers and rode unharmed into Gates's camp after thirty-six hours in the saddle.

Acting on Bryan's information, General Gates promptly selected the most strategic position in Stillwater to deploy his army. The Americans set up defenses on Bemis Heights along the Hudson River. Their artillery placements and fortifications essentially allowed them control of all military movements in the nearby Hudson Valley.

Days after Bryan's report to Gates, General Burgoyne's army slammed into the Americans at Stillwater. In the Battle of Freeman's Farm (First Saratoga), the British made no headway and suffered heavy casualties.

For the next eighteen days, the two armies remained in place. Then on Tuesday, October 7, the conflict resumed at the Battle of Bemis Heights (Second Saratoga). This time, the Americans routed the Redcoats and Hessians, forcing them into retreat. Pressing their advantage, Gates's soldiers encircled the fleeing army of Burgoyne. Unable to fight their way out, the British were forced to capitulate. On October 17, Burgoyne formally surrendered the surviving sixty-three hundred soldiers in his army.

The importance of the two American victories cannot be overstated. The British were forced to give up their plan to capture Albany, the head of navigation of the Hudson; the American states in the North were spared further British incursions out of Canada; and France decided to intervene in the war on behalf of the Americans.

Sadly, the man who risked his life to enable the American army to claim the crucial victories never received remuneration or recognition for his service. When General Gates got his report from Alexander Bryan, the extreme urgency of the situation caused him to forget to acknowledge his scout's invaluable contribution. In subsequent official reports of the battle, Gates made no mention of Bryan's daring exploits.

Following the war, Bryan returned to life as an innkeeper. In 1787, he purchased a new inn in Saratoga Springs just across from the famous High Rock Spring. Just three years earlier, George Washington had attempted to buy the site because of the medicinal qualities of the springs.

Until his retirement many years later, Alexander Bryan owned and operated the Bryan Inn on Maple Avenue in Saratoga Springs. Over time, his son, John, replaced the original log building with a more substantial stone structure. It was subsequently converted into a private residence and used in that manner until the Olde Bryan Inn was opened as a restaurant in the last quarter of the twentieth century.

For more than two hundred years, Alexander Bryan has hung around to ensure that patrons receive the hospitality that has made this place a legend.

When the Veitch family made its home in the building from 1954 to 1979, the ghosts of the Revolutionary War scout and a female made their presences known from time to time.

While doing his homework in the area where the bar is now located, one of the Veitch children was overwhelmed by the feeling that he was being watched in the otherwise empty room. As he looked around, he suddenly heard a phantom male voice.

His two sisters also experienced the ghostly presences of Bryan and a lady thought to be a member of his family. One of the Veitch sisters came home from high school early one day and went up to her bedroom, located adjacent to a bathroom. No sooner had she entered her room than the next-door shower began running. A subsequent search of the entire building revealed no other human presence.

One evening, the same teenage girl was awakened by someone calling her name. When she opened her eyes, she was startled to see a female ghost in a high-necked Victorian dress by her bed. Until the revenant finally vanished, the girl sat up in her bed in a trancelike state.

On a separate occasion, the other Veitch sister, Karen, was brushing her hair in front of a mirror when she noticed the spectral image of a woman standing behind her. Terrified, she turned around, only to discover no one there.

Years later, after the residence was converted into a restaurant, one of the Veitch grandchildren, unaware of the haunted nature of the building, made a visit to the upstairs restroom during the course of the evening meal. Upon returning to his table, the child appeared pale as he announced he had seen the apparition of a woman floating as if she were trying to walk upstairs—at a place where no staircase existed!

Restaurant employees observed a similar occurrence involving another young patron. While dining one night, a woman attempted to take her granddaughter to the ladies' room on the second floor. Her grandchild, exhibiting great fear, refused to go because she saw a spectral woman in a green dress on the steps.

Staff members at the Olde Bryan Inn, quite familiar with the female ghost, have chosen to name her Eleanor. Because Alexander Bryan's family owned the property until the twentieth century, the lady in the green gown is thought to be the apparition of one of his relatives.

But what concrete evidence suggests the ghost of old Alexander still calls the inn home?

Unexplained occurrences are attributed to the spirit of the master of the inn. Water runs in the sink in the men's room when the second floor is devoid of human occupants; objects move about the bar area after closing hours; wait staff have felt phantom hands on their backs and invisible brushes against their cheeks and arms. Do these manifestations evince Alexander's desire to ensure that the restaurant continues the longstanding tradition of hospitality he established?

To keep staff members on their toes, their ghostly host causes a commotion from time to time. One evening about midnight, long after closing, employees were cleaning up when the downstairs chandelier began swinging back and forth without explanation. As they stared in amazement, the lights went out.

On occasion, the actual ghost of Alexander Bryan has appeared to human eyes. During the Veitch family's occupancy, one of the girls walked into the bathroom late one night, only to find the ghost of Bryan sitting atop a white horse. She noted that the apparition carried a lance in its hand. Scared out of her wits, she raced back to the safety of her bedroom.

Since that time, numerous customers have reported seeing the spectre of a man dressed in clothing of the Revolutionary War era in the men's room. Likewise, an archaeologist digging in the portion of the dining room known as "the Livery" encountered a ghost of similar appearance.

To honor the resident ghosts and the Bryan family, the restaurant's owners have added several special items to their menu. Guests at this haunted restaurant at Saratoga Springs can sample Eleanor's Roast Turkey Melt and Alexander Bryan's Crab and Lobster Cake. If a ghostly figure stops by their table, they should not be alarmed. It's most likely old Alexander, the innkeeper whose hospitable spirit toward customers of all political persuasions enabled him to become one of the unsung heroes of the American Revolution.

The **Olde Bryan Inn** is open for lunch and dinner seven days a week. Its address is 123 Maple Ave., Saratoga Springs, N.Y. 12866; the telephone number is 518-587-2990.

Terror in the House of Skene
WHITEHALL, NEW YORK

*Every man must now perceive how essential it may be to
the King's service to continue vigorously the pursuit of a flying
enemy.*

BRITISH GENERAL JOHN BURGOYNE,
WHILE HEADQUARTERED
AT THE MANOR HOUSE OF
COLONEL PHILIP SKENE

Colonel Philip Skene (a despised officer in the British army), his
wife, her lead-lined coffin, a castle, and a ghost all come into play in this
macabre story set in the Adirondack Mountains of New York.

Following his service to the king in the colonial wars in America,
the English-born Skene assumed his military career was over. He put
down roots on his reward from the Crown, a fifty-six-thousand-acre
tract along Wood Creek, a tributary of Lake Champlain in eastern New
York. There, he built the town of Skenesborough (now Whitehall) and
constructed a magnificent multistory mansion for his wife, Katherine
(a British heiress), and their three children. He settled into what he

expected to be a long life of luxury funded by his wife's fortune and the profits from the numerous enterprises on his landholdings. But his dream soon dissolved into harsh reality as a result of his wife's death, her will, and the exigencies of the Revolutionary War.

Described by contemporaries as a husky fellow with dark eyes and a jowly face, Skene was not well liked by a number of the people who settled in his town. Many were suspicious of him. When questioned as to whom they hated the most, most early residents of Skenesborough would name the devil. Their second choice was invariably "old Skene."

Apparently, Skene was distrusted by members of his own family as well. Katherine, concerned that her husband would run through her fortune if she preceded him in death, wrote a will in which her estate was not bequeathed to Skene. Instead, it contained a provision that established an annual income for her husband "as long as my body lies above ground."

At an unknown date prior to the Revolutionary War, Katherine died at the mansion. Anxious to comply with her will, Skene had his wife's body embalmed in vinegar and placed in a fine lead-lined wooden coffin with exquisite metal embellishments. Rather than burying the coffin, he had it propped against a basement wall. Thus, he was able to enjoy a hefty annual stipend from Katherine's sizable estate.

In 1775, when hostilities between the American colonies and Great Britain threatened to erupt into full-scale war, Skene, ever loyal to his native land, sailed to London, where he convinced Lord North, the prime minister, that the rebellion could be quickly ended with the threat of military force led by veterans of the French and Indian War, like Skene himself. So impressed was Lord North that he sent Skene home with two new Royal appointments. He was named colonel and governor of Ticonderoga and Crown Point, British forts on the shores of Lake Champlain.

In America, Skene did not receive a warm homecoming. When his ship made port in Philadelphia, he was taken into custody. Supporters of American independence considered Skene a significant threat and promptly dispatched him to a prison in Connecticut, where he remained until October 1776.

During Skene's absence, American soldiers resided in his town. They captured the colonel's private schooner, the *Katherine*, renamed it the *Liberty*, hastily fitted it with cannons, and put it into service on Lake Champlain as one of the first vessels in the infant United States Navy. At Skene's stone palace, American raiders happened upon Katherine's coffin. In desperate need of metal for musket balls, they stripped the coffin of its lead and other metal. Before unceremoniously interring Mrs. Skene's body on the estate grounds, they stripped the corpse of its jewelry. But just as the graverobbers prepared to return to their military duties, they were horrified when the translucent ghost of Katherine Skene suddenly emerged from the freshly dug grave. As they watched in terror, the ghost vanished as a ball of glowing light. So frightened were they that they begged their commander to be relieved from nighttime guard duty on the grounds of the Skene house. This would not be the last appearance of the apparition.

Upon his release from prison, Skene sailed once again for England. There, he was informed that General John Burgoyne was on his way to America, where he was to lead an expedition in the Lake Champlain region. Skene then returned to New York and joined Burgoyne at Crown Point. Over the months that followed, the colonel served as Burgoyne's principal Loyalist adviser. Area Loyalists, jealous of Skene's influential position, held him in disdain.

On July 8, 1777, just two months before First Saratoga, Skene, in the company of General Burgoyne and his army, came home to Skenesborough. Burgoyne set up his headquarters in the heavily vandalized mansion. Skene was dismayed to discover his wife's desecrated and empty coffin. No one knows whether Katherine's ghost appeared to her husband. Skene was further mortified when Sir Frederick Haldimand, one of Burgoyne's generals, ordered the estate put to the torch as the British army departed.

In the wake of Burgoyne's capitulation at Second Saratoga, Skene was taken as a prisoner of war. Upon his release, he fled to England, where the British government compensated him for some of the losses he had suffered as a result of his unwavering loyalty.

Following the war, folks in Skenesborough were anxious to rid themselves of the memory of the man who had done his best to prevent America from breaking from Great Britain. They changed the name of the town. But the site of his burned home remained haunted. Stories circulated that Katherine's skeleton could be seen walking about the ruins of the house, which sat on the heights overlooking the village and the adjacent waterway.

In 1874, Joseph Potter, a justice of the New York State Supreme Court, erected a massive Gothic granite castle near the site of the destroyed colonial mansion. Ironically known to this day as Skene Manor, the nine-thousand-square-foot palace survives as the home of the ghost of Katherine Skene. Over the years, visitors have reported seeing her disembodied hand, a gaudy jewel adorning one finger, floating about an interior fountain.

Just after World War II, the castle was converted into a restaurant. Its owners, well aware of the haunted nature of the site, decided to add a prop to enhance the spooky ambiance. They placed a coffin in the bar. Nearby, a fountain flowed with water. To entertain patrons, a hand complete with a ring was rigged to rise from the fountain.

But Katherine's ghost had the last laugh. One day while several diners were being amused by the rising hand, their attention was suddenly attracted to the doorway, where they observed the apparition of a full-skirted matron sporting a large bauble on her hand. This phantom was not a part of the show, for it vanished into thin air. Still other patrons reported seeing a skeletal hand wearing a ring turn a doorknob in the room.

After the restaurant closed in the late 1980s, the manor reverted for a time to a private residence. In one of its ten bedrooms, a gentleman awoke one evening to the sounds of someone walking down the hallway of the otherwise empty floor. Fearful for his safety, he pushed a bed over to block the door to his chamber. In the morning, he discovered that the bed had been returned to its original position.

In 1995, an out-of-state businessman announced plans to move the castle from its site atop Skene Mountain to a location outside New York. A nonprofit corporation, Whitehall Skene Manor Preservation, Inc., was established to save the house. Known affectionately as "Save Our Skene," or "SOS," the organization subsequently purchased the castle and has embarked upon a restoration project.

During the ongoing renovations, a lady visiting Whitehall happened to see a woman waving frantically from a window on the second floor of Skene Manor. Concerned that she might be witnessing an emergency, the lady drove up to the main entrance and knocked on the door until a workman opened it. He informed her that no human being lived in the house. In the course of their conversation, the entire ceiling in the room where the laborer had been working fell to the floor with a crash. Longtime residents claimed that the waving ghost was that of Katherine Skene, trying desperately to prevent another tragedy at the old homesite.

Among Katherine's last wishes was that her body lie above the ground. Try as he might to honor that wish, her husband was kept from doing so by the Revolutionary War. But today, little doubt remains that the ghost of Katherine Skene is alive and well above and beyond the grave.

Skene Manor is open to the public on a schedule that changes from time to time. Its address is 8 Potter Terrace, Whitehall, N.Y. 12887; the telephone number is 518-499-1906.

No Peace Here
STATEN ISLAND, NEW YORK

You are hereby commanded to receive into your custody
the body of Col. Christopher Billop, prisoner of war, herewith
delivered to you, and having put irons on his hands and feet, you
are to chain him down to the floor in a close room in the said jail,
and there so detain him, giving him bread and water only for
his food.

ELISHA BOUDINET, COMMISSARY OF
PRISONS FOR THE STATE OF NEW JERSEY,
NOVEMBER 6, 1779

September 11 is a day etched in the history of New York City and
the American republic. On that date in 2001, the twin towers of the
World Trade Center were destroyed by terrorists. And on that date in
1776, the only face-to-face attempt at peace between the Americans and
the British during the Revolutionary War took place at a seventeenth-
century stone house on the southern end of Staten Island. Known alternately as the Conference House, the Billop House, and Bentley Manor,

the historic two-story structure survives as one of the oldest buildings in New York City. On its interior and about its grounds, ghosts from the Revolutionary War era abound.

Captain Christopher Billop, an English sea captain, constructed the house in the last third of the seventeenth century. His grandson, also named Christopher, was born there in 1738 and assumed ownership in the years leading to the American Revolution. Once hostilities began, Billop, an avowed Loyalist, was commissioned as a colonel of the Richmond County militia. Regarded by the British high command as an officer of great courage, energy, and zeal, Billop was only too happy to offer his home to Lord Richard Howe as the site of the so-called Peace Conference of September 1776.

At the time, the British controlled New York City and Long Island, while the Americans held sway just across the water in New Jersey and Pennsylvania. Lord Howe was convinced that British forces would ultimately prevail in the clash of arms. Anxious to prevent further bloodshed, he floated the proposal of a peace conference whereby the colonies would be persuaded to lay down arms and return to the British Empire, with greater rights and without punishment. In Philadelphia, members of the Continental Congress reluctantly voted to send three delegates—Benjamin Franklin of Pennsylvania, John Adams of Massachusetts, and Edward Rutledge of South Carolina—to the meeting.

For three hours on September 11, 1776, the trio of American envoys politely listened to Howe's entreaties at the Billop House. Finally, Ben Franklin took the floor and offered the American response. He reminded Howe that, two months earlier, the colonies had declared themselves to be thirteen states independent of British rule. Then he clearly annunciated the American position: no peace would be forthcoming until Great Britain recognized American independence. With that, the conference concluded. The three Americans were returned to the relative safety of Perth Amboy, New Jersey, on Lord Howe's private barge, and the war resumed.

For the remainder of the conflict, the master of the stone home thereafter known as the Conference House served as a partisan officer for the Crown in New York City and environs. Meanwhile, American operatives just across the bay in New Jersey were anxious to get their hands on the hated Christopher Billop.

Their opportunity came on June 23, 1779, when a band of Patriots raided the Conference House. Legend has it that they were notified of Billop's presence through a candle signal provided by a servant girl. Billop was spirited out of his house through a basement tunnel that led to the shore of the bay. Once across the water in New Jersey, the captured Loyalist was imprisoned under the harsh conditions described in the quote at the beginning of this story.

Not until the day after Christmas was Colonel Billop released in a prisoner-of-war exchange. He hastily made his way home, where he confronted his servants to ascertain the person in league with the Americans. Convinced that a fifteen-year-old house helper had alerted Patriots in the steeple of St. Peter's Church at Perth Amboy, the outraged Billop pushed—and some say stabbed—the girl to death as the two quarreled on the staircase of the mansion.

When the British capitulated in 1781, Billop abandoned the Conference House and fled with members of his family to New Brunswick, Canada. There, he held a number of important political positions until his death in Saint John in 1827. But on Staten Island, his spirit and several others have continued to haunt his old house.

For much of the nineteenth century and into the twentieth, the Conference House was devoid of human occupation and sat forlornly, hastening toward ruin. The ghosts there reigned until the 1920s, when a preservation association was created to restore and preserve the landmark. Now open to the public, the stately edifice serves as the centerpiece of Conference House Park. On the first floor are two large rooms, one a parlor and the other a dining room. The staircase down which the teenage servant fell to her death leads to the second floor, which houses a master bedroom, a child's room, and Colonel Billop's study. An attic and basement, both massive in size, complete the mansion. Early

American furnishings abound, but the only pieces original to the house are a storage bench, a book, and a letter belonging to Colonel Billop.

Employees and visitors have experienced a variety of paranormal phenomena throughout the house: flashing lights; auras; hot and cold spots; moving objects; phantom footsteps and knocks; disembodied screams, laughs, murmurs, moans, sighs, and pitiful pleas; and apparitions. Most of these occurrences are thought to be related to Colonel Billop and the servant girl who died at his hands.

The heavy footsteps of a man wearing boots with spurs have been heard when the second floor is empty of staff and guests. Could Billop yet be at work in his study?

On the anniversary of the servant girl's murder, a caretaker witnessed the colonel's ghost race up the stairs toward a young female apparition standing on the landing. When the house is closed for the evening, the sounds of a struggle between the two ghosts echo out toward the bay, followed by the screams of a female.

Without question, the most frequently encountered spirit at the Conference House is that of the murdered servant. Her nighttime presence is manifested in an unexplained light that frequently beams from the same window that alerted Patriots during the Revolutionary War. Witnesses have reported seeing a teenage girl peering from an upstairs window when the house was locked tight. Some years ago, a candlelight vigil was conducted on the stairway where the young lady tumbled to her death. As one of the participants related, the candle held by the person adjacent to the storyteller suddenly went out. None of the other candles even flickered.

Employees and volunteers have experienced the servant's spirit without seeing it. A caretaker was busy one day vacuuming the house when she heard a singing female voice over the roar of her machine. She turned off the cleaner, made a thorough inspection of the dwelling, and found no one about. On another occasion, a housekeeper felt a gentle tap on her shoulder while working alone in the place.

In the child's room upstairs, a yarn-spinning demonstration was set up on Friday afternoon in preparation for its premiere the following day. Though the door to the room was secured, strange things took place over the course of the night. When the door was unlocked Saturday morning, the room was in total disarray. Yarn and other materials were strewn about. No other reasonable explanation being available, the mess was attributed to the ghost of the servant.

Perhaps some of the strange disturbances are caused by Colonel Billop's ghost. It has been blamed for the candlesticks that are often overturned, the paintings that mysteriously move on the walls, and the odd indentation that appears on an upstairs bed covering. The colonel's invisible presence has spooked more than one guest near the entrance to the basement tunnel where he was shepherded as a prisoner of war.

Numerous accounts exist of a red-coated soldier prowling the main floor. While dusting the furniture there, a housekeeper was terrified when she unwittingly ran her hand "right through a British soldier." In the 1970s, the young son of the caretakers of the Conference House awoke from a nap and announced to his parents that a soldier wearing a red coat had roused him and patted him on the head.

The ghosts of Colonel Billop and his wife have also been witnessed taking a nightly stroll about the grounds. Several years ago, two teenage girls inquired about a costume party that had taken place at the Conference House the previous evening. When they were informed that the house had not been used on the night in question, their faces turned ashen. In a voice evincing fear, one of the girls stated that while she and her friend were walking the bay shore below the mansion, they had seen a couple attired in eighteenth-century clothes walking hand in hand around the house.

Yet other haunts from the Revolutionary War are at work at Conference House Park. A number of British soldiers who died from war wounds and disease were laid to rest under the basement of the house and on its grounds. Their spectral figures have been encountered near the burial sites. An old well on the grounds, long covered over and dry by the time of the American Revolution, is haunted. A small child died of smallpox on Staten Island during the war. His bereaved parents, fearful that British soldiers would kill them to prevent the spread of the contagion, sealed their son's body in the well. To this day, the ghost of the unfortunate lad roams the old Billop estate.

Ben Franklin, John Adams, and Edward Rutledge departed the Conference House on the night of September 11, 1776, well aware that there would be no peace between Great Britain and America. If the haunts that continue to dwell in the ancient mansion have their way, there will be no peace here in the foreseeable future as well.

The address for the **Conference House** is 7455 Hyland Blvd., Staten Island, N.Y. 10307; the telephone number is 718-984-0415.

Other "Spirited" Revolutionary War Sites in New York, Briefly Noted

BEAR MOUNTAIN—SINNIPINK (HESSIAN) LAKE

An expeditionary force of British regulars, Hessians, and Tories departed Stony Point on Monday, October 6, 1777, on a march to the north, where it was to attack Patriot outposts at Bear Mountain. Heavy fighting took place on the east bank of Sinnipink Lake, located at the foot of the mountain. Sir Henry Clinton and General John Vaughan ordered wave after wave of Hessians to the initial assault. Repulsed by the Americans garrisoned at Fort Montgomery and Fort Clinton, the German troops suffered more than 250 dead. Not until Clinton sent forward his regulars did the British prevail.

In the aftermath of the slaughter, the victors tossed the bodies of their dead comrades into the deep waters of Sinnipink Lake, which became alternately known as Hessian Lake or Bloody Pond. Numerous eyewitnesses have since seen the ghosts of tall, pale Hessian soldiers in metal helmets and tall boots charging into a phantom battle along the shore of the picturesque lake on the west side of the Hudson River.

The lake is accessible at Bear Mountain State Park. The address for the park is N.Y. 9W, Bear Mountain, N.Y. 10911; the telephone number is 845-786-2701.

BROOKLYN—SITE OF GENERAL
WILLIAM HOWE'S HEADQUARTERS

At midnight on August 27, the anniversary of the Battle of Long Island in 1776, the ghost of General William Howe can be seen prowling the streets near the site of his headquarters at Thirty-third Street and Third Avenue in Brooklyn. Perhaps his spirit continues to celebrate the British victory that forced the Americans to abandon New York City.

BROOKLYN—WALLABOUT NEIGHBORHOOD

Melancholy ghosts thought to represent some of the many Americans who perished aboard British prison ships anchored in the East River are said to aimlessly wander the riverbanks between the Williamsburg and Manhattan bridges. They are witnessed particularly in the old Wallabout neighborhood near the historic Brooklyn Navy Yard.

FORT EDWARD—UNION CEMETERY

On Monday, July 27, 1777, the young, attractive Jane McCrea was excited about a planned meeting with her fiancé, David Jones, a Loyalist officer attached to General John Burgoyne's army at nearby Fort Edward on the Hudson. As she awaited her assignation, Jane walked to the home of a neighborhood friend, Sarah McNeil. There, the two ladies were savagely attacked by Indian warriors assigned to Burgoyne's command. After Jane was shot and scalped, her lifeless body was thrown into a ravine.

Jane's grave is located in Union Cemetery not far from the home where she was brutally assaulted. Both the private home and her grave are said to be haunted by Jane's ghost. The address for the cemetery is N.Y. 4, Fort Edward, N.Y. 12828.

HUNTINGTON—OLD BURIAL HILL CEMETERY

This ancient burial ground dates to 1712. Originally, it adjoined the frame First Presbyterian Church, which was torn down on Tuesday, November 26, 1782. British soldiers dismantled the structure and used its wood to construct Fort Golgotha, an installation commanded by Colonel Benjamin Thompson, a British officer who also called himself Count Rumford.

To add insult to the injury already perpetrated on the local Presbyterians, who were staunch supporters of American independence, Colonel Thompson ordered the tombstone of the Reverend Ebenezer Prince moved to the front of his tent. The Redcoat officer reasoned that each time he left his tent, he would have the distinct pleasure of treading on "the old Rebel." The much-loved Prince, a devout Patriot, had served as minister of the church from 1763 until his death in 1779.

Just four months after Thompson's actions, the British abandoned the post. The current First Presbyterian Church was built at the site in 1784. The spirits of both Colonel Thompson and the Reverend Prince linger in the cemetery.

The address for Old Burial Hill Cemetery is Main St. and Nassau Rd., Huntington, N.Y. 11743.

NEW YORK CITY—ALICE AUSTEN HOUSE MUSEUM

Known as Clear Comfort when it was constructed in 1690, this farmhouse later became the home of Alice Austen, the noted female photographer of the nineteenth century. During the Revolutionary War, an American soldier was hanged here by Redcoats and Tories. His ghost roams the grounds. It is often seen swinging the gallows rope in its spectral hand.

The house and grounds are open to the public. The address is 2 Hylan Blvd., Staten Island, N.Y. 10305; the telephone number is 718-816-4506.

NEW YORK CITY—CHURCH OF
ST. ANDREW CEMETERY

Constructed in the first decade of the eighteenth century, the Church of St. Andrew was sequestered by the British army for use as a headquarters and hospital during the fight against the colonies. In the nearby church cemetery, the ghost of a teenage soldier wearing Revolutionary War clothing and a tricorn hat wanders about the graves. Its head is wrapped with a bloody bandage. Area residents believe the spectre to be the spirit of a young musician or flag bearer who fell in one of the nearby wartime skirmishes.

The address for the Church of St. Andrew is 40 Mill Rd., Staten Island, N.Y. 10306.

NEW YORK CITY—D'AGOSTINO RESIDENCE HALL

Aaron Burr (1756–1836) was a national hero long before he was elected vice president of the United States. His extraordinary bravery as an officer during the Revolutionary War was displayed at far-flung places from Canada to New Jersey. Ironically, he is best known for killing Alexander Hamilton, who had also served as a staff officer of General George Washington.

On the campus of New York University, D'Agostino Residence Hall stands on the site once occupied by Burr's private stables. His ghost has been observed roaming the halls of the building.

The address for D'Agostino Residence Hall is 101 West Third St., New York, N.Y. 10012; the telephone number is 212-998-6508.

NEW YORK CITY—MORRIS JUMEL MANSION

Aaron Burr is thought to maintain a ghostly presence in this magnificent mansion, constructed in 1765 by British colonel Roger Morris. During Burr's brief residence here, his life was turbulent. He moved into the stately dwelling upon his marriage to its high-spirited owner, Eliza Jumel, in 1833, just a year after she had killed her previous husband, Stephen. From the outset, her marriage to Burr was deeply troubled. Eliza accused the seventy-seven-year-old former vice president of adultery. Divorce followed a year later. Eliza's gloomy ghost can often be seen shouting from the third-floor windows.

Because New York City was occupied at various times by each army, British and American soldiers used the mansion by turns throughout the conflict. General George Washington was headquartered here for several weeks in the autumn of 1776. On the upper floor, an unidentified ghost dressed in a Revolutionary War uniform has been observed by tour groups on several occasions.

The mansion, open to the public, is located at the corner of Edgecombe Avenue and 160th Street. The address is 1765 Jumel Terrace, New York, N.Y. 10032; the telephone number is 212-923-8008.

NEW YORK CITY—NATHAN HALE PLAQUE

A commemorative plaque affixed to the Old Biltmore Hotel building marks the spot where Nathan Hale, one of the most famous American heroes of the war, was hanged as a spy on Sunday, September 22, 1776. His spirit is believed to abide at the site. Passersby sometimes experience overwhelming sensations of despondency and violence.

The plaque is located at the corner of Forty-third Street and Vanderbilt Avenue in Manhattan.

NEW YORK CITY—SUGAR HOUSE WINDOW

The Sugar House, constructed in 1763, was used by the British as a prison during their Revolutionary War occupation of New York City. Patriot prisoners' gaunt, pale faces could often be seen peering from the barred basement window that looked out onto the busy city. Following the war, pedestrians were haunted by phantom hands stretching into the street from the window, as if pleading for freedom.

When the old prison was replaced by the Rhinelander Building in 1862, the historic window was transferred to the façade of the new structure as a memorial to the suffering Americans. When the Rhinelander gave way to the existing police building, the window was again incorporated into the new construction. Even now, a low-lying mist often forms near the window, and shadowy figures emerge from it.

The haunted window memorial can be seen at the Police Plaza and Municipal Building at the lower end of Manhattan near the Brooklyn Bridge. The address is 1 Police Plaza, New York, N.Y. 10038.

NEW YORK CITY—TRINITY CHURCH

Alexander Hamilton died in 1804 from wounds sustained in his infamous duel with Aaron Burr. He was buried in the churchyard of historic Trinity Church in the heart of New York City. His grave could not hold the spirit of the great soldier and statesman. Over the years, Hamilton's ghost has been observed near his elaborate tomb.

Trinity Church is located near Wall Street and Broad. The address is 74 Trinity Pl., New York, N.Y. 10001.

ORISKANY—ORISKANY BATTLEFIELD
STATE HISTORIC SITE

When the British army unleashed a savage assault against Fort Stanwix (five miles east of the town of Rome) on Wednesday, August 6, 1777, Brigadier General Nicholas Herkimer quickly rallied a force of eight hundred Mohawk Valley militiamen to aid the beleaguered Americans. As Herkimer's advance elements galloped toward the fort through the marshes surrounding Oriskany Creek, they were ambushed by a four-hundred-man detachment of Indians and Tories commanded by Joseph Brant, a British officer. The bloody clash included hand-to-hand combat. Herkimer and a dozen of his officers fell. The general's leg wound led to his death ten days later. Despite their heavy losses, the militiamen prevailed, killing more than a hundred Oneida Indians. Ultimately, the ambushers retreated in defeat.

The battlefield is now part of a state historic site. A marker at the spot where General Herkimer was wounded is sometimes surrounded by orbs and glowing white objects. A ghostly white figure has been observed nearby. On other portions of the site, shadowy figures have been seen wandering the landscape. In the woods where so many men fell that day, an awful stench of unexplainable origin has been experienced by park personnel and visitors. In the men's restroom at the site, doors open and close without visible reason and blowers come on to dry phantom hands. Area residents sometimes hear moans and cries and the occasional sound of musket fire coming from the old killing ground.

The address for Oriskany Battlefield State Historic Site is 7801 N.Y. 69, Oriskany, N.Y. 13424; the telephone number is 315-768-7224.

OSWEGO—FORT ONTARIO

In 1777, British forces abandoned Fort Ontario, a colonial installation built in the 1750s on Lake Ontario at the mouth of the Oswego River. American soldiers burned the fort a year later, but the Redcoats rebuilt it in 1782. It is haunted by a spectral officer known as Colonel Fykes. Fykes died of disease here just after the British reconstructed the fort.

Portions of the fort can be seen at Fort Ontario State Historic Site. The address is 1 East Fourth St., Oswego, N.Y. 13126; the telephone number is 315-343-4711.

PELHAM MANOR—PELHAM DALE

Located just north of the Bronx, the village of Pelham Manor overlooks Long Island Sound and boasts two pre–Revolutionary War homes. One of them, Pelham Dale, is a magnificent multistory house constructed of stone between 1750 and 1760. Tradition has it that the venerable structure played a prominent part in a ghost story from the war for independence. On the chilly evening of October 16, 1776, a four-thousand-man British landing force commanded by Sir William Howe was moving toward Pelham Manor when it was observed by an Indian maiden on a nearby island. The young lady raced along a well-worn trail and across the bridge connecting her island to Pelham Manor. There, she called at Pelham Dale, the home of David J. Pell, to spread the alarm that the British were coming.

American forces under John Glover, though only 750 strong, sprang into action and achieved a significant victory at the Battle of Pell's Point the following day. According to local legend, the ghost of the Indian heroine continues to make her heroic run on October nights. Her lightning-fast feet can be heard pounding on the forest floor.

Pelham Dale, a private residence, stands at 45 Iden Avenue in Pelham Manor.

PLEASANTVILLE—BUTTERMILK HILL

John André, the British officer who conspired with General Benedict Arnold to relay American war secrets to the British army, passed through this town northwest of New York City with valuable documents secreted in his boot. Just outside Pleasantville, he lost his way near what is now the corner of Bedford Road and Choate Lane. American scouts patrolling the area near Buttermilk Hill took custody of André and sent him on the road to execution as a spy. His ghost is said to haunt the area where he fell into the hands of the Americans.

ROME—FORT STANWIX NATIONAL MONUMENT

Continental troops commanded by Colonel Elias Dayton rebuilt the colonial-era Fort Stanwix in June 1776. Fourteen months later, the determined but heavily outnumbered garrison held on against a savage attack by the two-thousand-man force of British lieutenant colonel Barry St. Leger until rescued by eight hundred regulars led by General Benedict Arnold. Legend has it that the Stars and Stripes flew in battle for the first time at Fort Stanwix during the fierce clash in August 1777.

Members of its Revolutionary War garrison dwell in supernatural form at the reconstructed fort. Spectral figures attired in their blue Continentals have been spotted patrolling the eighteen-acre site. In one of the barracks, visitors and employees have encountered a one-legged man who vanishes before them. Phantom sounds such as disembodied footsteps, laughter and chatter from invisible beings, and the swish of an invisible broom permeate the compound. Unseen musicians play drums and fifes.

The address for Fort Stanwix National Monument is 112 East Park St., Rome, N.Y. 13440; the telephone number is 315-336-2080.

STILLWATER—FREEMAN'S FARM

On Friday, September 19, 1777, at the Battle of Freeman's Farm (First Saratoga), General John Burgoyne decided to split his ten-thousand-man army into three columns. At midday, the British center ran headlong into the five hundred Virginian riflemen of Colonel Daniel Morgan at the farm of John Freeman, a British sympathizer. Fighting raged across the fertile fields. By day's end, more than seven hundred men were killed or wounded.

At night, strange lights and unexplained orbs float across the fields where the soldiers suffered and died. Some claim the glowing orbs are the spirits of battlefield casualties. At the site of an American field hospital, visitors have heard ghostly screams and the phantom voices of men in great pain.

The address for Saratoga National Historic Park is 648 N.Y. 32, Stillwater, N.Y. 12170; the telephone number is 518-664-3349.

STONY BROOK—COUNTRY HOUSE RESTAURANT

This popular Long Island eating establishment is haunted by the ghost of a young lady executed as a spy by the British during the war. Identified as Annette Williamson, the woman was buried on the property after her captors hanged her. Inside the restaurant, Annette's spirit makes its presence known in a variety of ways. Her phantom touch has been felt on the stairway. Kitchen staffers have watched in awe as a towel floated before their eyes. Even skeptics have become believers in Annette's ghost. One such person had a glass of wine thrown in his face by an invisible hand.

The Country House Restaurant is housed in a building dating from 1710. The address is N.Y. 25A, Stony Brook, N.Y. 11790; the telephone number is 516-751-3332.

STONY POINT—POORHOUSE

This nondescript colonial house, now a private home, is haunted by two British soldiers executed by General Anthony Wayne on the eve of his victory at the Battle of Stony Point on Friday, July 16, 1779. Built as an almshouse, the place was being used as a British sentry post when General Wayne surprised the two Redcoats as he prepared for his perilous and highly secret attack. After quickly burying the men, Wayne proceeded to lead a stunning American victory that took all of fifteen minutes to complete.

In the 1970s, an exorcist attempted in vain to rid the poorhouse of its British ghosts. In the surrounding forests, witnesses have seen and heard the ghost of the famed general mounted atop his trusted steed.

TARRYTOWN/SLEEPY HOLLOW—PATRIOT'S PARK

Located on the dividing line between the villages of Tarrytown and Sleepy Hollow, Patriot's Park features a statue erected to the memory of

John Paulding, one of the three Patriot militiamen who arrested British spy John André. On Saturday, September 23, 1780, Paulding, Isaac Van Wart, and David Williams came upon André as he was making his way to the British line with invaluable intelligence obtained from Benedict Arnold. Dressed as a civilian, the British officer aroused the suspicions of Paulding and his comrades, who promptly took him into custody. Legend has it that Paulding's ghost dwells in the park, apparently still celebrating his significant contribution to American independence.

Patriot's Park is located adjacent to the Warner Library. The address is U.S. 9 (North Broadway), Tarrytown/Sleepy Hollow, N.Y. 10591.

New Jersey

ME
(WAS N. MA.)

VT

NH

NEW JERSEY

NY

MA

CT

RI

PA

NJ

MD

DE

VA

NC

SC

GA

SHADED AREA SHOWS
COLONIAL AMERICA

Spooky Ringwood Manor
RINGWOOD, NEW JERSEY

It is a common observation here that our cause is the cause of all mankind, and that we are fighting for their liberty in defending our own.

BENJAMIN FRANKLIN

Some American officers made important contributions to the Revolutionary War effort without leading troops on the battlefield. So it was with General Robert Erskine (1735–80), who produced badly needed iron for the American military and drew maps used by General George Washington and his high command. Erskine made his home at Ringwood Manor, a substantial estate in northern New Jersey near the Saddle River. He died during the war from an illness contracted while doing cartographic work in the field. Acting on his wishes, family and friends buried him in a brick tomb on the grounds of the estate. But the general's ghost escaped. Today, it dwells at Ringwood Manor with several other phantoms from the Revolutionary War era.

After his arrival in America in 1771, the Scottish-born Erskine began management of three significant iron-producing plantations in an ore-rich area near the New Jersey border with New York. Because it was located on the military route between West Point, New York, and Morristown, New Jersey, Ringwood Manor was ideally positioned to expedite its iron products to the Continental Army. Metal from Erskine's enterprises was used to fabricate the famous chain across the Hudson River, a navigational hazard constructed by the American military in 1778 to hamper British water traffic.

Erskine was a multitalented man who developed a friendship with George Washington during the early stages of the war. Cognizant of Erskine's superb skills as an engineer, Washington commissioned him as geographer and surveyor to the United States Army on July 27, 1777. Over the next three years, Erskine produced a prodigious number of maps and sketches that proved invaluable in developing American war strategy.

His colonial manor house was built around 1762. On numerous occasions during the war, Washington called on General Erskine at Ringwood. Significantly expanded and altered over the years, the mansion serves today as the centerpiece of Ringwood Manor State Park.

After her husband's death, Mrs. Erskine continued to reside in the manor house, where she entertained officers and soldiers who traveled the nearby military route. James Thacher, a Continental Army surgeon, described her social graces: "Mrs. Erskine is a sensible and accomplished woman; lives in a style of affluence and fashion; everything indicates wealth, taste, and splendor; and she takes pleasure in entertaining the friends of her late husband with generous hospitality." On April 19, 1783, the very day that hostilities ceased between Great Britain and America, George Washington enjoyed her company at Ringwood Manor.

Strange, eerie occurrences give credence to the belief that the ghosts of General Erskine and his wife are in residence in their venerable home. A spectral figure carrying a blue lantern about the corridors may be the spirit of the old mapmaker. And Mrs. Erskine's ghost is believed to be the source of the mysterious disembodied footsteps and the doors that suddenly slam throughout the fifty-one-room house. Visitors have reported strange cold spots in her former chamber.

Outside the manor house, the bizarre clopping of large numbers of phantom hooves is sometimes heard. Unlike the Revolutionary War era, when scores of horses were maintained on the estate, few are in the area today.

Located down the hill from the mansion is a majestic pond with mirrorlike waters. Behind it is the estate cemetery, best visited while the sun is high in the sky. When darkness begins to cover the historic landscape, a phantom sentry in a Revolutionary War uniform guards the old entrance gate. If you are able to gain passage, you can walk among some four hundred graves of area pioneers, eighteenth-century iron makers, and Revolutionary War soldiers.

Near the tomb of General Erskine, several French soldiers from the command of the Viscount de Rochambeau are buried in an unmarked grave. Their spectres have been observed and their French words heard in the stillness of the place.

If you happen to see a ball of blue light in the cemetery, you are most likely near General Erskine's grave. Take notice of the missing bricks. Rational minds would attribute the damage to vandals or the ravages of time. But some say Erskine attempted to claw his way out of the grave. As the legend goes, when the first brick fell, his spirit came rushing out. On dark, misty nights, the ghost of the old mapmaker can be seen sitting atop his tomb. More than one visitor has unwittingly been escorted back to the manor house by the general's kindly, congenial spirit.

Ringwood Manor was a welcoming place for freedom fighters during the Revolutionary War. Today, its ghosts still roll out the welcome mat for visitors to a place where the American cause was immeasurably aided without a shot being fired.

The address for **Ringwood Manor** is Sloatsburg Rd., Ringwood, N.J. 07456; the telephone number is 973-962-2240.

Ghosts from the Heat of the Battle
MONMOUTH, NEW JERSEY

*[General Washington] swore that day till the leaves shook on
the trees. Charming! Delightful! Never have I enjoyed swearing
before or since.*

GENERAL CHARLES SCOTT

On June 13, 1778, General George Washington struck his headquarters at Valley Forge, Pennsylvania, and put his army of thirteen
thousand men on a desperate march. Intelligence had revealed that the
British army commanded by Sir Henry Clinton had left Philadelphia
en route to the New Jersey coast, where the fifteen thousand Redcoats
were to be ferried to New York. Determined to catch and seriously damage the enemy juggernaut, Washington hurried his army forward. At
Monmouth, located midway between Trenton and the Jersey shoreline,
the two armies collided on June 28. By nightfall, the largest one-day
battle of the entire war and the last major engagement in the North was
at an end. Today, the battlefield is little changed from that hot, bloody
day in the early summer of 1778. Visitors to the place now preserved as

Monmouth Battlefield State Park are likely to encounter ghosts from the horrific clash, whether a troop of skeletal Hessian warriors, a Continental soldier, or a true American heroine.

On the eve of the battle, Major General Charles Lee, who had recently rejoined the Continental Army in a prisoner exchange, was selected by Washington to command the field operations at Monmouth, much to the chagrin of the officers and soldiers in the army. Lee was in large measure distrusted by the rank and file.

Washington ordered General Lee to attack Lord Cornwallis, who commanded the rear of Clinton's army, in the early-morning hours of June 28. Despite urgent appeals from General Anthony Wayne, Lee did not commence his attack until nine o'clock. Cornwallis and his men fought back with great distinction, holding their ground until reinforcements of British regulars and Hessians arrived. With the element of surprise lost, the Americans found themselves in serious trouble as Lee sounded the retreat for his panicked charges.

Drawn to the sound of the fighting, Washington galloped to the scene and asked why his soldiers were scurrying to the rear. The reply was universal: "Ask Lee. He ordered it." According to the Marquis de Lafayette, Washington called Lee "a damned pultroon" and proceeded to reorganize and rally his army to fight a fiercely contested battle that continued until darkness covered the landscape. The searing heat took an unimaginable toll on the soldiers and animals in both armies.

Amid the blistering temperatures, an angel of mercy appeared. Mary Ludwig Hays, born in New Jersey in 1754, was an artillery wife. She had traveled with her husband, John, following his enlistment in the Continental Army in 1775. At Valley Forge, they suffered the brutal winter together, only to march to Monmouth to take part in the grim spectacle played out there that fiery June afternoon.

As the artillery of her husband and his comrades belched lethal fire toward the enemy, Mary realized that someone must provide water to cool the big guns and soothe the fatigued warriors. Disregarding the deafening blasts of muskets and field pieces, her striped skirt blowing in the wind, she rushed onto the battlefield with pitcher after pitcher of lifesaving water. Soldiers who witnessed her actions referred to her as "Molly Pitcher," a heroic nickname she would forever carry.

On each trip to the field, Molly ministered to the wounded and comforted the dying after dispensing her water. At one point, she placed a badly wounded American soldier on her back and struggled to carry him to safety. In the course of the battle, Mary saw her husband fall at his gun. After briefly treating John's nonfatal wound, she rose, took the rammer staff, and assumed charge of the cannon. Only once before had an American woman—Mary Corbin at Fort Washington in 1776—manned a piece of artillery in combat.

The site of Molly Pitcher's heroics is part of the 1,810-acre Monmouth Battlefield State Park. Visitors are free to roam the ground where more than 130 soldiers died of sunstroke alone. The number of victims would have been much higher had it not been for the selfless acts of Molly Pitcher that day. And even now, her ghost remains on duty at the site. More than one park guest has been offered water by a spectral lady dressed in the clothing of bygone days. On one hot summer day, a family thanked the staff at the park museum for providing a guide in full costume at Molly Pitcher's well. Perplexed, the staff noted that no one in the park was dressed as Molly Pitcher.

Adjacent to the battlefield stands the white frame, two-story Old Tennent Church, which served as a field hospital on the day of the battle. Surgeons and nurses waded in blood up to their ankles in the old sanctuary, where limbs were amputated without anesthesia. Now, unexplained sounds emanate from the place.

Under a tree in the churchyard, an American soldier enjoying a brief respite from the battle was hit by an enemy cannonball, which carried away his entire arm and shoulder. His ghost has been observed wandering the grounds.

Visitors to the battlefield will do well to leave the place as the sun begins to set, the very time of day when hostilities ceased here in 1778. They should be forewarned that soldiers in ghost form make twilight appearances. The first encounter with this phantom force occurred in September 1779. At the end of a tiring day in the field, several farmers making their way past the Monmouth battleground en route to their homes were intrigued when their dogs raced off toward the forest surrounding the site. Just before they reached the woods, the dogs came to a sudden halt. They turned around, began whimpering, and returned to their masters, tails between their legs. Anxious to determine why their dogs were spooked, the farmers hurried to the edge of the forest. There, they were horrified to see a group of Hessian ghosts, fleshless skeletons dressed in full military uniforms, prepared for combat.

Casualties at the Battle of Monmouth were about even for both sides. Because Sir Henry Clinton was forced to retreat from the field, the Continental Army proclaimed itself the victor. Most military historians have subsequently deemed the engagement a draw. But if eyewitness accounts are to be believed, Hessian ghosts at Monmouth remain ready and willing to do battle again, when and if the Red and Blue decide to take up arms.

For more information, contact **Monmouth Battlefield State Park,** 347 Freehold Rd., Manalapan, N.J. 07726; the telephone number is 732-780-5782.

A Traitor, a Spy, and a Martyr: Ghosts All
NAVESINK HIGHLANDS, NEW JERSEY

Those who expect to reap the blessings of freedom must, like men, undergo the fatigue of supporting it.

THOMAS PAINE

Famous Sandy Hook Bay, an arm of Raritan Bay, borders the northern coast of New Jersey. Towering above the bay are the Navesink Highlands, a range of hills offering a splendid view of the historic waters that have sheltered military vessels since colonial times. The heights above Sandy Hook as well as the beach below remain home to the ghosts of a trio of men from the American Revolution.

Charles Lee, the general who drew insulting comments from George Washington at the Battle of Monmouth (see 128-31), was born in 1731 in England to a high-ranking British officer. He saw combat prior to the American Revolution in the colonial wars. In 1773, he settled in Virginia and aligned himself with the movement toward independence. His gift of oratory enabled him to rise in prominence—so much so that the Continental Congress appointed him a major general, second

in rank to only Washington and General Artemas Ward of Massachusetts. Before Lee accepted the appointment, he successfully demanded
that Congress compensate him for his family estates in England, which
would be confiscated by the British government.

During the latter half of 1776, Lee's reluctance to cooperate in
the New Jersey campaign raised suspicions that he was anxious to take
Washington's job. Consequently, in a letter of December 9, 1776, to
General Horatio Gates, Washington noted about Lee, "*Entre nous* a
certain great man is damnably deficient."

Four days later, Lee was captured by British soldiers at Basking
Ridge, New Jersey. William Howe, then the British commander in
chief in America, refused to accede to requests that Lee be transported
to England to be tried for treason. Instead, the prisoner was detained in
New York for nearly sixteen months. There, unbeknownst to Americans
for more than seventy years after the war, Lee provided his captors with
a secret plan to "unhinge the organization of American resistance" by
subjugating the middle colonies. Since his captors put little stock in his
suggestions, Lee went through the war as an undetected traitor.

Upon his exchange in April 1778, he rejoined the American army
at Valley Forge. Washington's renewed confidence in him proved mis-
guided when Lee performed abysmally at Monmouth. A court-martial
was convened in the aftermath of the battle, and Lee was suspended
from command for a year. On January 10, 1780, the Continental Congress dismissed him from military service.

After Lee died at his Virginia estate in 1782, his ghost began appearing on the New Jersey shoreline. To this day, a gaunt, haggard, pale
spectral figure dressed in Revolutionary War attire peers east toward the
Atlantic. At times, Lee's ghost is observed standing atop the Navesink
Highlands, as if watching for his rescue by ship from his native land.
After all, his spirit must be anxious to leave the country he attempted
to destroy in its infancy.

Though it has not been reported in the company of Lee's apparition, another Revolutionary War ghost is often encountered about the

Navesink Highlands. John Honeyman (1729–1822) was a renowned spy for George Washington. As legend has it, his spirit stands on the hills above Sandy Hook Bay in a lonely vigil to fulfill Honeyman's last mission for his general. "Let me know when the British fleet leaves New York," Washington asked of him.

Born in Ireland, Honeyman was the son of a farmer of Scottish descent. Like Charles Lee, he first came to North America to fight for Great Britain in the French and Indian War. On the voyage across the Atlantic, Honeyman saved Colonel (soon to be General) James Wolfe from serious injury or death. Wolfe tripped on a steep stairway of the ship, and the young private rushed to catch him. So grateful was Wolfe that he made Honeyman his personal bodyguard. Just a year later, Honeyman bore the body of the mortally wounded general from the field at the decisive British victory at Quebec City.

Upon receiving his honorable discharge from the British army, Honeyman settled in Pennsylvania. As the disagreement between Great Britain and the colonies grew, he was drawn to the cause of independence. When he moved to Philadelphia in 1775, Honeyman, a butcher by trade, met George Washington, who came to admire his modesty and lack of pretension. Washington was delighted when Honeyman accepted his invitation to serve as a special agent for the American cause.

In November 1776, Washington ordered the Continental Army to retreat across New Jersey into Pennsylvania. But he was determined to return. Meanwhile, his operative, Honeyman, was at work in Trenton, posing as a Tory merchant. There, he gained invaluable intelligence. In a ruse designed to safely deliver his information, Honeyman arranged to be "captured" by the American army. Upon his "escape" from Washington's clutches, the spy made haste back to Trenton, where he promptly reported to Colonel Johann Rall, the commander of the large Hessian force defending the city. Upon being advised by Honeyman that Washington's army was too demoralized to launch an attack, Rall authorized his men to stand down in order to enjoy the forthcoming Christmas festivities. Honeyman quickly departed the city, setting the stage for one of the most dramatic chapters in American history.

At eleven o'clock on the bitterly cold Christmas night of 1776, the ragged, shoeless Continental Army loaded into boats to cross the icy Delaware River en route to a showdown in Trenton. At eight the following morning, the twelve-hundred-man Hessian garrison was rudely awakened by Washington's attack force. In less than ninety minutes, the American rout was complete. Historian George Otto Trevelyan opined about the surprise attack, "It may be doubted whether so small a number of men ever employed so short a space of time with greater or more lasting results upon the history of the world."

John Honeyman, the man behind the scenes at Trenton, rendered invaluable service as Washington's spy for the remainder of the war. And his ghost seeks to continue in that role. Dressed as an unassuming Tory, it stands on the Navesink range, intent on carrying out its one final mission.

If, while traversing the highlands, you fail to come across the ghost of the traitor or the spy, perhaps you will encounter that of the American martyr who was hanged here during the war.

Captain Joshua Huddy (1735–82) was a New Jersey native who aligned himself with the American cause from the outset of the struggle for independence. As a militia captain, Huddy led daring raids in which his soldiers killed Loyalists and looted their residences in his home county of Monmouth.

In August 1780, Huddy was granted a license to operate a privateer, the *Black Snake*. A month later, Loyalist raiders captured him after a two-hour gunfight at his home. Following a miraculous escape, Huddy was given command of a small fort on the Toms River designed to protect an important saltworks.

On March 1, 1782, Tory forces overwhelmed Huddy's small garrison and once again took him prisoner. This time, there would be no escape. Huddy was promptly charged with the murder of Philip White, a noted Loyalist refugee. Turned over to British authorities, he was transported to New York City to await prisoner exchange. However, friends of Philip White convinced William Franklin (the son of Benjamin Franklin and the last Royal governor of New Jersey) to gain custody of Huddy. Soon thereafter, Captain Huddy was confined in leg irons on a prison ship anchored in Sandy Hook Bay.

Governor William Franklin gave his approval to Huddy's execution without benefit of trial. On April 12, 1782, the condemned man was taken ashore on a beach shadowed by the Navesink Highlands. His execution was carried out by Loyalists under the direction of Captain Richard Lippincott. Before the noose was placed around Huddy's neck, his detractors pinned a note on his chest: "Up Goes Huddy for Philip White." Eyewitnesses described Huddy as calm and brave. He shook hands with Lippincott and muttered that he would "die innocent and in a good cause."

The following morning, Patriots on patrol discovered Huddy's body dangling from the tree. They cut it down and transported it to Old Tennent Church near the Monmouth battlefield, where it was interred.

George Washington was outraged over the tragic affair. So was Sir Henry Clinton, who condemned the execution as a "barbarous outrage against humanity." To redress the injustice, area Patriots demanded that Captain Lippincott be turned over to them. When the demand was rejected, they selected Charles Asgill, a captured British officer, to die in Lippincott's stead. Only after Asgill's mother persuaded the French foreign minister to intervene was his life spared.

Many a visitor to the Jersey Shore below the Navesink Highlands has been startled to see the spectre of a Revolutionary War officer striding the beach. Observers have noted that as the ghostly figure draws near, it suddenly turns and walks away after listening to the voices of the living. All those without a British accent are safe. The phantom captain is on an apparent search for his executioners. On some days, the apparitions of two men dressed in clothing of the Revolutionary War era have been encountered along the same stretch of beach. They are thought to be the ghosts of Huddy and Charles Asgill, the man who almost paid with his life for the captain's death.

Charles Lee, John Honeyman, and Joshua Huddy—three names etched in the Revolutionary War history, and the supernatural history, of the United States of America.

The **Navesink Highlands** may be viewed at the Twin Lights of Navesink Lighthouse Historic Site, located just off N.J. 36. The address is Lighthouse Road, Highlands, N.J. 07732; the telephone number is 732-872-1814.

The Curse and Ghost of Mary Post
MAHWAH, NEW JERSEY

*When the sword is once drawn, the passions of men observe
no bounds of moderation.*

ALEXANDER HAMILTON

Since the founding of the Boy Scouts in the first decade of the
twentieth century, scout camps have been perhaps the most popular
places in America to listen to ghost stories. Many of the haunted tales
told around campfires over the years have been purely fictional. On the
other hand, some have had a basis in fact. One such tale was that of
Mary Post, recounted over the decades to scouts in the Ramapo Mountains of northeastern New Jersey at Camp Glen Gray, which served as
a scouting complex from 1917 to 2001. Scouts were especially terrified
because the story was played out on the site of the camp during the
Revolutionary War. Long before Boy Scouts began camping here, area
residents whispered the tale of the local woman Americans executed as
a spy in the summer of 1777.

Legend aside, the land upon which the Boy Scout camp was constructed played a prominent role during the Revolutionary War in New Jersey. In the vicinity of the existing parking lot, two historic roads, Cannonball Trail and Mary Post Road, meander through the extensive complex, now operated by Bergen County as a public camping and recreational facility. During America's fight for independence, the Cannonball Trail served as a vital route for soldiers and supplies for the Continental Army. It offered a direct link between Morristown, an important winter headquarters for General Washington in central New Jersey, and West Point on the Hudson.

One of the prominent landmarks on the route was the Mary Post Inn, located near the junction of Mary Post Road and Cannonball Trail. Its proprietor was described by contemporaries as a beautiful, young, vivacious brunette. American officers including members of George Washington's staff stayed overnight at the inn from time to time as they accompanied troops and supply shipments. There, they relaxed and enjoyed outstanding food, drink, and lodging. Their hospitable hostess was only too happy to engage the officers in conversation. Sometimes, too much drink resulted in loose lips.

Beginning late in 1776 and continuing well into the summer of 1777, British forces operating out of New York City repeatedly ambushed American supply shipments along the Cannonball Trail in the Ramapo Mountains. As concern grew among George Washington's inner circle, questions arose as to why the British always seemed to know where and when to strike. Lieutenant Colonel Alexander Hamilton, Washington's aide-de-camp, suggested Mary Post might be a spy for the enemy.

Acting on his suspicions, the officer who would subsequently serve as America's first secretary of the treasury directed Patriot operatives to tail Mary Post. Hamilton's worst fears were realized. Under the cloak of darkness, the pretty spy mounted her horse and galloped off to New York City, where she spent the night with her lover, Major Carlton McDonnell, a British officer known for his cruelty to Americans. In the course of her frequent liaisons with McDonnell, Post yielded to his demands for the confidential information she had obtained from her guests.

Rather than arrest Mary Post on the evidence supplied by American agents, Hamilton was authorized by Washington to lay a trap and let the innkeeper "convict" herself. Thus, during the first week of August 1777, Hamilton called at the inn and requested that Mary close her place for an evening so the Americans could hold a high-level strategy meeting. Only too happy to grant the request, she agreed to make the inn available on Monday, August 11, 1777.

As Mary served the meal, Hamilton and his fellow officers conversed about an enormous shipment of equipment and supplies that would pass the inn eight days hence. Mary listened intently. One night later, she sped away to renew her tryst and to bear the news planted by Hamilton and his associates.

On Tuesday, August 19, an entire British division descended upon the Cannonball Trail near the inn, fully expecting to capture an American supply convoy. Instead, the Redcoats were overwhelmed by an elite unit of Continentals personally selected by General Washington.

A day later, American regulars arrested Mary Post at her inn. Not long after she was taken into custody, an angry band of armed local Patriots interceded. They wrested the woman from the Continentals and proceeded to mete out their own form of justice. Venting their rage, members of the mob brutally beat her at a spot a hundred yards from her inn. Some of the men affixed a hanging rope on a nearby young maple tree.

The hapless spy, bleeding profusely, was strung up as the crowd multiplied. For nearly fifteen minutes, she clung to life as the rope ever so slowly tightened about her neck. Her tormenters jeered at, taunted, and tortured her, seeming to enjoy every second of her pain and terror.

When the end was apparent, Mary Post spoke weakly in a melancholy voice. She cursed the maple tree on which she was hanging and swore revenge against the Americans who executed her and the British who failed to come to her rescue. As she struggled for her final breaths, she warned that anyone who caused harm to the hanging tree would come to understand the "true meaning of pain and suffering through injury, insanity, or death."

No one in the assemblage took the curse seriously, considering it to be nothing more than the ranting of a spy caught in the act. Little did they know that the maple tree would indeed be a source of death, misery, and strange, unexplained incidents.

Tales of the eerie malediction were handed down over the generations in the Ramapo Mountains. When Camp Glen Gray opened in 1917, the Mary Post Maple survived as a mature tree within its confines. Over the years that followed, an unbelievable series of tragic events occurred at the tree.

A scoutmaster cut a limb from the old maple in 1923 in an attempt to demonstrate to his pack that there was nothing to the curse. Just three days later, he and his entire family perished in a house fire.

Sixteen years later, a camp official attempted to fell the Mary Post Maple. Determined to dispel the legend, he slammed a sharp ax into the tree trunk. Again and again he chopped, until the ax flew back and sliced into his neck. He died from the wound.

A camper harmlessly (or so he thought) carved his initials into the maple on a summer day in 1940. When he fell asleep in his tent that evening, he was fine. But he awoke the following morning to excruciating pain. His leg had sustained a compound fracture while he slept.

Almost fifteen years later, a camp worker attempted to defy the curse of Mary Post by chopping pieces from the maple to sell as souvenirs. No sooner had he completed the feat than he began to suffer terrible nightmares. Ultimately, the nightmares led to complete insanity that necessitated hospitalization in a mental institution for the remainder of the man's life.

By 1969, the Mary Post Maple was badly diseased. Its condition and age forced New Jersey officials to decide that the tree should be brought down before it toppled onto a nearby structure. Two men assigned to the duty arrived at the campground on the evening before they were to do the job. As they turned in for the night, one of the workers expressed his concern about the Mary Post legend, but the other dismissed it as rubbish. During the night, the scoffer died in his sleep of a brain hemorrhage. His companion fled the scene without completing his assignment.

Six years passed. The tree still stood but was no longer alive. But was the curse? On Friday, February 13, 1980, a brave group of thirteen individuals including three young Boy Scouts assembled at the old maple to tempt the age-old curse. Chain saws buzzed until finally the tree crashed onto the snow-covered landscape. A portion was salvaged and can now be seen in the park headquarters.

Of the thirteen who participated in the tree cutting, three subsequently died. One was killed in a horrible automobile wreck two weeks after the event. Another perished in a skiing accident. The third died of a liver malady after imbibing large quantities of alcohol on the second anniversary of the day the maple was taken down.

The other ten participants were not spared misfortune. Each sustained major nonfatal injuries within twelve months of the tree removal.

Area folks thought they were finally finished with the evil of old Mary Post. *Au contraire!* Not long after the tree fell, campers and locals alike began to observe the ghost of the female spy looming about the place where she was executed. At Lake Vreeland, located near the site of the old inn, Mary's spectre is often seen floating above the water, particularly on autumn nights. Her apparition has also been encountered in the nearby forests.

Some people argue that the Revolutionary War legend and the ghostly sightings are nothing more than folklore, claiming the "real" Mary Post was not born until the nineteenth century. If you care to spend the night at Camp Glen Gray, you can be the judge. As for the ghost of a gorgeous young lady attired in blouse, skirt, and apron of the

Revolutionary War era, it is merely a character from a campfire tale designed to scare Boy Scouts munching s'mores. Or is it?

Camp Glen Gray is now a public overnight camping and recreational facility. Its address is 200 Midvale Mountain Rd., Mahwah, N.J. 07430-2700; the telephone number is 201-327-7234.

The Sourlands Spook
EAST AMWELL TOWNSHIP, NEW JERSEY

Whatever we obtain too cheap, we esteem too lightly; it is
dearness only that gives every thing its value.
THOMAS PAINE, DECEMBER 19, 1776

In January 1932, world-famous aviator Charles Lindbergh moved
his family into Highfields, an expansive twenty-three-room manor
house he had constructed in the Sourland Mountains of western New
Jersey. Less than three months later, the nation reacted in horror when
Lindbergh's son was abducted from the estate, located on a densely
forested mountain ridge seventeen miles east of the Delaware River on
the Pennsylvania border.

Lindbergh chose to build his home in an isolated area with a longstanding reputation for being haunted. Charles Sutphin, a native of
the Sourlands, once described the spooky aura: "Queer things are seen,
queer things are heard, and queer things happen in the wilderness of
the trees and the blue-jingler rocks of the Sourland Mountains where

Colonel and Mrs. Lindbergh have built their home. Ghosts have plenty of reason for haunting that section. Nine murders have been done there since I can remember."

One of the most prominent peaks in the Sourlands is Knitting Betty's Rock, just northeast of the Lindbergh estate. Named for a Revolutionary War woman who turned spy for the Continental Army after her fiancé died in the early stages of the war, this famous natural feature and the surrounding landscape have long been haunted by the ghost of Betty Wert, executed by the British in 1778 after the Battle of Monmouth.

Though no Revolutionary War battle was fought in the Sourlands, the area played an important role in the struggle for independence. John Hart, one of New Jersey's five signers of the Declaration of Independence, was forced to take refuge here when British troops raided his home in the latter portion of 1776. As General George Washington prepared to confront the British army of Lord Howe in New Jersey, he camped his army in the Sourlands on June 23, 1778. A day later, Washington convened a council of war at the Hunt House, an extant two-story dwelling less than two miles south of Knitting Betty's Rock. There, Washington, General Charles Lee, General Anthony Wayne, General Nathanael Greene, and the Marquis de Lafayette developed the American strategy subsequently used in the days leading up to the Battle of Monmouth. Some of the American high command's crucial information came directly from the espionage of Betty Wert.

At the onset of the war, spying was the last thing on the mind of Elizabeth "Betty" Wert. She stayed behind in her native Sourlands as her intended answered the call to arms against Great Britain in the wake of the clashes at Lexington and Concord in Massachusetts. Day by day, she waited for his return, whiling away the time by knitting atop the promontory now bearing her name. From her lofty perch, Betty reasoned she would catch the first sight of the triumphant return of her beau.

But death, whether by battle or disease, came to the young man as he served his new country. After a period of grieving, Betty grew angry. She sought a means of revenge and of serving her fellow Americans as the British army pushed to make good on its threat to cut New Jersey in half. Because of her excellent knowledge of the central part of the state, George Washington enlisted Betty as a spy.

During the first half of 1778, the pretty brunette exposed herself to peril as she rode about the area as an undercover agent for the Continental Army. On the eve of the Battle of Monmouth, Betty vanished. Tories in central New Jersey, smarting over recurrent indignities suffered at the hands of Patriots, had grown increasingly suspicious of her. They took her captive and turned her over to British authorities.

Condemned as a traitor and spy, Betty was incarcerated on a prison ship in Raritan Bay and then at Sugar Hill, the infamous British prison in Harlem. She was subsequently beheaded in New York City, after which her executioner displayed her head on a pike in the Battery. Her headless body was dumped into the water near Sandy Hook.

Over the ensuing years, Betty Wert's ghost has been observed on countless occasions in a variety of forms.

Horsemen, pedestrians, and motorists have reported the apparition of a beautiful young woman with flowing brown hair on Knitting Betty's Rock. According to numerous reports, the ghost sits on the peak, peacefully knitting until it fades from view.

One day in 1983, a twenty-three-year-old man traveling the Sourlands on business noticed a gorgeous brunette wearing a long blue dress and resting upon the rocky ledge. Attracted by her beauty, he brought his vehicle to a screeching halt and jumped out to introduce himself, only to see the vision of loveliness vanish before his eyes.

Encounters with a darker, more sinister form of Betty's ghost have also occurred. Many settlers of the Sourlands in the post–Revolutionary War era observed the apparition of the decapitated Betty sitting upon her rock. Her head, resting in her lap, spun round and round.

In the 1920s, sightings of an even more frightening nature were reported after a local man with deep roots in the Sourlands was found decapitated. The culprit was never discovered, but folks in the area attributed the death to a horrid wraith roaming the countryside. Eyewitnesses described the spectre as a lighted, translucent, headless female body, inside which was a sewing pouch fashioned from human skin. Speculation was rampant that Betty was exacting revenge on descendants of the Tories who killed her in 1778.

A springtime drive through the haunted Sourlands offers spectacular vistas in an area yet preserved from the rampant development so prevalent in New Jersey. If on your visit you happen to see the apparition of the lovely female sitting atop a rock ledge, recall that bittersweet day in the spring of 1775 when she kissed her boyfriend goodbye and watched as he marched off to fight for an independent America. But if you happen to see a vengeful headless ghost walking along the highway or peering down from a nearby hill, remember that dark day in the late spring of 1778 when area Tories set their neighbor, a pretty young American spy, on the road to an excruciating death.

Knitting Betty's Rock is visible just north of Highfields (the former Lindbergh estate) ten miles northwest of Princeton, New Jersey.

Other "Spirited" Revolutionary War Sites in New Jersey, Briefly Noted

BELLEVILLE—BELLEVILLE DUTCH REFORMED CHURCH

This historic church, organized in the last decade of the seventeenth century, saw extensive action during the Revolutionary War. Patriot soldiers used the steeple as an observation post from which to monitor enemy movements. Area militiamen killed in action were buried under the church basement, and sixty-seven soldiers who survived the war were later interred in the adjacent cemetery. So popular was the church with one American freedom fighter buried here that his ghost offers phantom organ recitals in the empty sanctuary.

The address for Belleville Dutch Reformed Church is Main St. and Rutgers St., Belleville, N.J. 07109.

BERNARDSVILLE—BERNARDSVILLE PUBLIC LIBRARY

Phyllis Parker, a ghost of the Revolutionary War era, has been witnessed here since 1877. During the war, the building operated as the Vealtown Tavern. Tradition has it that Phyllis, the daughter of owner John Parker, fell in love with Dr. Byram, one of her father's tenants. In a short time, the romance blossomed into marriage, but the newlyweds' happiness was brief. Mad Anthony Wayne took custody of Dr. Byram and put him to death as a spy. His corpse was delivered to the Vealtown Tavern in a pine box. Unaware of her husband's fate, Phyllis opened the makeshift coffin. When her eyes beheld the gruesome sight, she suffered an emotional breakdown from which she never recovered. For the remainder of her life, her weeping, wailing, and moaning were the norm in the building.

The old structure, incorporated into the local library, is now used as a public meeting room. The melancholy cries of Phyllis Byram can yet be heard in the place where she opened her husband's coffin. On occasion, her ghost has been observed hovering about the room.

The address for the Bernardsville Public Library is 2 Morristown Rd., Bernardsville, N.J. 07924; the telephone number is 908-766-0118.

ELIZABETH—UNION COUNTY COURTHOUSE AND FIRST PRESBYTERIAN CHURCH CEMETERY

An imposing monument in the First Presbyterian Church Cemetery marks the graves of a team of husband and wife Patriots, the Reverend James and Hannah Caldwell. It is said that Hannah cannot rest in her grave. Her spirit walks about the cemetery and the adjacent county courthouse, perhaps because her life was cut short by a British bullet.

On Wednesday evening, June 7, 1780, British and Hessian troops under the command of Hessian general Wilhelm Knyphausen poured into the streets of what is now Elizabeth. The out-of-control soldiers, reeling from their afternoon defeat at nearby Connecticut Farms, pillaged and set fire to homes in their quest for revenge. At the manse on Caldwell Street, Hannah waited patiently with her children for the return of the reverend, a field chaplain with the Continental Army. Suddenly, a bullet smashed through a window and struck her. She was killed instantly.

Her melancholy ghost is sometimes observed looming near her grave site. On other occasions, it floats forlornly through the corridors of the Union County Courthouse next door.

The address for the Union County Courthouse is 2 Broad St., Elizabeth, N.J. 07207.

ENGLISHTOWN—VILLAGE INN

Now painted blood red, the clapboard Village Inn, built around 1726, is in the heart of Englishtown just blocks from the battlefield of Monmouth. George Washington maintained his headquarters in the inn during the famous battle. In its aftermath, he sat at a table here and penned the orders for the court-martial of General Charles Lee as a result of his subordinate's inept conduct of the early stages of the fighting.

Several ghosts from the Revolutionary War haunt the venerable structure. Phantom Continental soldiers have been heard running up the steps. Lights flicker off and on without scientific explanation.

The former inn is now the home of the Battleground Historical Society. The address is 2 Water St., Englishtown, N.J. 07726; the telephone number is 908-446-9760.

FARMINGDALE—OUR HOUSE RESTAURANT

George Marriner constructed this building in 1747 for use as a tavern. For the remainder of the eighteenth century, it served in that capacity, operating alternately as Marriner's Tavern and Our House Tavern. During the Revolutionary War, a lawless group of fellows known as the Fagen Gang used it as a place to socialize and plot their mayhem against Patriot families. To rid the area of the incorrigibles, Lee's Light Dragoons arrived at the tavern from Monmouth on Thursday, September 23, 1779. They summarily hanged Lewis Fenton, one of the Fagens, in front of the tavern. His ghost is thought to linger here.

The modern restaurant housed in the old tavern serves as the venue for Fenton's supernatural activities. Pictures mysteriously move on the walls; unexplained noises echo throughout the structure; phantom foot-steps tread across the floors; doors creak and close without the touch of a human; and lights turn on and off by themselves.

The address for Our House Restaurant and Banquet Facility is 420 Adelphia Rd., Farmingdale, N.J. 07727; the telephone number is 732-938-5159.

GLENDORA—GABRIEL DAVIES TAVERN

During the colonial era, this tavern was popular with boatmen making their way to Philadelphia, twelve miles distant. When the Revolutionary War engulfed the area, General George Washington designated the attic as a military hospital. For a time, the place was known as the Hillman Hospital House. The original floor in the attic bears bloodstains dating from the fight for independence. Ghosts from that time haunt the site.

Now restored and preserved as a historical showplace, the building, constructed around 1756, has been investigated by numerous professional ghost-hunting teams. Among the supernatural occurrences attributed to Revolutionary War ghosts are the disembodied footsteps in the attic, the phantom sounds of human suffering, and the mysterious lights that glow from the windows of the empty building.

The old tavern is open to the public on occasion. Its address is Fourth Ave., Glendora, N.J. 08029; the telephone number is 856-939-2699.

GREAT BAY—MULLICA RIVER

Ten miles north of Atlantic City, the Mullica River empties into Great Bay on the New Jersey coast. Along the banks of the river, a lonely Patriot ghost continues to signal the approach of the British with his phantom voice.

In the spring of 1778, Sir Henry Clinton, vexed over the successful operations of American privateers on the Mullica River and other coastal waterways, dispatched a seven-hundred-man expeditionary force to Tuckerton, a port village north of Great Bay. From their headquarters, the Redcoats enjoyed success in their initial attacks against Patriot pirates. Determined to raid the enemy ironworks at Batsto, located up the Mullica in the New Jersey Pine Barrens, the British raiders impressed a local fisherman, Nathaniel Cowperthwaite, into service as a river pilot. As soon as an opportunity presented itself, Cowperthwaite, a strong supporter of American independence, grounded the enemy vessel, jumped into the river, and swam ashore, where he ran along the Mullica screaming, "The British are coming!"

Even now, those words are heard from the ghost of New Jersey's Paul Revere as it ambles up and down the banks. Boaters and fishermen on the Mullica frequently hear the eerie call to arms from an apparition wearing the clothes of a colonial fisherman.

N.J. 563 crosses the picturesque Mullica approximately ten miles south of historic Batsto in the heart of the Pine Barrens.

HANCOCK'S BRIDGE—JUDGE WILLIAM HANCOCK HOUSE AND JOHN HANCOCK'S BRIDGE

As spring approached in 1778, a small contingent of militia troops was dispatched to John Hancock's Bridge in a desperate effort to prevent the British from crossing Alloway Creek, a tributary of the Delaware River in southwestern New Jersey. Hot on the heels of the meager force of Patriots was a three-hundred-man detachment of Redcoats and Tories of the Queen's Rangers, commanded by Major John G. Simcoe.

In the predawn hours of Saturday, March 21, many of the Patriots were sleeping in the expansive brick house located within sight of the bridge. Constructed before 1740, the dwelling was owned by Judge William Hancock, a justice of the peace loyal to King George III. Before the sun rose that first day of spring, Simcoe's troops eliminated the guards at the bridge, killed the sentinels at the house, and brutally attacked the sleeping Americans inside. In the course of the massacre, upwards of forty Patriots, primarily teenagers and middle-aged men, were bludgeoned and bayoneted to death. Judge Hancock also died in the attack.

Ghosts of the slaughtered Patriots are still observed patrolling the Hancock House and its grounds. The screams and moans of the victims can sometimes be heard inside the home.

The Hancock House is open to the public. Its address is 3 Front St., Hancock's Bridge, N.J. 08038.

HUDSON PALISADES—BLACKLEDGE-KEARNEY HOUSE

As he began his chase of General George Washington in New Jersey, Lord Cornwallis arrived at Closter Landing on the Hudson in November 1776. He promptly set up his headquarters near the river's edge at the Blackledge-Kearney House, which now serves as a museum in the Palisades Parks Conservancy. By all accounts, the British commander enjoyed the house and its outstanding natural setting so much that he never wanted to leave—and indeed he did not. Both the house and grounds are haunted by the ghost of the famous Redcoat general.

Upon his arrival here, Cornwallis immediately put his soldiers to work with pickaxes to blaze a road through the wilderness. To this day, local fishermen claim that they see the general's ghost making its way up the road from his former headquarters building. They say that the spectral British officer shouts orders laced with profanity to an unseen contingent of soldiers.

To reach the Blackledge-Kearney House, turn off U.S. 9W onto Alpine Approach Road and follow it past the park headquarters to the river. The telephone number is 201-768-1360.

LITTLE EGG HARBOR—
WEST CREEK AND ISLAND BEACH STATE PARK

Though Lord Cornwallis had surrendered to George Washington at Yorktown almost a year earlier, hostilities were yet at a fever pitch along the New Jersey coast in the fall of 1782. One of the most notorious of the lawless Tory bands on the south-central New Jersey shoreline was that of John Bacon. Operating from a hideout on the barrier island now home to Island Beach State Park, the outlaws brutally attacked unsuspecting Patriots in the waning days of the war. One such incident, known as the Long Beach Massacre, left behind a party of ghosts.

On an autumn day in 1782, seven Patriots were working on the beach to salvage a sizable cargo of tea from a British ship that had grounded on the treacherous Barnegat Shoals. While taking a brief respite, the men were murdered by John Bacon and his followers. Upon learning of the massacre, area Patriots formed a posse that vowed to "bring home the Bacon." The culprits were subsequently hunted down and killed one by one.

On foggy nights near the mainland coastal community of West Creek, a party of ghosts suddenly forms. The armed mob of spectral men in colonial dress chases a fleeing apparition about the sandy landscape until it overtakes the lone ghost, beats it, and shoots it. Then the phantoms fade into the mist.

West Creek is located on Little Egg Harbor along U.S. 9.

METUCHEN—AYERS-ALLEN HOUSE

Built around 1740, the Ayers-Allen House has long been regarded as one of the most haunted places in New Jersey. Its ghosts seem to have originated during the Revolutionary War, when it was a tavern. Zachariah Allen and his wife, Catherine, were hospitable hosts who served soldiers and townspeople ale and ginger cakes. But after tragedy unfolded in and around the house as the war progressed, it acquired a haunted reputation. Unexplained noises and cold spots throughout the home are attributed to the two ghosts that have been observed roaming the place. One is a soldier dressed in a Revolutionary War uniform, the other a Hessian who hanged himself on the second floor. On the grounds, eyewitnesses have spotted the apparition of a woman wandering about looking for her child, who was killed by British soldiers.

The privately owned Ayers-Allen House is located on Dunham Avenue in Metuchen.

NATIONAL PARK—WHITALL HOUSE

During the fall of 1777, Americans crafted a crude outpost, Fort Mercer, near the east bank of the Delaware just downriver from Philadelphia. Constructed in the orchard of James and Ann Whitall, a modest Quaker family, the fort was the site of the Battle of Red Bank on Wednesday, October 22, 1777. Ghosts of the soldiers who fought, bled, and died in the clash haunt the site today.

Here, a two-thousand-man Hessian army under the command of Count Emil von Donop unleashed a savage attack on the four-hundred-man garrison of Colonel Christopher Greene. In what an eyewitness described as "one of the most glorious stands ever made by Patriots," more than two hundred Hessians were killed, while the Americans lost thirty-seven. Wounded and dying men from both armies were taken to the nearby Whitall farmhouse, which was converted into a field hospital for the two weeks following the bloodshed.

The home is open to the public as a memorial. Visitors have heard the voices, cries of pain, and labored breathing in the rooms where badly injured troops once received care. Cold spots abound, as do the spectres of soldiers from both armies.

The address for Red Bank Battlefield and the Whitall House is 100 Hessian Ave., National Park, N.J. 08063; the telephone number is 865-853-5120.

PATERSON—GARRET MOUNTAIN RESERVATION

The seventy-seven-foot-high Great Falls of the Passaic River is one of America's most magnificent natural landmarks. George Washington, Alexander Hamilton, and the Marquis de Lafayette stopped to lunch near the breathtaking falls during the Revolutionary War. Hamilton took note of the enormous water power generated at the site. Later, while serving as secretary of the treasury, he authorized the development of Paterson as the first industrial city in America.

Not far from the falls is Garret Mountain Reservation, a 568-acre natural area where the Continental Army camped during a respite from fighting in New Jersey. A ghostly sentinel dressed in a blue Revolutionary War uniform has been encountered at the entrance to the park around closing time. Vehicle lights are said to shine right through the spectral soldier, who holds an injured arm.

Garret Mountain Reservation is a public recreational facility. Its address is Mountain Ave., West Paterson, N.J. 07424; the telephone number is 973-881-4832.

PINE BARRENS—BATSTO

Located at the southern edge of Wharton State Forest in the famed New Jersey Pine Barrens, the colonial village of Batsto served as an important supply center for the Continental Army. It is also the place where one of America's most famous supernatural creatures has been sighted since the Revolutionary War.

Of the many accounts of the origin of the Jersey Devil—a creature with horns, a tail, wings, and a horselike head—one has its origins in the American Revolution. A teenage girl from Leeds Point, a community near Great Bay, fell in love with a British soldier dispatched with his unit to the Mullica River to rid the area of Patriot operatives. Local residents sternly opposed the love affair and condemned their neighbor as a traitor. When she became pregnant, a curse was placed on the unborn child. It was born as the legendary creature that has long made its home in the Pine Barrens. Countless eyewitnesses, many in the Batsto area, have caught sight of the strange beast over the years.

Information on historic Batsto is available from Batsto Village, 31 Batsto Rd., Hammonton, N.J. 80307; the telephone number is 609-561-0024.

PINE BARRENS—MULLICA RIVER

The Pine Barrens encompass more than 1.1 million acres. Two marked graves in the remote wilderness are claimed to be the burial sites of one of New Jersey's most colorful Revolutionary War figures. Joe Mulliner, acclaimed "the Robin Hood of the Pine Barrens," was executed as a robber and traitor during the war. His remains were interred in the Pine Barrens. Today, he dwells in the spooky wasteland in ghost form.

Though two of his brothers fought with distinction for the American cause, Joe maintained his allegiance to Great Britain. Operating in and about the Pine Barrens, Mulliner and his band of merry criminals robbed and pillaged in a polite, humane way, refusing to physically injure their victims. Patriot authorities finally got their hands on Joe during the summer of 1781. They tried him in Burlington for high treason. Soon after his conviction, he was sent to the gallows. But the "spirited" fellow could not rest in the grave.

Hikers in the Pine Barrens traverse the trail that once served the stagecoaches held up by Mulliner and his men. Laughter has often been heard booming from the woods surrounding the ancient trail. Sometimes, a shadowy figure armed with eighteenth-century pistols is observed approaching the walkways in the wilderness. Old Joe's ghostly form has also been encountered on the footpaths along the river.

Batsto, the Revolutionary War–era village in the Pine Barrens, is located on the banks of the Mullica River. N.J. 542 passes through the village.

PORT MONMOUTH—SPY HOUSE MUSEUM

Constructed in 1683, this three-story wooden edifice survives as one of the oldest buildings on the New Jersey shoreline. Long regarded as the most haunted place on the state's coast, the old Spy House is home to a number of ghosts, some dating from the Revolutionary War.

When the fight for American independence began, the Patriot owners of the building converted their private home into an inn. In short order, it became a gathering spot for British sailors making their way ashore from the nearby harbor for food, spirits, and fellowship. Meanwhile, Patriot operatives, alerted by the tavern owners, watched the activities. While the British tars were at the inn, the Americans raided their ships. Thus, the place acquired its longstanding name.

Among the ghosts sighted here is that of Lord Cornwallis, who enjoyed the hospitality of the inn's owners. The apparition of an unidentified British sea captain with a full beard has also materialized in the building. Described as a stern-looking fellow, the ghost peers out toward the Atlantic with a spyglass before vanishing into thin air.

The address for the Spy House Museum is 199 Port Monmouth Rd., Port Monmouth, N.J. 07758; the telephone number is 732-787-1807.

PRINCETON—PRINCETON UNIVERSITY

During the Revolutionary War, both armies quartered troops at Nassau Hall, a Princeton University landmark constructed around 1756. The building suffered damage as a result: the library was ransacked; priceless furniture and ornamental woodwork were used to stoke fires; and the organ in the prayer hall was rendered useless. Rearguard military action took place at the architectural masterpiece when General George Washington defeated the British army at the Battle of Princeton on Friday, January 3, 1777. During the fighting, an American cannonball smashed through a window in the prayer hall and demolished a portrait of King George II.

Supernatural reminders of the war abound at Nassau Hall in the form of several soldier ghosts. One of the apparitions is that of a dying British soldier most often observed in the basement.

The university is located on Nassau Street in Princeton.

RIVER EDGE—STEUBEN HOUSE

Completed in 1713, this stately twelve-room sandstone structure housed American troops throughout the Revolutionary War. General George Washington used it as his headquarters in 1780. A year later, New Jersey confiscated the property from its owner, John Zabriski, an unrepentant Loyalist.

On December 23, 1783, a life estate in the house and forty surrounding acres was presented by the New Jersey legislature to Major General Baron von Steuben as a gift for his service to the cause of American independence. After the general's death, the property was repurchased by Zabriski, but Steuben's spirit remained in residence. Perhaps the most famous sighting of the general's ghost occurred in 1951, when a visitor encountered Steuben sitting in the living room. Suddenly, the apparition spoke. It inquired about General Washington and the state of the new country. When the bewildered lady informed the ghost of the year, it vanished without further comment.

The address for the Steuben House is 1209 Main St., River Edge, N.J. 07661; the telephone number is 201-487-1739.

WAYNE—DEY MANSION

For most of July 1780, General George Washington used the Dey Mansion in New Jersey's Preakness Valley as his headquarters. Colonel Theunis Dey owned the Georgian masterpiece, erected in the middle of the eighteenth century. Among the other dignitaries who availed themselves of Dey's wartime hospitality were General Anthony Wayne, the Marquis de Lafayette, and Alexander Hamilton. Some of those illustrious guests continue to enjoy the mansion in ghostly form today.

The Dey Mansion is open to the public as a museum. Its address is 199 Totowa Rd., Wayne, N.J. 07470; the telephone number is 973-696-1776.

Pennsylvania

PENNSYLVANIA

ME
(WAS N. MA.)

VT
NH
MA
NY
CT
RI
NJ
PA
MD
DE
VA
NC
SC
GA

SHADED AREA SHOWS
COLONIAL AMERICA

Of Ben, Benedict, and Betsy: Haunted Philadelphia Freedom

PHILADELPHIA, PENNSYLVANIA

Yes, we must, indeed, all hang together, or assuredly we shall all hang separately.

BENJAMIN FRANKLIN

Philadelphia has long prided itself on being the birthplace of American independence. After all, the Declaration of Independence was adopted in the city on July 4, 1776. Among the fifty-four signers of that document was a famous Philadelphian regarded by many historians as the genius behind the concept of an independent America. Benjamin Franklin (1706–90), an eminent scientist and inventor, witty author, printer, political activist, statesman, and diplomat, was the American epitome of the Renaissance man. After Franklin's death in Philadelphia in 1790, his spirit never abandoned his home. His ghost has been encountered in several of Philadelphia's historic haunts. So, too, have the spirits of some of the other key players in the Revolutionary War drama that unfolded in the City of Brotherly Love, among them Mr. and Mrs. Benedict Arnold, the Marquis de Lafayette, and Betsy Ross.

One stop in haunted Philadelphia is the Powel House, located at 244 South Third Street. Now open to the public, this exquisite Georgian brick mansion was constructed in 1765. Acquired by Philadelphia mayor Samuel Powel four years later, the magnificent multistory town house survives along the city's so-called Mansion Row as one of its most haunted places.

An ardent supporter of American independence before and during the war, Samuel Powel, nicknamed "the Patriot Mayor," opened his home to Philadelphia's high society and important visitors to the city. George Washington, Ben Franklin, John Adams, and the Marquis de Lafayette were among the distinguished men who appreciated the hospitality at the Powel House. In fact, some of the visitors so enjoyed the welcome that their ghosts continue to extend their visits.

Several apparitions of Continental soldiers and the ghost of Lafayette have been observed ascending the grand mahogany staircase.

The ghost of the enigmatic Benedict Arnold has been witnessed in the drawing room. In May 1778, Arnold, a rising star in the Continental Army, was given command of Philadelphia. Eleven months later, he took as his second wife Peggy Shippen (1760–1840), a Philadelphia socialite and the daughter of the chief justice of Pennsylvania.

Some historians have speculated that Peggy may have initiated the negotiations between her husband and her former lover, John André, that culminated in General Arnold's subsequent treasonous acts. Considered a Loyalist by friends and family in Philadelphia, she reportedly provided vital information to the British before her marriage. Peggy reveled in the festivities at the Powel House. Her ghost can be found in the drawing room and other places throughout the mansion.

In 1965, while visiting the Powel House, the wife of respected historian Edwin Coutant Moore witnessed the ghost of a lovely young lady wearing a splendid lavender and beige gown. According to Mrs. Moore, the phantom beauty was smiling as she fanned herself in the drawing room. Suddenly, the ghost tapped its foot twice and vanished.

Not until later was the spectral lady identified. Mrs. Moore, searching for an authentic colonial gown to wear to a ball, was stunned when she came across the gown worn by the ghost she had seen in the Powel House. Upon inquiry, Mrs. Moore learned that it had once belonged to Peggy Shippen Arnold, who had last worn it to a gala at Mayor Powel's mansion.

Among the ghosts identified over at Independence Hall, one of the nation's greatest historic edifices, is that of Benedict Arnold. Perhaps the general's restless, remorseful spirit longs to abide where America celebrates the victory in which he might have played an important part.

Also keeping the spirit of '76 alive at Independence Hall is Ben Franklin. His ghost sometimes roams the corridors of the magnificent brick landmark of Georgian design, where George Washington was appointed commander in chief of the Continental Army in 1775 and where the Declaration of Independence was signed a year later. In the very room in which a copy of the Declaration is now displayed, Franklin's apparition, dressed in the clothing of his time, has been seen studying the document he helped draft.

Rangers from the National Park Service (the administrator of Independence Hall) have been spooked by Franklin's spirit when the building is closed to the public. While working in the northwestern portion of the structure one night in June 1994, an employee stood in shock as a mist seeped through the main entrance. In an instant, the mist took the form of Ben Franklin attired in a long, dark-colored coat, white breeches, and a tricorn hat.

Another ranger, responding to the sound of footsteps in the second-floor gallery when the hall was closed, found no living human about. Just as he reached the top of the steps, he experienced intense cold and a musty smell. As he stepped onto the gallery floor, he observed a strange mist. In a split second, it took the form of Ben Franklin, only to vanish almost as quickly as it had appeared.

Ben Franklin's supernatural presence has been felt and seen in many other places in the city as well. It was in Philadelphia that Franklin established the first public lending library in America. Little wonder, then, that his spectre haunts the library of the American Philosophical Society, which he founded. As early as 1844, Franklin's ghost knocked a cleaning lady and her armload of books to the floor. Some pedestrians even claim to have watched in awe and bewilderment as Ben's statue, located in front of the building, jumped from its pedestal in order to parade down the historic streets of the city. Ben's ghost has also been seen resting on the front steps of the library. Eyewitnesses have noted that the apparition appeared to be deep in thought—until it suddenly disappeared.

When Franklin died at age eighty-four on April 17, 1790, more than twenty thousand mourners paid their respects at his wake in Philadelphia. He was interred at historic Christ Church Burial Ground in the heart of the old city. His grave marker reads simply, "Benjamin and Deborah Franklin." Ben's ghost is alive and well near what was intended to be his final resting place.

Around eight-thirty on a July evening during the two hundredth anniversary of the signing of the Declaration of Independence, a local nurse had a strange encounter with Franklin's ghost while waiting for a bus at the corner of Fifth and Arch streets, within eyesight of Ben's grave. As she enjoyed the beautiful sunset, something struck her neck and fell to the sidewalk with a pinging sound. She looked down and found a penny. Observing no one about, the nurse was pondering the source of the coin when another penny struck her, and then another. She happened to glance at Franklin's grave, upon which countless Americans have thrown pennies as an homage to the man who proclaimed, "A penny saved is a penny earned." Unnerved by the pennies, the lady hurried to another bus stop. Over the years, similar occurrences have taken place near Franklin's penny-laden grave.

At 239 Arch Street, not far from the Franklin plot, stands the two-and-a-half-story Betsy Ross House, where the American heroine lived during the Revolutionary War. Now open to the public as a national shrine, the historic nine-room building attracts more than a quarter-million guests annually, ranking it just behind Independence Hall and the Liberty Bell in popularity among visitors to Philadelphia.

Here, Betsy Ross, an upholsterer by trade, sewed the first American flag at the behest of George Washington. When she died, she was buried in the home's courtyard. Her spirit still haunts the premises.

Most often, her ghost has been observed or sensed sitting at the foot of her bed. A psychic investigation of the place identified the apparition as that of Betsy. Her countenance is one of sadness and gloom. Most likely, the ghost of the legendary lady is yet grieving over the two husbands she lost fighting for the nation symbolized by the banner she crafted.

A visit to historic Philadelphia offers an opportunity to see the places where Patriots labored to birth the American republic. On your visit, you may be lucky enough to come face to face with some of their ghosts, the true spirits of Philadelphia freedom.

All of the sites haunted by Ben, Benedict, and Betsy are open to the public. The address for **Powel Hall** is 244 South Third St., Philadelphia, Pa. 19106; the telephone number is 215-627-0364. The address for the **American Philosophical Society Library** is 105 Fifth St., Philadelphia, Pa. 19106; the telephone number is 215-440-3400. The address for **Independence Hall** is Chestnut St., Philadelphia, Pa. 19106; the telephone number is 215-965-2305. The address for **Christ Church Burial Ground** is Fifth St. and Arch St., Philadelphia, Pa. 19106; the telephone number is 215-922-1695. The address for the **Betsy Ross House** is 239 Arch St., Philadelphia, Pa. 19106; the telephone number is 215-686-1252.

Spectres of a Devastating Defeat
CHADDS FORD, PENNSYLVANIA

Incline to the right! Incline to the left! Halt! Charge! The balls plowing up the ground. The trees cracking over one's head. The branches riven by the artillery. The leaves falling as in autumn by the grapeshot.

> UNIDENTIFIED BRITISH OFFICER AT
> THE BATTLE OF BRANDYWINE

On September 11, 1777, the Continental Army, commanded by General George Washington, clashed with the British army of General Sir William Howe in a bitter battle along the banks of the Brandywine River in southeastern Pennsylvania. At the Battle of Brandywine, the largest land battle of the Revolutionary War, Washington was embarrassed by Howe, who marched his army of Redcoats and Hessians on to capture Philadelphia two weeks later. Visitors have experienced supernatural reminders in the form of phantom horses and riders, ghost soldiers, and eerie screams and other unexplained sounds at the site of the battle, which has been little disturbed by time.

Late in July 1777, General Howe dispatched a mighty armada of more than 250 ships laden with approximately 17,000 troops from Sandy Hook, New Jersey, to a landing spot on the northern end of Chesapeake Bay just fifty miles south of Philadelphia. Concerned that Howe had his sights trained on the American capital, Washington marshaled his forces to intercept the invaders at the Brandywine River, a significant waterway that Howe's army had to cross on its march toward Philadelphia. Reckoning that Howe would attempt to cross at Chadds Ford (located near where U.S. 1 runs today), the American commander placed the bulk of his army there on the high ground of the east bank on September 11. Smaller contingents of Americans were assigned to the other fords in the vicinity save Jeffries' Ford.

To execute Washington's defense, an impressive array of officers deployed their troops along the river: General Nathanael Greene, General Anthony Wayne, General John Sullivan, General John Armstrong, General William Maxwell, and the Marquis de Lafayette, who would see his first battlefield action in America.

In advance of the anticipated showdown, Howe's scouts reported to the British commander that Chadds Ford was swarming with American troops commanded by Generals Wayne and Greene, while Jeffries' Ford was unprotected. Unwilling to risk a frontal confrontation with Wayne, Howe devised a strategy to take advantage of his adversary's failure to defend one of the fords. He divided his army to flank the Americans. Hessian general Wilhelm Knyphausen was directed to use his seventy-five-hundred-man column to keep Wayne and Greene busy at Chadds Ford. Meanwhile, Lord Cornwallis, accompanied by Howe, was ordered to send his eight thousand soldiers across the river at Jeffries' Ford. Once that force was on the east bank, the American army would be flanked.

The fog enveloping the Brandywine the hot morning of September 11 offered cover for the British columns as they set out for the two river crossings. Howe's plan worked perfectly. By early afternoon, Cornwallis had flanked the Americans near the Birmingham (Quaker)

Meeting House. In the face of eight thousand enemy bayonets, the Continentals and their militia comrades desperately fought to extricate themselves from the trap. General Greene brought reinforcements from Chadds Ford. General Wayne, left with but thirty-five hundred men, gallantly defended his position until his charges were overwhelmed by Knyphausen's Germans storming across the river.

Muskets blazed and artillery belched deadly fire for the balance of the day as the two armies continued their bloody work. Only when darkness covered the river, tinged red from blood, did the battle come to a close. Washington ordered his defeated army to retreat, while Howe instructed his charges to camp for the evening on the battleground and surrounding farms.

By candlelight, Captain John André noted in his journal why the badly damaged American army was allowed to limp away in the darkness: "Night and fatigue the soldiers had undergone prevented any pursuit." Several of André's superiors lamented that Howe could have ended the American Revolution then and there if only the British had a few more hours of sunlight.

Adjacent to the battlefield stands the Birmingham Meeting House, little changed today from September 1777. At the height of the battle, Cornwallis sequestered the church as a hospital. Wounded soldiers from both armies were treated there by military surgeons and comforted by local Quaker nurses. The pews and floorboards still carry the bloodstains.

The casualties at Brandywine reached nearly fifteen hundred. Joseph Townsend, a young Quaker boy from the area, described the landscape in the days following the battle: "The inhabitants found it necessary to call in the assistance of their neighbors to rebury many of the dead, who lay exposed to the open air and ravages of beasts and wild fowls, having in consequence of the late heavy rains, been washed bare, and some of them had never been interred."

Today, a monument in the stately cemetery at the Birmingham Meeting House memorializes the unknown British and American troops who died at Brandywine and were buried in a common grave nearby. The ancient stone walls surrounding the graveyard served as the first line of defense for the Americans when Cornwallis attacked.

Given the suffering at Brandywine, visitors can have little doubt the battleground and environs are haunted. Woeful moans, unearthly cries, and anguished screams often emanate from the meeting house. And some witnesses have observed spectral figures in eighteenth-century military uniforms walking past the windows of the church turned hospital.

All about the battlefield, phantom soldiers and horses with and without riders traverse the historic landscape. Revolutionary War reenactors have been spooked by soldiers of another time. Some years ago, a thirty-year veteran of reenacting was taking a break with his artillery crew during a commemoration of the battle when he noticed someone approaching from the nearby river marsh. As the figure drew closer, it appeared to be a boy of sixteen to eighteen dressed in a dirty, tattered British uniform. In the words of the eyewitness, the stranger "stunk like rotten vegetation." Speaking in eighteenth-century English, the boy was hard to understand. He appeared to be confused as he inquired about the location of his unit. Then he ambled away and disappeared before the astonished reenactor. Was he the ghost of a Redcoat who fought here in 1777?

Area residents and visitors have caught sight of a smoky gray stallion, sans rider, that has roamed the Brandywine Valley since the American Revolution. All efforts to corral the beautiful horse have led to the same conclusion: the animal is a phantom. In the late twentieth century, several friends were riding horses near the battlefield when they observed the steed running about as if it were lost. Anxious to rope it and take it to safety, they backed the horse into a grove of trees from which there could be no escape. But before the horse could be taken, it dissolved before the eyes of its would-be rescuers.

Amid the disappointing defeat at Brandywine, Mad Anthony Wayne rendered a stellar performance for the Americans. True to his nickname, the native Pennsylvanian galloped up and down his lines with great abandon in an attempt to exhort his men to prevent the Red-coats and Hessians from crossing the river. His dynamic energy and commanding presence can still be felt at Brandywine in ghostly form.

On moonlit nights as summer prepares to give way to autumn, a Revolutionary War officer on a magnificent white horse can be observed riding along the river. Dressed in a long blue coat with brass buttons, white knee breeches, and a three-cornered hat, the rider is armed with a sword that clangs in the quiet of the place. Witnesses have identified the shade as that of Mad Anthony Wayne. Spectral rider and horse pass though trees and obstacles as they speed into a blur of light.

Nighttime motorists along U.S. 1 in the vicinity of Chadds Ford have come face to face with this phantom horseman. As their head-lights illuminated the startling spectacle, some have had to swerve to avoid a collision. But a quick glance in the rearview mirror has always revealed a black, lonely, vacant road. Mad Anthony has once again van-ished into the night in his endless quest to revitalize his charges.

The well-preserved battlefield at Brandywine offers a glimpse of the place where George Washington suffered one of his worst defeats. Historic structures, markers, and monuments bring the great battle to life—and so do the ghosts.

The address for **Brandywine Battlefield Historic Site** is U.S. 1, Chadds Ford, Pa. 19317; the telephone number is 610-459-3342.

Haunted Reminders of Sacrifice and Suffering

VALLEY FORGE, PENNSYLVANIA

*Naked and starving as they are we cannot but admire the
incomparable patience and fidelity of soldiery.*

GEORGE WASHINGTON AT
VALLEY FORGE, FEBRUARY 16, 1778

Perhaps no place in the original thirteen colonies calls to mind
the sacrifices of Americans during the Revolutionary War more than
Valley Forge, Pennsylvania. Ironically, no significant confrontation between the armies took place here. Yet the indescribable human misery
experienced at Valley Forge during the harsh winter of 1777–78 has
long stood as one of the great lessons of patriotism in American history.
The landscape, little changed since the eighteenth century, remains the
dwelling place of the ghosts of men who endured a multitude of hardships in order that the Continental Army could survive to fight and win
on future fields of battle.

In the wake of the skirmish with the British at Whitemarsh,
Pennsylvania, during the first week of December 1777, General Washington decided to end the fighting for the winter. He immediately put
his twelve thousand hungry, ragged, tired Continentals on the march to
the site selected for the army's headquarters. When the initial wave of

emaciated American soldiers reached Valley Forge, twenty-two miles northwest of Philadelphia, bitterly cold winds were already blowing. The first order of business was to dig in and prepare defensive lines to protect against British attackers. In the midst of the work, the nearby Schuylkill River froze. Six inches of snow blanketed the encampment.

Tents were soon replaced by more than a thousand crude huts, which offered a bit more protection from the elements. Compounding the soldiers' problems was a scarcity of food. Subsistence was ultimately reduced to "firecake," a rather bland concoction of flour and water. Impassioned pleas for meat were heard throughout the camp on a daily basis. As the winter wore on, food for the army's horses became almost nonexistent. Hundreds of animals perished from starvation or froze to death. Diseases wrought by exposure to the cold, hunger, and unsanitary conditions swept through the army. More than two thousand soldiers died in makeshift hospitals. At the height of the suffering, a dejected George Washington was forced to concede, "If the army does not get help soon, in all likelihood, it will disband."

Soon, the dark winter nights of despair would turn into bright spring days for the Continental Army. By February, the winter, though yet difficult, moderated. A month later, empty stomachs were filled when General Nathanael Greene, the newly appointed head of the Commissary Department, made sure that food and other provisions poured into Valley Forge. Then, in April, as the soldiers regained their strength, Baron von Steuben, a foreign officer known for his ability to train and discipline troops, began to transform the surviving Americans into an efficient fighting force.

By the time Washington ordered the surviving Continentals to break camp on June 19, 1778, his army, once bloodied, weary, and despondent, was ready, willing, and able to take on the enemy. At Valley Forge, the Continentals won a war of will and prepared to win battles on the field against the most professional army in the world. In less than ten days, the American juggernaut would render a magnificent performance in the devastating heat at Monmouth, New Jersey.

For generations, visitors to Valley Forge have encountered numerous spirits at the place where the Continental Army rose from the
ashes. In 1895, a reporter for the *Philadelphia Press* described the supernatural nature of the historic landscape: "It is said that the spirits of
the dead Revolutionary soldiers flit along the hillsides on stormy nights
and visit the shadowy spots where they gathered around the campfire[,]
and that ghostly campfires have been flickering among the trees on
starless nights."

Are these the ghosts of soldiers who died as a result of bitter conditions during the war? No one knows for sure. Surprisingly, only one
grave is marked at Valley Forge, that by a single headstone etched with
the initials *J. W.* In 1975, the United States Veterans Administration
considered developing a cemetery at Valley Forge National Historical Park, but the idea was dismissed because the necessary excavation
would have disturbed unmarked burial grounds. One known burial site
is located near Outer Line Drive as it makes its way from Wayne's
Woods. By 1896, this hilly area had eroded to the point that the bones
of soldiers buried in crouched positions (because they had literally fro-
zen to death) were exposed.

Maybe the spirits of those unfortunate men cannot rest. Park
guides and patrons sometimes see soldiers wearing Revolutionary War
uniforms on days when no reenactors are in the park. Countless visitors
have reported a common unnerving experience: the sight of a lifeless
body with a noose around its neck dangling from an ancient tree. Upon
returning to the scene with help, the terrified eyewitnesses have been
mortified to find that the dead man has vanished. This recurrent phantom is thought to be the spectre of a spy executed by the Americans
during the war.

Other unusual experiences and sensations are commonly reported
by park patrons. Their feet sometimes burn and feel numb. Inside the
reconstructed huts of General Peter Muhlenberg's brigade, they have
encountered abnormal cold spots even during the heat of summer.

Two of the apparitions in the park have been identified. George

Washington's ghost inhabits the stone house of Isaac Potts, which the general used as his headquarters during the encampment. And the ghost of General Anthony Wayne gallops on his phantom horse, Nab, in the vicinity of the statue erected in his memory.

When darkness descends, frightening things begin to happen at Valley Forge. The crack of muskets and the roar of artillery echo in the distance. Maybe these are the sounds from Steuben's intense training program. Ghost soldiers of the Continental Army cluster around burning campfires in a desperate attempt to once again survive the cold winter. On stormy winter nights, spectral shoeless troops in tattered uniforms walk the snowy landscape in an apparent search for shelter and warmth.

Few supernatural encounters at Valley Forge have been more mystifying than the experience of a history teacher in the 1970s. On a cold winter evening, the teacher slipped on a denim coat and set out on a walk along the park's perimeter to gain an appreciation of some of the hardships faced by his forefathers in 1777–78. In the course of his walk, he unwittingly received a lesson in the supernatural.

Suddenly appearing from the darkness was a young soldier attired in a Revolutionary War uniform that was little more than rags. At first glance, the strange-looking fellow seemed to be a reenactor in authentic dress. But when the soldier prodded his "captive" with a bayonet, the teacher grew concerned, feeling that the reenacting was going a bit far. Nonetheless, for safety's sake, he decided to accompany the soldier through a wilderness area that looked out of place amid the well-landscaped grounds of the national park.

The two made their way to the grounds where Mad Anthony Wayne's command had camped. But instead of seeing the general's statue, the teacher was bewildered when he witnessed crudely built shelters and roaring fires, around which were scores of Continental soldiers in wretched condition.

The sharp tip of the bayonet directed the teacher into one of the largest huts. Inside, soldiers were sitting around a table upon which a lamp burned. Addressing the man who seemed to be in command, the confused teacher explained that he had been on a casual walk when he was "kidnapped" at bayonet point by the young reenactor, who was still standing in the room.

Then the officer spoke: "Your name, sir? Are you a British spy?"

Highly annoyed by what he perceived as a game gone too far, the man lost his temper and screamed that he was a history teacher and wanted to return to his motel. After explaining that the Revolutionary War had ended two hundred years earlier, he began to move toward the door. Bayonets altered his decision.

His fears began to subside as the officer told the soldiers he did not believe the man in strange clothes was either a teacher or a spy. But when the soldiers asked why General Washington had not announced the war's end, the teacher once again exploded: "We won the war! George Washington served as our first president. Don't you know your history?"

With that, the officer declared once more that the unusual man did not seem to be a British agent. He directed the young soldier to escort the man back to the place where he had found him. To the other soldiers in the room, the officer noted, "Gentlemen, this incident shall be forgotten by all who are present."

Back at the place where he had been "captured," the relieved teacher turned to speak to his escort. But the soldier from a different time faded away.

The fledgling United States and its war-weary army were sternly tested during that bleak winter at Valley Forge. But through suffering, perseverance, and iron will, the new nation prevailed. And the spirits that roam this haunted piece of historic ground bear supernatural testimony to one of the crowning achievements of the American spirit.

The address for **Valley Forge National Historical Park** is 1400 North Outer Line Dr., King of Prussia, Pa. 19405; the telephone number is 610-783-1077.

The "Mad" Search for His Bones
U.S. 322 BETWEEN MEADVILLE
AND RADNOR, PENNSYLVANIA

Waiting, are they? Well, let 'em wait!

GENERAL ANTHONY WAYNE,
AFTER BEING TOLD BY HIS ATTENDING
PHYSICIANS THAT THE ANGELS
WERE WAITING FOR HIM

Care to see a ghost from the Revolutionary War? Well, if you traverse the long route of U.S. 322 from Meadville in western Pennsylvania to the historic village of Radnor, just south of Philadelphia, on New Year's Day, chances are you will spot a soldier ghost. And not just any soldier ghost, but the spectre of Major General Anthony Wayne, who gallops across his native state on his birthday every year on a desperate search to recover his bones.

Born January 1, 1745, in eastern Pennsylvania as Isaac Wayne, Mad Anthony was educated as a surveyor in Philadelphia at his uncle's academy. In the decade before the Revolutionary War, Ben Franklin dispatched the young surveyor to Canada to map some of the land owned there by Franklin and his associates.

At the onset of the war, Wayne held two significant positions—colonel of the Fourth Pennsylvania Regiment and member of the Pennsylvania legislature. His daring exploits and effervescent personality as a Continental Army officer were the inspirations for his unusual nickname. Though the intrepid general had many bright days during the Revolutionary War, his greatest hour occurred at Stony Point, New York, where he led American forces to an almost miraculous victory on July 16, 1779. There on the cliffs of the Hudson, Wayne inspired his soldiers to dare an extremely dangerous bayonet charge in the dark of night. By war's end, grateful Americans had come to regard Major General Wayne as one of George Washington's most able commanders.

With peace came a return to politics, which included Wayne's service in the Second Congress of the United States. One of his biggest admirers was President George Washington, a personal witness to his brilliance on many battlefields. Accordingly, on March 5, 1792, Washington convinced Wayne to return to military life as commander in chief of the tiny American army.

At the time, the Northwest Indian War was going badly for the troops fighting in America's frontier territories against Indians who had sided with the British in the Revolutionary War. Wayne immediately took command of an elite unit, the Legion of the United States. On August 20, 1794, an American victory masterminded by General Wayne at the Battle of Fallen Timbers in Ohio effectively ended the war. In its aftermath, Wayne played an instrumental role in negotiating a peace treaty with the Indians that enabled Ohio to enter the union in 1803.

In December 1796, Wayne stopped at Fort Presque Isle (in what is now Erie, Pennsylvania) on his way home following a visit to Detroit. While he was at the fort, a serious attack of gout accompanied by intense stomach pains disabled the general. As his condition worsened, military physicians from Pittsburgh were summoned. By the time they arrived, nothing could be done to save the general. He died on December 15. At his request, his body was buried at the foot of the fort's flagstaff.

Throughout history, some have speculated that General Wayne died as the result of a curse—Trotter's Curse. As the story goes, Wayne was headquartered at Fort Lafayette near Pittsburgh in 1792 during the early stages of his campaign against the Indians in Ohio. Known for his fondness for drink, the general was in a drunken stupor at the fort when Sergeant John Trotter reasoned that he could steal a short trip to his home in nearby Murrysville before his commander sobered up. But during Trotter's absence, the inebriated general called for him. The missing soldier was declared a deserter. Wayne ordered three of his officers to hunt Trotter down and shoot him on the spot.

The three-man detail found Trotter while he was making his way back to the fort. When they informed him of his death sentence, the terrified fellow requested a Bible and read from Psalm 109, invoking the vengeance of God on the killers of an innocent man. Just before the executioners pulled their triggers, Trotter proclaimed a curse on all those associated with his murder.

Upon their return to Fort Lafayette, the three officers related the unsettling details of their experience to General Wayne. He was overcome with guilt and fell into a state of deep depression.

Over the next four years, the tragedies that befell all four officers were attributed to Trotter's Curse. One of the three executioners became a hopeless alcoholic who believed that Satan, in the form of a mad dog, was following him. The second was afflicted with a serious case of diabetes, which left him in a constant state of thirst. The third lost his mind, convinced he was possessed by devils. And General Wayne, of course, died in excruciating pain.

Mad Anthony remained in his grave near Erie until 1809, when his seriously ill daughter, Margaretta (who would die the following year), implored her brother, Isaac Jr., to bring their father's body to their home in Radnor for burial at St. David's Church. Acceding to his sister's request, the general's son set out on the arduous 380-mile journey in a sulky. Much of his trip followed the route of what is now U.S. 322.

Upon his arrival in Erie, Isaac Jr. enlisted the aid of Dr. John Wallace, the physician who had attended General Wayne on his deathbed. As the earth was removed from the burial plot, both men expected to find little more than bones in the coffin. They were shocked at what they saw when the lid was removed: a well-preserved corpse with a chalklike appearance. Only one leg exhibited significant decay.

Isaac Jr. faced a dilemma. His small, two-wheeled buggy would not accommodate a full dead body. Dr. Wallace offered a solution. Assisted by four men, the physician cut the corpse into numerous pieces and put them into a cauldron of boiling water. Once the dead flesh was boiled away from the bones and the concoction cooled, the bones were neatly packed in a box and loaded onto the sulky. Before Isaac Jr. left on the long trip home, the cauldron, its remaining contents, and the tools used to dismember the body were tossed into General Wayne's plot and covered with earth.

During the return to Radnor, bumpy roads caused a number of the bones to spill from the box. When he finally arrived home, Isaac Jr. was dismayed to learn that he had lost most of his famed father. Nonetheless, the remaining bones were reburied at St. David's Church in a well-marked grave, where Wayne's children assumed the general would lie forever at rest. Not so!

Every year on January 1, America's most often seen Revolutionary War ghost rides the route of U.S. 322 in Pennsylvania, scouring the roadside in a "mad" search for his long-lost bones.

The cauldron in which Mad Anthony Wayne's corpse was boiled and the chair in which he died are on display at the **Erie County History Center**. Its address is 419 State St., Erie, Pa. 16501; the telephone number is 814-454-1813.

Other "Spirited" Revolutionary War Sites in Pennsylvania, Briefly Noted

ALTOONA—FORT ROBERDEAU

In the spring of 1778, General Daniel Roberdeau, one of Pennsylvania's delegates to the Second Continental Congress, volunteered to superintend the construction of this fort, also known as "the Lead Mine Fort." The frontier-style compound protected the extensive nearby lead-mining and smelting operations, which provided critically needed ammunition for American guns. Area residents often fled to Fort Roberdeau for refuge from British and Indian raiders.

One of the soldiers garrisoned at the fort hangs around in spectral form. His ghost, the shadowy figure of a Revolutionary War sentinel, has been observed about the grounds.

A reconstructed stockade fort serves as the centerpiece of Fort Roberdeau Historic Site. The address is Rural Route 3, Box 391, Altoona, Pa. 16601; the telephone number is 814-946-0048.

BENSALEM—PEN RYN

Construction on this magnificent mansion on the banks of the Delaware River commenced in the middle of the eighteenth century. During the Revolutionary War, Pen Ryn was the country home of the affluent Bickley family, known to be loyal to the British Crown. Eyebrows were raised when young Robert Bickley introduced his family to his intended, a beautiful young lady from a family of Patriots. Robert's father, unable to contain his emotions, screamed his disapproval and ordered the girl never to set foot in the house again. Over the weeks that followed, Robert and his father argued incessantly. Finally, on Christmas Eve, the disconsolate Robert walked down to the river and flung himself into the cold waters of the Delaware.

Legend has it that each December 24 since Robert's death, his pathetic ghost has been observed walking on the historic trail from the river to the estate. Loud phantom knocking on the doors and windows of the house—thought to be spirited attempts to reason with the elder Bickley—usually follows Robert's spectral appearances. A female ghost adorned in a black cape rides about the grounds on a coal-black steed. Thought to be Robert's girlfriend, the angry ghost uses her whip to strike at anyone who approaches her. On other occasions, she has ridden through horrified observers. When her horse nears the mansion, the spectre offers blood-curdling screams.

Pen Ryn, privately owned, is used for corporate meetings and weddings. Its address is 1601 State Rd., Bensalem, Pa. 19020; the telephone number is 215-633-0600.

BENSALEM—TREVOSE (GROWDEN) MANOR

This fine estate, built around 1730, always had a welcome mat out for Patriots during the fight for American independence. In the years leading up to the conflict, Joseph Growden, its owner, served as speaker of the Pennsylvania legislature. When war came, Growden was only too happy to share his home with noted men like George Washington and John Adams. For a time, General James Wilkinson used the grand structure as his headquarters.

Trenches were built behind the manor to protect American soldiers as they warded off British raiders. To this day, the distinct sound of fire from phantom muskets can be heard at the trenches.

Without question, the most famous resident ghost here is that of Benjamin Franklin, a close friend of Joseph Growden. Franklin was not only one of the greatest statesmen in eighteenth-century America but also one of its most outstanding scientists. It was on the grounds of Trevose Manor where Franklin flew his kite in an attempt to catch the electricity generated by lightning. His ghost, kite in hand, has been sighted here.

Trevose Manor is owned by Bensalem Township. Its address is Old Trevose Rd. (Neshaminy Blvd.), Bensalem, Pa. 19020; the telephone number is 215-639-6575.

HESSTON—PHILLIPS' RANGERS MONUMENT

A tall monument of native stone stands near a picturesque stream in a peaceful Bedford County forest as a memorial to the brave American soldiers who died here in the summer of 1780. Given the horrendous violence, it is little wonder that the site is haunted by spirits from the Revolutionary War.

On Saturday, July 15, 1780, Captain William Phillips and a dozen of his intrepid rangers made their way into the Woodcock Valley, where they were dismayed to find the abandoned cabins of area settlers. As twilight approached, the scouting party decided to take shelter in one of the structures. While Phillips and his soldiers slept, a large band of Indians encircled their position. Upon waking the following morning, the commander realized he was in an untenable situation. Hoping to avert the wholesale slaughter of his men, Captain Phillips agreed that he and his teenage son would turn themselves over to the British as prisoners of war. But instead of releasing the other ten men, the Indians tied the rangers to trees and slashed, mutilated, and tortured them before unleashing a flurry of death arrows.

Within days, a relief expedition led by Colonel John Piper came upon the grisly scene. Bodies bloated by the summer heat were cut down and buried in a common grave at the site. One hundred fifty years later, when construction of the existing monument commenced, workers found the bones of nine of the victims.

According to eyewitnesses, on July 16 each year, the ghostly forms of Indians and rangers can be observed at the place of the executions. On occasion, a lonely, shadowy figure thought to be the spirit of Captain William Phillips is seen at the monument standing guard over the men whose lives he tried in vain to save.

The address of Phillips' Rangers Monument is Pa. 26, Hesston, Pa. 16647.

HORSHAM—KEITH HOUSE AT GRAEME PARK

Graeme (pronounced Gram) Park, a forty-two-acre historical site owned by the state of Pennsylvania, has as its centerpiece the stately Keith House, built around 1732. Named for Sir William Keith, a colonial governor, the multistory stone structure was acquired as a summer home by Dr. Thomas Graeme in 1739. Dr. Graeme, an early supporter of American independence, died in 1772. His daughter, Elizabeth, a poet and a highly educated woman for her time, inherited the house and grounds.

As the colonies moved toward war, Maggie, as she was known, began a series of relationships with men whose political leanings were diametrically opposed to those of her late father. First was a sultry affair with William Franklin (Benjamin Franklin's illegitimate son), a strident Loyalist who served as the Royal governor of New Jersey. And then when the British army captured nearby Philadelphia, Maggie entered into a tryst with Henry Hugh Fergusson, a poor Scottish immigrant serving with the British occupation forces. Though they married,

Fergusson abandoned Maggie and returned to Europe at war's end.

Maggie's heartbroken ghost can be found in the Keith House and about its well-landscaped grounds. The smell of lilacs, Maggie's favorite flower, has been detected in her bedroom. Security alarms sound in the chamber when no human is about. On moonlit evenings, Maggie's ghost walks the historic paths within sight of her home. Sometimes, her ghost is joined near the pond by a male spectre thought to be that of Henry Hugh Fergusson, who has returned to reclaim his war bride.

Yet another wraith roams near the Keith House. This headless ghost is said to be that of a servant of the estate who was decapitated by a British raider.

The address for Graeme Park is 859 County Line Rd., Horsham, Pa. 19044; the telephone number is 215-343-0965.

MALVERN—GENERAL WARREN INN

Opened in 1745, this historic hostelry was known as the Admiral Vernon Inne until 1825. In the early stages of the Revolutionary War, it was a popular hangout for British and Tory troops.

Lord Charles Grey, anxious to ascertain the whereabouts of General Anthony Wayne's camp, captured a local blacksmith and tortured him on the third floor of the inn on the night of Saturday, September 20, 1777. Upon gaining the information he sought, General Grey used the inn to plan the military foray now known as the Paoli Massacre. Just after midnight the following day, the Redcoats attacked Wayne's sleeping soldiers a mile from the inn and savagely bayoneted more than fifty of them to death.

The ghosts of Revolutionary War soldiers are sometimes heard running through the old inn. It is unknown whether they are the spectres of victims of the nearby massacre or the British troops who dwelled here. One of the rowdy military spirits haunts the bar area by blowing on the necks of female patrons and turning the television upside down.

The address for the General Warren Inn is Old Lancaster Hwy., Malvern, Pa. 19355; the telephone number is 610-296-3637.

MERION—GENERAL WAYNE INN

Until it was converted into the Jewish Faith Center in recent years, this building, erected in 1704, served as an inn and/or restaurant throughout most of its history. Located on the outskirts of Philadelphia, the inn hosted officers and soldiers from both armies during the war. General Anthony Wayne, for whom the building is named, frequented the place, as did Ben Franklin, George Washington, and the Marquis de Lafayette. Franklin established the first area post office in this building in 1763. A subsequent guest was Edgar Allan Poe, the famed writer rumored to be the illegitimate grandson of Benedict Arnold. Here, Poe penned portions of "The Raven."

By that time, the place already had a spooky aura. A ghost seen then and now is that of a German soldier killed in the basement by Patriot fighters hidden there. The Americans gained secret access to the cellar via a tunnel. After killing their Hessian adversary, they buried his body under the tunnel. The green-coated revenant has prowled the basement and other areas of the structure for years.

The address for the General Wayne Inn is 625 Montgomery Ave., Merion, Pa. 19066.

NEW HOPE—LOGAN INN

Dating from 1727, this historic hostelry was a popular stop for soldiers fighting along the nearby Delaware River during the Revolutionary War. The ghosts of some of those troops have been observed strolling the dining room and the corridors of the second floor.

Without question, the most famous ghost here is that of a former officer who stayed at the inn following his duel with Alexander Hamilton in

1804, just seven days after the twenty-eighth anniversary of the Declaration of Independence. Aaron Burr continues to dwell here in spectral form.

The address for the Logan Inn is 10 West Ferry St., New Hope, Pa. 18938; the telephone number is 215-862-2300.

NEWTOWN—THE GEORGE SCHOOL

Long recognized for its excellent academic program, this Quaker academy boasts a beautiful, historic campus. Among the oldest buildings is the Tate House, built in 1756. It now houses the academy's teaching staff, as well as a ghost created by a doctor—or a mad scientist.

During the Revolutionary War, the structure served as the home and office of Dr. James Tate, the son of the man who built it. After a Hessian soldier succumbed to disease, Dr. Tate claimed the buried corpse by unearthing it under the cloak of darkness. He then transported the body to the laboratory at his home, where he proceeded to dissect it for special experiments. Once Dr. Tate was finished with the cadaver, he interred it under the basement floor.

To this day, disembodied feet are heard running up the steps from the basement, as if someone is attempting to escape the dank confines. It has long been maintained that when a person walks across the Hessian's grave with a burning candle, the flame will go out.

The address for the George School is 1690 Newtown Rd., Newtown, Pa. 18940; the telephone number is 215-579-6500.

NORTH WALES—JOSEPH AMBLER INN
(JOHN ROBERTS HOUSE)

In many parts of America, the Revolutionary War played out as a civil war. And so it was in the North Wales community. Today, a victim of the uncivil conduct among neighbors haunts one of the beautiful colonial houses in this pretty Bucks County town.

John Roberts, an affluent Quaker, lived with his family in this fine stone dwelling. His gristmill in North Ardmore was a popular site during the war because of the copious provisions produced there. But Roberts was disliked by his Patriot neighbors, who believed him to be a Tory. Not only did he make frequent trips to British-controlled Philadelphia, but it seemed that the farms of local Patriots were always pillaged by Redcoat raiders not long after he returned to North Wales. Rumors also circulated that Roberts secretly added ground glass to the flour he sold to American military forces.

On Friday, October 10, 1777, the red-hot anger of area Patriots boiled over. They carried out a raid on the Roberts residence, anxious to punish their traitorous neighbor. In the nick of time, Roberts escaped into the country, but his less fortunate son was shot and badly wounded. One of Roberts's farm laborers, a man named Fishburn, was mistaken for the hated Tory. The mob took custody of the man, placed a noose around his neck, and executed him on the spot.

A ghost attired in colonial clothing has inhabited the old house over the years. Speculation claims that it is the spirit of either John Roberts or his farm hand, Fishburn.

On November 23, 2003, the Roberts House was carefully moved two miles to the twelve-acre site of the Joseph Ambler Inn. Ambler was Roberts's father-in-law. The relocated house was incorporated into the bed-and-breakfast complex. Guests have yet to determine whether or not the Revolutionary War ghost joined in the move.

The Joseph Ambler Inn encompasses five historic structures. Its address is 1005 Horsham Rd., North Wales, Pa. 19454; the telephone number is 215-362-7500.

PHILADELPHIA—ALLENS LANE

One of the most historic avenues of Philadelphia, Allens Lane is haunted by a headless Revolutionary War ghost that gallops up and down the street on foggy nights. In one hand, the apparition holds the reins; in the other, it carries its severed head.

PHILADELPHIA—CLIVEDEN MANOR

Located on a peaceful six-acre tract, this massive mansion served as a portion of the battleground in the grim fighting on Saturday, October 4, 1777, during the Battle of Germantown. Constructed in the 1760s by Benjamin Chew, the last Royal-appointed chief justice of the Pennsylvania Supreme Court, the house was filled with British soldiers at the time of the battle. The blazing muskets and sharp bayonets of the Redcoats enabled them to hold off the attacking Americans. Today, the thick outer walls of the Georgian estate bear scars from the cannon and musket fire. And the ghosts of some of the fifty-three Continentals killed as they stormed the house are said to haunt the tree-shaded grounds.

In the hours leading up to the battle, one of the British soldiers broke under the pressure and severed the head of an elderly lady who had taken refuge at the house. According to local legend, the deranged Redcoat raced onto the grounds holding the head by its hair. Visitors to Cliveden have encountered the spectre of the headless victim as it wanders about the home in search of its head.

Cliveden Manor, a National Trust museum, is open to the public. Its address is 6401 Germantown Ave., Philadelphia, Pa. 19119; the telephone number is 215-848-1777.

PHILADELPHIA—FORMER FIRST NATIONAL BANK
OF THE UNITED STATES

Alexander Hamilton, George Washington's invaluable staff officer and secretary of the treasury, was one of the guiding forces in the creation of a national bank, first headquartered in this building located in the heart of old Philadelphia. Soon after Hamilton died from wounds sustained in his infamous duel in 1804, his ghost began to appear in the bank building. Seven years later, the haunting caused such a stir that a priest was summoned to bless the place. Since that time, the ghost has been sighted infrequently.

The address of the old bank building is 102 Third St., Philadelphia, Pa. 19106; the telephone number is 215-597-8974.

PHILADELPHIA—FORT MIFFLIN

Several ghosts haunt this storied military fortress (also known as Mud Island Fort), erected by the British on the Delaware River in 1771 to protect Philadelphia. In the early days of the war, Continental Army soldiers wrested the compound from the Redcoats. Beginning in October 1777 and extending over a five-week period, the four-hundred-man garrison of determined Americans made one of the greatest stands in military history against an enemy army five times as large. As a result, General Washington was able to move his army to Valley Forge. When Fort Mifflin was decommissioned in 1954, it was the oldest fort in continuous use in the United States.

The ghost of a lone Revolutionary War soldier is often sighted standing guard by a fireplace in the fort's dungeon.

The address for Fort Mifflin is 1 Fort Mifflin Rd., Philadelphia, Pa. 19153; the telephone number is 215-685-4167.

PHILADELPHIA—GRUMBLETHORPE

John Wister, a successful Philadelphia importer, constructed this spectacular multistory stone house in 1744. His family was not in residence during the Battle of Germantown. Instead, the house served as the headquarters of James Agnew, a British general in the army of Lord Cornwallis.

In the course of the free-for-all, a civilian sniper by the name of Hans Boyer fatally wounded Agnew as he stood in the front parlor of the mansion. His blood still stains the floor there. Agnew's ghost haunts the house where he made the ultimate sacrifice for the British Crown.

Grumblethorpe is open for tours. Its address is 5267 Germantown Ave., Philadelphia, Pa. 19149; the telephone number is 215-843-4820.

PHILADELPHIA—WASHINGTON SQUARE

William Penn foresaw this piece of ground in the center of Philadelphia as a majestic park. But when the Revolutionary War ravaged the city, the land was needed as a burial ground for the four thousand American soldiers and the countless British and Hessian warriors claimed by the conflict in and around the city. The Tomb of the Unknown Revolutionary Soldier stands here today as a memorial to the nameless heroes interred in a mass grave.

For many years, a kindly Quaker lady known as Leah maintained a lonely vigil in the cemetery in a one-person effort to ward off graverobbers and desecrators. Since her death, her vigilant spirit has continued the patrol she commenced long ago.

Ghosts of the Revolutionary War soldiers buried here are said to haunt the place as well. These shadow people have made Washington Square so spooky that most of Philadelphia's homeless refuse to sleep on the property.

Washington Square is located at Locust and Sixth streets in the heart of Philadelphia.

WARMINSTER—CRAVEN HALL

American casualties from the Battle of Crooked Billet—fought on Friday, May 1, 1778, at nearby Hatboro—were brought to a field hospi-

tal at Craven Hall. Some of the soldiers treated in the pre–Revolutionary War manor house died and were interred in the ancient cemetery
at the rear of the structure. The ghost of one of these men is said to
haunt Craven Hall. On occasion, a young fellow dressed in the clothes
of a colonial militiaman has been witnessed peering from a first-floor
window and beating on the glass in an apparent attempt to leave the
place for home.

The address for Craven Hall is 599 Newton Rd., Warminster, Pa.
18974; the telephone number is 215-675-4698.

YORK—CAMP SECURITY

In 1781, the Continental Congress authorized the construction of
a prisoner-of-war camp on a 270-acre farm near York. Hundreds of
British and Hessian troops from the armies of Burgoyne and Cornwallis were herded into the facility. Harsh weather and a fever epidemic
claimed many of the prisoners during the bitter winter of 1782–83.
Their bodies were buried in an adjoining valley.

Before the last of the prisoners left, rumors circulated that the
ghosts of the men who perished here roamed the makeshift graveyard
on Christmas Eve. Their phantom voices, it was said, jeered their commanders for the battlefield losses that had led to their incarceration and
eventual death. Even now, the trail leading to the graves is patrolled by
the ghosts of the defeated soldiers.

Deemed the last intact prisoner-of-war facility of the American
Revolution, Camp Security is ranked by the National Trust for Historic
Preservation as eleventh on the list of the most endangered sites in
the United States. For more information, contact the Friends of Camp
Security, P.O. Box 20008, York, Pa. 17402; the telephone number is
717-755-4367.

YORK—PENN COMMON

This public square in the heart of old York is haunted by the ghosts of men executed here at the direction of General Anthony Wayne during the Revolutionary War. The men were condemned as deserters and plotters against the general. Mad Anthony personally marched the unlucky seven to Penn Common, also known as York Square, where each of them died before a firing squad. Three of their number roam the square in spirit form today.

Market and George streets intersect in the center of historic downtown York. Penn Common is five blocks southwest of the intersection.

Delaware

ME
(WAS N. MA.)

VT
NH
NY
MA
CT RI
DELAWARE
PA
NJ
MD
DE
VA
NC
SC
GA

SHADED AREA SHOWS
COLONIAL AMERICA

Ghost Writer

DOVER, DELAWARE

Then join in hand, brave Americans all!
By uniting we stand, by dividing we fall.
JOHN DICKINSON, "THE LIBERTY SONG" (1768)

In one of the great ironies of American history, John Dickinson, the renowned statesman known as "the Penman of the Revolution," refused to sign the Declaration of Independence. In the Continental Congress of 1776, Dickinson, a political moderate, found himself among a multitude of firebrands who were hell-bent on fighting a war with Great Britain to gain the independence of the American colonies. But before and after the Declaration, a free American nation had no stronger advocate than Dickinson. His voluminous writings, dating from the decade before the Declaration to the ratification of the Constitution, were respected by his contemporaries and reflected Dickinson's passion for an independent, unified nation. At the John Dickinson House in Dover, Delaware, the ghost of the Patriot wordsmith continues to do what Dickinson did best—write for the cause.

Born on his father's extensive tobacco plantation in Talbot County,

Maryland, John Dickinson (1732–1808) moved with his family to the magnificent house that bears his name at the age of seven. In 1757, he established a law practice in Philadelphia, where he quickly became enmeshed in the growing controversy between the colonies and Great Britain. Furor over the enactment of the Stamp Act in 1765 led Dickinson, then a member of the Pennsylvania legislature, to write and publish a pamphlet, *The Late Regulations Respecting the British Colonies. . . .* This highly influential piece urged colonists to seek repeal of the measure. His admiring legislative colleagues selected Dickinson as a delegate to the Stamp Act Congress, where he drafted subsequent resolutions adopted by that body.

A series of Dickinson's newspaper articles called "Letters from a Farmer" was published and widely circulated in 1767–68. In the articles, the author criticized British taxation laws and urged peaceful resistance. On June 18, 1768, the *Boston Gazette* published Dickinson's "The Liberty Song," considered the first patriotic song written in America. This masterpiece won Dickinson the respect and admiration of Bostonians and inspired them to continue their opposition to British colonial policies.

In 1771, the Pennsylvania legislature adopted a petition drafted by Dickinson and addressed to the king of England. Three years later, Dickinson served as chairman of the Committee of Correspondence when it called for the First Continental Congress to convene. He was a member of the august body when it met in Philadelphia in 1774. Likewise, he was a member of the Second Continental Congress in 1775–76. Despite his belief that independence could be obtained in a peaceful resolution with Great Britain, Dickinson was chosen to prepare the Declaration of the Causes of Taking Up Arms. The final draft, primarily the product of Dickinson's pen, was passed by Congress on July 6, 1775, as was Dickinson's "Olive Branch Petition." His words in the former read, "The arms we have been compelled by our enemies to assume, we will, in defiance of every hazard, with unabating firmness and perseverance employ them for the preservation of our liberties being with one mind resolved to die free men rather than to live as slaves."

Because of his belief that the colonies were not ready to fight a full-scale war with Great Britain, Dickinson was not a member of the committee selected to prepare the Declaration of Independence. When the historic proposal came before Congress for consideration, Dickinson, also known as one of the superior orators of the body, engaged in a heated debate with John Adams, one of the chief proponents of the Declaration. Dickinson argued that the colonies should engage in war only as a last resort. He reasoned that if all peaceful entreaties for independence ultimately failed, the colonies would be better positioned to enter into a military conflict of unknown duration against the mightiest power in the world.

His convictions compelled Dickinson to vote against the Declaration, but upon its adoption, the American cause had no greater champion. His congressional colleagues, cognizant of his skills with the pen, chose Dickinson to draft the Articles of Confederation, which were duly adopted on Saturday, November 15, 1777.

Although it was Dickinson's reasoned opinion that the pen was mightier than the sword, he was one of only two members of the Second Continental Congress (Thomas McKean of Delaware being the other) to see military action during the war. Dickinson, already colonel of a battalion assigned to defend Philadelphia, fought in 1777 in Elizabethtown, New Jersey, and at the Battle of Brandywine.

Dickinson returned to the Continental Congress in 1779. Two years later, he was elected president (governor) of Delaware. From 1782 to 1785, he held the same position in Pennsylvania. In 1787, Delaware sent him to the Continental Congress, called for the purpose of framing a federal constitution. There, Dickinson championed the cause of the smaller states.

A year later, when it became apparent that the states were reluctant to adopt the constitution as originally proposed, Dickinson once again put his pen into action. Under the pseudonym of Fabius, he wrote and published an extremely important series of letters circulated throughout

America. In them, he urged readers to support ratification of the new constitution. Due in large part to Dickinson's leadership, Delaware and Pennsylvania became the first two states to ratify the United States Constitution.

Today, visitors can tour the Delaware home of the hero regarded by historians as one of America's most influential founders and a statesman who stood at the forefront of Revolutionary War thought. Inside the lavish edifice, constructed around 1740, guests can view the rooms and some of the furnishings used by "the Penman of the Revolution." And if they maintain a sharp ear and a keen eye, they might just witness the ghost of old John Dickinson.

Staff members assigned to administer the site for the state of Delaware are reluctant to discuss Dickinson's presence and the strange goings-on at his plantation house, known as Poplar Hall. So are law enforcement officers who have been spooked upon receiving a call to the old mansion after dark. They maintain that some of the things seen and heard there are too mysterious to discuss. Efforts by paranormal investigators to inspect the place have likewise been rejected by authorities.

Nonetheless, numerous supernatural occurrences observed throughout the house suggest that John Dickinson still resides here in phantom form. Tape recordings in the tiny, otherwise empty Book Room, located near the main entrance hall, have revealed the distinctive sound of a quill pen scratching out words on parchment. Also audible on the tape are the sounds of paper being crumpled and tossed across the room.

John Dickinson was known to be fond of afternoon naps during his life at Poplar Hall. On occasion, employees and volunteers have walked into his chamber, devoid of human occupants, only to find tousled covers on his bed.

Should another crisis confront the American republic, the ghost of one of its founders seems ready to compose words that might again serve as the conscience of the people, just as the flesh-and-blood John Dickinson did during the American Revolution.

The **John Dickinson Plantation** is open to the public. The address is 340 Kitts Hummock Rd., Dover, Del. 19901; the telephone number is 302-739-3277.

A Ghost Story within a Ghost Story
NEWARK, DELAWARE

Let us raise a standard to which the wise and honest can
repair; the event which is in the hands of God.

GEORGE WASHINGTON

From the time it was published in 1820, Washington Irving's "The Legend of Sleepy Hollow" has amused and terrified generations of Americans. The classic story about a scary, headless Hessian horseman set during the Revolutionary War remains one of the greatest ghost tales in American history. Though based on New York Dutch legends, Irving's story was purely fictional. Similarly, an American casualty at the only Revolutionary War battle in Delaware became the subject of an instant legend. Within a few days, however, the legend took the form of a true headless horseman, one that still rides the road near historic Cooch's Bridge in an endless search for Redcoats and its head.

Following the disembarking of Sir William Howe's massive army at the mouth of the Elk River in northern Maryland in late August

1777, George Washington and the Marquis de Lafayette hurried south from New Jersey to marshal forces in and around Wilmington, Delaware. From there, Washington made his way to Elkton, Maryland, where he personally reconnoitered the movements of the enemy. Once he was satisfied that Howe had his sights on Philadelphia, the American commander rode north to Wilmington, where he decided to use small bands of Continentals and militiamen to harass the British army on its march north until he could devise a strategy to interpose the bulk of the Continental Army as a roadblock.

One evening during his sojourn in Wilmington, General Washington happened upon a modest grain merchant and his teenage son as they were hard at work unloading a wagon of grain intended for the American war effort. When informed that Charles Miller, Sr., had supplied the Americans with foodstuffs for almost a year without compensation, Washington, greatly moved, extended his gratitude to the humble man.

Mr. Miller informed the general that he was doing all he could to help America win the war before it could claim his sixteen-year-old son, Charlie Jr. The younger Miller instantly informed both men that he was ready for combat. But Washington assured the boy that he was playing an important role by providing vitally needed food for the soldiers. Just before riding away, he told the teenager that he knew he could be depended upon to fight for liberty when the time came. Unbeknownst to both of them, that time was near.

On August 28, Washington combined nine hundred handpicked Continental marksmen from New Jersey, Pennsylvania, Virginia, and North Carolina into a fighting unit under the command of Brigadier General William Maxwell. For one of the first times in the war, if not the very first, soldiers from various states would fight in a truly national unit. Together with three local militia battalions, these men would serve as the greeting party for the British vanguard pressing north.

As word spread that the British were coming, the impetuous Charlie Miller, Jr., mounted his white horse and galloped off to join the militia forces assembling near Cooch's Bridge, just south of Newark. Located in a swampy area near a three-way fork in the road leading from Elkton through Newark to Wilmington, the bridge offered a convenient crossing for the British if they were not intercepted by the Americans.

Early on the morning of September 3, the nine-thousand-man column commanded by Lord Cornwallis made its appearance on what is now Del. 896. Leading the massive army were Hessian jägers, highly respected sharpshooters. A half-mile south of Cooch's Bridge, Maxwell's small force ambushed the Hessians. Greatly outnumbered, the American regulars and militiamen fell back to the bridge to make a final stand.

Despite their numerical superiority, the British infantry forces were unable to flank the feisty defenders, who fought from the swamps and the banks of the stream, gorged from two days of heavy rain. Not until Cornwallis brought the artillery forward did the British begin to make headway. Attempting to continue the fight, the militiamen took cover behind the rock walls surrounding the nearby church on Welch Tract Road. One of the Americans there was poor Charlie Miller, Jr.

As the British cannons unleashed their deadly fury, one of the balls hit the ground, bounced, decapitated the teenager, and smashed into the church wall. (The imprint of the lethal ball can yet be seen.) Eyewitnesses claimed Charlie's headless corpse mounted a horse and galloped off in a northerly direction.

Not long after Charlie was killed, the overwhelmed Americans fell back in an orderly fashion. Cornwallis did not offer chase. Rather, he set up headquarters in the Cooch House, a majestic three-story home that stands today within sight of the cannon and monument marking the battlefield. For five days, the Redcoat army camped here. Cornwallis's aide, Major John André, sketched a map showing British soldiers surrounding the house.

News of Charlie's tragic death quickly spread throughout the area. Rumors were also rampant that the British guests at the Cooch House were taking advantage of their "hosts." In an attempt to spook the invading army, a story was circulated that a headless American horseman would soon appear in the British camp, intent on exacting revenge. In a short time, the tale had its intended effect. Cornwallis's troops were noticeably jittery when they picked up the march to the Brandywine River on September 8.

Two days later, as George Washington prepared his defenses at Chadds Ford, Pennsylvania (see 168-73), British snipers were already about. Washington's height and imposing presence immediately attracted the attention of the Redcoat marksmen, who took deadly aim with their muskets. But before they could fire, a sword-wielding headless horseman charged from the forested area behind the general, passed directly through Washington, and galloped toward his would-be assassins. Bullets fired at the phantom horseman missed their mark. With one deadly sweep, the horseman's sword carried away the heads of the pickets. Washington and his attendants stood in utter disbelief as the apparition disappeared into the darkness along the riverbank.

The following day, British and American troops observed the same decapitated soldier ghost storming the lines, sword in hand, as the two armies fought the Battle of Brandywine. Several British artillerymen lost their heads to the ghost's razor-sharp weapon.

The modern replacement for Cooch's Bridge is visible less than a mile from the football stadium of the University of Delaware. When darkness overtakes the site of the battle, the distinct sound of horse's hooves can be heard pounding down old Welch Tract Road or across the bridge. A headless apparition riding a spectral white horse has been seen on foggy nights. Its revenge secured at Brandywine, the ghost seems to have unfinished business at Cooch's Bridge.

Should you desire to help Charlie's ghost find its head, be sure to wear blue clothing. At the least, you should not show up in red. After all, this phantom hates red coats!

Cooch's Bridge is located along Del. 4 near its junction with Del. 896 in Newark.

Other "Spirited" Revolutionary War Sites in Delaware, Briefly Noted

DOVER—WOODBURN

Charles Hillyard, a colonel in the Revolutionary War, built this magnificent Georgian mansion in 1790 on land his family acquired from William Penn. In 1965, the Delaware legislature appropriated funds to purchase, restore, and use Woodburn as the residence for the governor.

Long before the chief executive of Delaware began living in the imposing brick structure, Woodburn acquired a reputation for being haunted. Four spooks are known to share the mansion with the governor. One of them is a happy ghost. Attired in a Revolutionary War uniform and powdered wig, it effortlessly floats about the spacious home from time to time. The spirit is also said to be responsible when wine mysteriously vanishes from glasses on the premises. Perhaps the ghost, believed to be that of Colonel Hillyard, is celebrating because Woodburn was chosen as the home of the governor of the first state to ratify the Constitution.

Woodburn is open to the public. Its address is 151 Kings Hwy., Dover, Del. 19901; the telephone number is 302-739-5656.

SMYRNA—BELMONT HALL

One of Delaware's most historic homes, Belmont Hall was acquired by the state in 1987. The original portion of the brick structure was built in 1686. As Delaware and its sister colonies moved toward war with Great Britain, the spectacular house came into the ownership of Thomas Collins, an outspoken advocate for American independence. A brigadier general of the Delaware militia and the speaker of the state legislature, Collins welcomed some of the most influential statesmen of the mid-Atlantic—John Dickinson, Thomas McKean, Allan McLane, Caesar Rodney—to Belmont Hall throughout the war. He subsequently served as governor of Delaware when the state ratified the Constitution.

Patriot soldiers garrisoned the house during the war to protect Collins and his family. Meanwhile, Mrs. Collins busied herself at the fireplace making bullets for Patriot muskets.

In 1777, British scouts hunting for General Collins took boats up Duck Creek to Belmont Hall. A lone American soldier was serving as lookout atop the widow's walk at the mansion. Redcoat marksmen made quick work of the young man. The badly wounded Continental stumbled down the winding steps and fell dead in a puddle of his own blood. His ghost has haunted the place from the day of his death.

The address for Belmont Hall is 512 Dupont Blvd., Smyrna, Del. 19977; the telephone number is 302-653-0135.

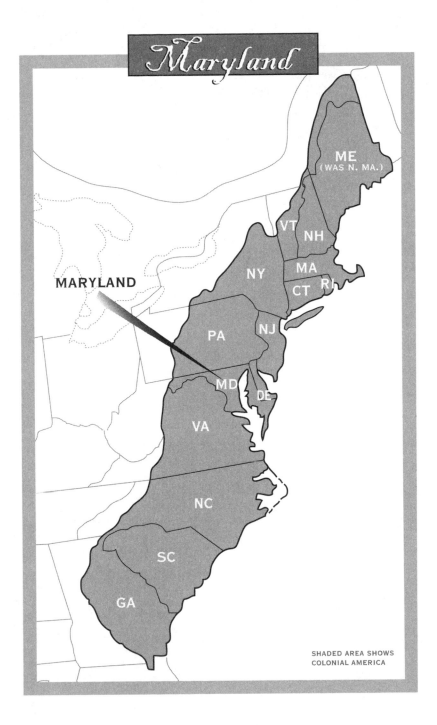

Maryland

MARYLAND

ME
(WAS N. MA.)

VT
NH
NY
MA
CT
RI
PA
NJ
MD
DE
VA
NC
SC
GA

SHADED AREA SHOWS
COLONIAL AMERICA

The Patriotic Spirit of Defiance
ANNAPOLIS, MARYLAND

One man with courage is a majority.

THOMAS JEFFERSON

Annapolis is one of America's oldest and most historic cities. It has been the capital of Maryland since 1694. From November 27, 1783, to August 13, 1784, it was the capital of the United States of America. Strategically located on Chesapeake Bay and the Severn River, the majestic waterfront town served as an important port during the American Revolution. Largely spared from military damage during the war, Annapolis boasts more extant colonial brick buildings than any other city in the United States. In one of those old landmarks, a rowdy Revolutionary War revenant continues to exhibit the defiant spirit that enabled the American colonies to become free American states. In the same building, the ghost of a more somber soldier yet waits for a ship to take him to a distant battlefield to fight for American independence.

During the Revolutionary War era, countless American statesmen and high-ranking military officers came to Annapolis on affairs of state. At crucial points in the war, troops, weapons, and supplies were loaded onto ships anchored at the port for shipment to Virginia and the Carolinas. In 1786, the city played host to the national convention that took crucial steps toward the formation of a federal constitution and government.

One of the favorite watering holes for visitors was the Middleton Tavern, located at the corner of Dock Street and Market Space. Among the noted men who called at the expansive three-story building constructed around 1740 were George Washington, Benjamin Franklin, Thomas Jefferson, the Marquis de Lafayette, James Monroe, and Tench Tilghman. It was from the Middleton Tavern that Tilghman, military secretary to George Washington, made his way to Philadelphia in October 1781 to deliver the news to the Continental Congress that Lord Cornwallis had surrendered at Yorktown, Virginia.

Today, the Middleton Tavern continues to operate as a restaurant and bar. From the outside of the Georgian building, patrons and passersby sometimes observe the apparition of a Revolutionary War figure moving by the front windows. Inside the massive wooden entrance doors, the supernatural experiences continue. In each of the four dining rooms, a spectre, nicknamed "Roland" by employees, is quite active. It takes dishes and glasses from shelves and throws them about the place one at a time; it knocks over tables, particularly dirty ones; it rearranges furniture to its liking; and it turns lamps upside down. Dressed in colonial garb, the phantom sometimes appears as a shadowy figure floating from dining room to dining room. No one has been harmed by its rough antics.

Who is this feisty spirit? Could it be the spirit of Thomas Jefferson, the fiery redhead whose outrage with Great Britain led him to draft the Declaration of Independence? Could it be the bespectacled Ben Franklin, who assisted Jefferson in drafting the document? Or could it be a nameless soldier yet celebrating the glad tidings delivered by Tench Tilghman in the autumn of 1781? Cigar smoking is not allowed inside the tavern. Nonetheless, when the building is empty of customers, the distinct smell of cigar smoke permeates the dining areas. Is this the phantom smoke of a victory cigar puffed when the glorious pronouncement of victory was made here by Washington's personal secretary?

Another apparition about the place is that of a lone Revolutionary War soldier peering out the windows overlooking the water, as if expecting the arrival of a naval fleet. Maybe this is the ghost of the Marquis de Lafayette, who in early March 1781 waited in vain in Annapolis with twelve hundred Continentals for French admiral Destouches and his armada. These American regulars and their young French commander were to be transported to Virginia to do battle with turncoat Benedict Arnold. Or maybe the soldier ghost at the window represents an unknown Continental who anticipated the appearance of the ship that would carry him to do battle, and perhaps die, at the Cowpens, Guilford Courthouse, or myriad other battlefields in the Carolinas.

Employees and patrons who have attempted to get close to the lonely spectre by the window have all reported that it disappears when approached.

Should you decide to enjoy the fine food and entertainment at the old Middleton Tavern, be on the watch for flying plates and glasses during the rollicking good fun had by patrons. This added commotion belongs to another time—the time when the American fighting spirit led to a grand celebration here and throughout the thirteen independent states.

The address for the **Middleton Tavern** is 2 Market Space, Annapolis, Md. 21401; the telephone number is 410-263-3323.

The Indefatigable Captain Jones
ANNAPOLIS, MARYLAND

I have not yet begun to fight.

JOHN PAUL JONES

More than one hundred years after he died and was buried in Paris, the naval hero of the American Revolution, John Paul Jones, came home to the United States in body and "spirit." Attended by great pomp, his remains were received by the United States Naval Academy in Annapolis on July 22, 1905. A magnificent marble and bronze crypt in the campus chapel now holds the bones of "the Father of the American Navy." But it cannot contain his indomitable spirit.

One of the brightest hours of early American naval warfare occurred off England east of Yorkshire on the night of September 23, 1779, when Captain John Paul Jones and his five-ship squadron encountered the British navy. At the Battle of Flamborough Head, the American commander, aware he might be outgunned, decided to revert to a strategy he had learned during his youthful days as a pirate. Accordingly, Jones locked his flagship, the forty-two-gun *Bonhomme Richard*, to the forty-four-gun British frigate *Serapis*. During the ensuing melee, Jones's deck guns and his sharpshooters in the rigging forced the crew of the *Serapis* to scurry below decks. It was at this stage of the battle that Jones uttered the enduring words, "I have not yet begun to fight!"

In the meantime, another American ship, the *Alliance*, drew alongside the conjoined vessels in an attempt to aid Jones and his crew. However, its broadside severely damaged both of the locked ships. Its ensign blown away by the blast, the *Bonhomme Richard* caught fire and began to slowly sink. One of the officers, fearing Captain Jones was dead, attempted to surrender to the commander of the *Serapis*. In response, the British officer demanded that the Americans strike their colors. But John Paul Jones, very much alive, rose to his feet and shouted words of defiance: "I may sink, but I'll be damned if I strike."

Throughout the night, the battle raged until the British surrendered to Jones. Unable to salvage the *Bonhomme Richard*, he climbed aboard the *Serapis* and sailed the prize of war to Holland, a nation sympathetic to the United States, despite its official neutral stance in the war.

Captain John Paul Jones—described by King George III as "the pirate Paul Jones, of Scotland, who is a rebel subject and a criminal of the state"—was instantly recognized as a hero in America and France. At Versailles, King Louis XVI bestowed the title of "chevalier" on Jones and further honored him with the *Ordre du Mérite Militaire*.

Following the war, Empress Catherine II of Russia offered Jones an opportunity to continue his career as a naval warrior. Retaining his American citizenship, he saw combat as a rear admiral, serving under the name of Pavel Dzhones. In 1790, after two years of service in the Russian navy, he settled in Paris, where he was appointed United States consul to gain release of American prisoners in Algeria.

On July 18, 1792, the lifeless body of the well-traveled forty-five-year-old hero was found in his third-floor apartment at No. 42 Rue de Tourron. A French admirer, Pierrot François Simmoneau, donated 460 francs for a lead coffin to hold Jones's body, which was preserved in alcohol supplied by the French government. It was interred in Paris at the Saint Louis Cemetery on land owned by the French royal family. After the French Revolution, the new government sold the property. Over time, the old graveyard was abandoned. It was subsequently used as a garden, a disposal site for dead animals, a hideaway for gamblers, and a development of stores and residences.

In 1895, more than fifty years after Jones's family in Scotland had first objected to the removal of the naval captain's remains to the United States, interest in bringing him home grew once more. General Horace Porter, the United States ambassador to France, initiated an intensive search for the grave at the site of the old cemetery. The work continued for nearly ten years until April 8, 1905, when the lead coffin was discovered. A subsequent autopsy by French physicians Capitan and Georges Papillault confirmed that the remains were those of John Paul Jones. Plans were promptly made to ship the body across the Atlantic to his adopted nation.

A new wooden casket adorned with the Stars and Stripes was reverently borne through the streets of Paris en route to the port at Cherbourg, where an armada of French and American naval vessels lay at anchor in tribute to Captain Jones. His casket was taken aboard the USS *Brooklyn*, which proceeded on the transatlantic crossing under the escort of three cruisers. As the four American warships neared the coast of the United States, they were joined by seven battleships from the United States Navy.

On the second day of summer in 1905, the body of Captain John Paul Jones arrived at Annapolis, where it was placed in the basement of Bancroft Hall at the Naval Academy. For almost eight years, Jones's coffin languished in a storage room. At length, a congressional appropriation provided the funds for the elaborate tomb at Annapolis in which the body was placed on January 26, 1913.

It seems, however, that the ornate crypt cannot hold the spirit of the famed officer who died far from the nation he helped to birth. Just ask the Naval Academy midshipmen assigned to serve as an honor guard at the tomb. On one such tour of duty, a young sailor was dumbfounded when he heard a distinct voice in the otherwise empty tomb chamber. The words were ever so clear: "What is your name, sailor?" Bewildered by the sound and yet bound to duty, the guard refused to answer and continued his patrol.

After a brief period of quiet in the crypt chamber, the voice repeated the words: "What is your name, sailor?" When the sailor turned his head to ascertain the source of the words, he saw the spectral form of a man dressed in an old naval uniform. Momentarily overcome with fear, he quickly regained his composure. He took the ghost to be none other than John Paul Jones beaming a wide smile. Then came the words a third time: "What is your name, sailor?"

Yielding to what he reckoned was a figment of his imagination or a voice from beyond the grave, the sailor gave his name. With that, the ghost nodded politely in acknowledgment and proceeded to the chapel doorway. Giving chase, the guard peered into the dying sunlight, but the ghost had vanished.

Other midshipmen and visitors to the Naval Academy Chapel have reported strange, almost unearthly sounds emanating from Jones's crypt, particularly after dark. And outside on the picturesque academy grounds, the apparition of Captain Jones has been observed roaming the place where America's naval officers have been educated since 1845.

Maybe John Paul Jones lives on in spirit here because he is anxious to oversee the schooling of the nation's finest sailors. Or maybe he is just glad to be home.

The address for the **United States Naval Academy** is 121 Blake Rd., Annapolis, Md. 21402-5000. Arrangements to tour the facility can be made through the United States Naval Academy Guide Service, 52 King George St., Annapolis, Md. 21402; the telephone number is 410-293-8697.

Other "Spirited" Revolutionary War Sites in Maryland, Briefly Noted

ANNAPOLIS—PACA HOUSE

In 1970, Paca House and Garden underwent a comprehensive restoration funded by state and federal grants. Now a showplace, Paca House was the home of one of Maryland's heroes of the American Revolution. William Paca, born in 1740, served his state as a member of the Continental Congress and as a three-term governor. He was one of Maryland's four signers of the Declaration of Independence. A portrait of Paca by Charles Willson Peale hangs in the house. Paca's ghost, attired in colonial dress, lingers as well. During the restoration project, night watchmen encountered the revenant so often that they were reluctant to continue their duties.

Paca House, constructed in 1765, is one of the most elegant landmarks in historic Annapolis. It is open to the public. The address is 186 Prince George St., Annapolis, Md. 21401; the telephone number is 410-267-7619.

ANNAPOLIS—SHIPWRIGHT STREET

A nighttime funeral procession for the last Royal governor of Maryland in 1784 has been eerily replayed over the centuries in Annapolis.

Robert Eden served the British Crown as governor of Maryland from 1769 to 1776. Anticipating the worst, Governor Eden fled to England just before the Declaration of Independence was adopted. Once military action concluded in America, the former governor ventured back to the Maryland capital, where he received mixed greetings in 1784. Less than twelve months later, Eden died in the home of Dr. Upton Scott at 4 Shipwright Street. Concerned that a public funeral during the light of day might lead Patriots to steal and desecrate the corpse, the physician and several residents of like mind decided to take the body to a cemetery outside the city under cover of darkness. On a fog-shrouded night, slaves carried the corpse down the incline from the house to the street and bore it to the dock. From there, a barge transported the coffin to St. Margaret's Cemetery.

When nights are deep and dark in Annapolis, people still witness the grim spectacle of slave ghosts shouldering the coffin down the ancient streets. No sounds come from the phantom cortege, led by the apparitions of Dr. Upton's household servants, who light the way with their lanterns. At the dock on Spa Creek, a ghost ship waits.

Eden's grave was subsequently moved to the center of Annapolis near the entrance to historic St. Anne's Episcopal Church at Church Circle. Nonetheless, the ghostly procession continues.

BUCKEYSTOWN—CARROLLTON MANOR

Born in Annapolis in 1737, Charles Carroll was one of the wealthiest of America's founding fathers. Upon his death in Baltimore in 1832, the nation lost its last signer of the Declaration of Independence.

Carroll built Carrolton Manor in Frederick County in 1765. His spirit continues to haunt the three-story brick edifice of late Georgian design. Residents and visitors have heard strange sounds in rooms devoid of humans. Dishes are banged against each other. Strange voices come from the kitchen after the house is dark for the night. These otherworldly activities have long been associated with Carroll, who split his time among his various estates.

Now in private ownership, the house is located at 5809 Manor Woods Road in Buckeystown.

ELKTON—ELK FORGE BED AND BREAKFAST INN AND RETREAT

As soon as the massive British army of General William Howe came ashore at the Elk River with designs on Philadelphia in August 1777, the area around Elkton swarmed with Redcoats. Some of the invaders made their way to the site now occupied by the Elk Forge Bed and Breakfast. There, they found an enterprise that produced pig iron and milled wheat. The invaders' demands for massive quantities of grain angered the miller, an unwavering Patriot. Anxious to bring discomfort to the insolent enemies, he added glass to the wheat he delivered to them. When his trick was discovered, the embittered Redcoats hanged him on the site.

The manor house, constructed around 1760, survived the war and now serves as a hostelry. It is also the home of the miller's ghost. A number of patrons have encountered the melancholy apparition of the man who gave his life fighting the enemy the best way he could.

The inn's address is 807 Elk Mills Rd., Elkton, Md. 21921; the telephone number is 410-392-9007.

FREDERICK—HESSIAN BARRACKS

Construction of this two-story stone building was authorized in 1777 by the Maryland legislature. Designed to house two battalions of

American troops, it became a prison for enemy soldiers as the Revolutionary War wore on. Hessian troops captured at Bennington, Saratoga, and Yorktown were incarcerated here. Many were not released until 1783. Twenty years later, Meriwether Lewis and William Clark used the structure to plan portions of their great expedition to the American West.

Located on the campus of the Maryland School for the Deaf, the historic building is haunted by the Hessians who suffered confinement here. The eerie moans and cries of their spirits reverberate from the building.

The address for the Hessian Barracks is 101 Clarke Pl., Frederick, Md. 21701.

FREDERICK—OLD CITY HALL

Located on historic Court Square in old Frederick, this stately brick structure was built following the Revolutionary War to replace the original courthouse, which stood on the same site. Citizens gathered here in 1765 to openly display their hatred of the Stamp Act by burning effigies of the Royal officials who enforced it. During the war, seven Tories were tried here. Following a highly publicized and emotional trial, all the defendants were convicted and sentenced to be hanged. Ultimately, three of their number met their fate on the gallows on the courthouse grounds, while their more fortunate fellows were deported.

The spirits of the hanged Tories continue to abide on the grounds. Shadowy figures have been seen around the execution site, and orbs and ectoplasms have been photographed by investigators.

The address for Old City Hall is 101 North Court St., Frederick, Md. 21701.

LAUREL—MONTPELIER MANSION

Major Thomas Snowden began construction of this Georgian brick mansion in 1781. His hospitable nature drew many of America's founders to the palatial house and well-landscaped grounds. While strolling the seventy-one-acre estate, modern-day visitors have sighted the ghosts of none other than Thomas Jefferson, George Washington, and John Adams.

The mansion is open to the public. Its address is 9650 Mulkirk Rd., Laurel, Md. 20708; the telephone number is 302-377-7817.

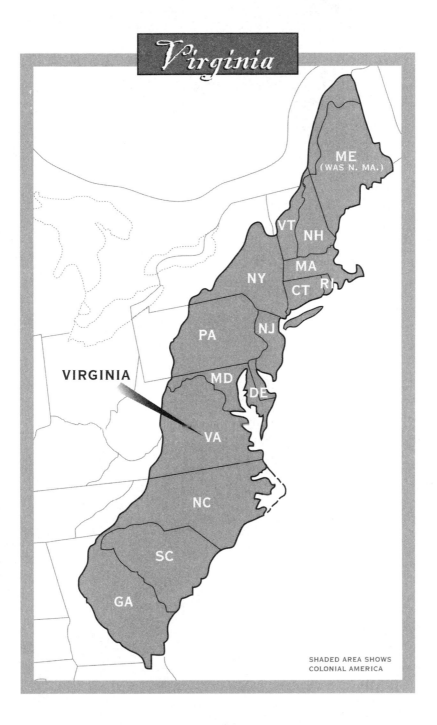

Virginia

ME
(WAS N. MA.)

VT
NH

NY
MA
CT RI

PA
NJ

VIRGINIA
MD
DE

VA

NC

SC

GA

SHADED AREA SHOWS
COLONIAL AMERICA

The Ghost of a Mad Housewife
ASHLAND, VIRGINIA

I know not what course others may take, but as for me, give me liberty or give me death.

PATRICK HENRY

Over the long, storied history of the United States, few Americans have been more renowned for their stirring words than Patrick Henry of Virginia. Not long after the First Continental Congress convened in Philadelphia in 1774, Henry (1736–99) rose to the floor and proudly proclaimed, "The distinctions between Virginians, Pennsylvanians, New Yorkers, and New Englanders, are no more. I am not a Virginian, but an American." Less than six months later, he delivered his celebrated "Liberty or Death" speech at St. John's Church in Richmond, wherein he prefaced his oft-quoted sentence with these words: "Gentlemen may cry peace, peace—but there is no peace. The war is actually begun! The next gale that sweeps from the north will bring to our eyes the clash of resounding arms! Our brethren are already in the field! Why stand we here idle? What is it that gentlemen wish? What would they have? Is life so dear, or peace so sweet, as to be purchased at the price of chains and slavery? Forbid it, Almighty God!"

Most Americans had little way of knowing that when Patrick Henry made some of his famous speeches, he was a troubled man in his personal life. During his service in the First Continental Congress, his wife, Sarah, was struggling with mental illness. She died in February 1775, just a month before her bereaved husband delivered his most famous address. Sarah Henry's ghost remains in residence at Scotchtown, the expansive home where she and her husband lived from 1771 until her death.

At the age of eighteen, Patrick Henry was already a failed merchant when he married sixteen-year-old Sarah Shelton. Her dowry—which included a six-hundred-acre farm, a house, and six slaves—enabled the newlyweds to establish themselves as young planters. Three years later, a devastating fire ravaged the plantation. Henry subsequently made a second attempt in the mercantile business and failed again. He then began to read law. In 1766, he embarked upon a legal career that flourished rather quickly in Hanover County and northeastern Virginia. Prosperity allowed Henry to purchase Scotchtown, to which he, Sarah, and their five children moved in 1771. The Georgian house, erected near Ashland in 1698, was one of the largest residences in colonial America.

Just months after the Henrys moved in, Sarah gave birth to a son. In the days that followed, she began to exhibit signs of mental instability, a condition that worsened until her death four years later. Few details of Sarah's illness survive. Speculation has centered on puerperal psychosis, a severe sickness that most often occurs after childbirth.

As his wife's condition deteriorated, Henry was forced to make a difficult decision about her care. He traveled to Williamsburg to tour the public hospital there. Disgusted by what he observed, he decided to keep his wife at Scotchtown, where he could ensure that her needs would receive special attention.

In the last year of her life, Sarah displayed what observers termed "a strange antipathy" toward her family. For her own safety and that of the family, she was "hospitalized" in two dungeonlike rooms in the basement of Scotchtown. A servant was assigned to monitor her behavior until it became necessary to restrain her in a "strait-dress," a device thought to be similar to a modern straightjacket.

When Sarah died, her body was buried on the estate in an unmarked grave, perhaps out of concern over neighborhood fears and misunderstanding of her sickness. Rumors were rampant that Mrs. Henry had been possessed by devils.

In 1777, just a year after he was elected the first governor of the commonwealth of Virginia, Patrick Henry chose to part with Scotchtown because it was the death site of the lady who had been his sweetheart from childhood. Sarah's ghost, however, has lingered for more than two centuries.

A great-great-great-granddaughter of Patrick and Sarah Henry once described Scotchtown as "haunted." Although she was reluctant to be specific, staff members at the historic estate agree with her assessment. They have been witnesses to the supernatural presence of Sarah Henry. An unlocked door leading to the basement has at times been difficult to open, almost as if someone were holding it on the other side. Pieces of historic furniture often move without the aid of human hands. A candle surviving from the days of the Henry family has been mysteriously moved when Scotchtown was closed for the night.

Sarah's ghost has enjoyed a "tea party," moving a tea caddy and removing the top of a teapot while the house was empty. Unexplained problems with the house's alarm system and motion detectors have reportedly brought law enforcement officers to the estate. Very much aware of Scotchtown's haunted reputation, the police always request that estate personnel be the first to enter the spooky structure.

On Halloween night in 1990, a policeman reported that a neighborhood woman had noticed a light, apparently a candle, shining from a window of Scotchtown. When the lady made her way onto the estate grounds, the light mysteriously went out. Then she caught a brief glimpse of a spectral woman walking past the window, candle in hand.

Before 1958, when the Preservation of Virginia Antiquities acquired and restored the old Henry estate, the dwelling suffered years of abandonment. While it hastened toward ruin, area residents regularly experienced frightening episodes there. During the 1930s and 1940s, they heard strange noises, including chains dragging across the floor.

Likewise, locals observed a female apparition dressed in a long white gown floating about the backside of the house. This ghostlike figure was witnessed by a group of adults and children for thirty seconds until it faded from view. Similarly, others spotted a female ghost making its way from the basement to the ancillary structures that once housed servants.

Visitors to the house in more recent times have also experienced the ghost of Sarah Henry. During one tour, a docent took a group into the room just above Sarah's basement quarters. As the tourists were listening to the sad story of Mrs. Henry's last years, terrifying shrieks and screams came from the "dungeon" where Sarah was confined. The visitors quickly scattered. Throughout the house, and particularly in Sarah's basement rooms, visitors often experience the unnerving feeling that someone is watching them from behind.

Should you tour Scotchtown, pay particular attention to the walls in the basement quarters. They need painting. But try as they might, professional painters have been unable to get even the best-quality paint to adhere to the walls in the two rooms where Sarah spent her last days. It literally burns off the surfaces. No scientific explanation has been offered for this anomaly.

When Sarah Henry grew ill at Scotchtown, she was robbed of the joy of motherhood, the pleasure of living at a magnificent estate, the opportunity of becoming the first first lady of Virginia, the excitement surrounding the birth of an independent American nation, and the companionship of the love of her life. Maybe Sarah's ghost yet abides at the old Henry homestead, searching for the happiness that should have been hers.

The address for **Scotchtown** is 16120 Chiswell Ln., Beaverdam, Va. 23015; the telephone number is 804-227-3500.

The Ghost of the Brooding Brother-in-Law
FREDERICKSBURG, VIRGINIA

We began a contest of liberty ill provided with the means for the war, relying on our patriotism to supply the deficiency. We expected to encounter many wants. . . . We must bear the present evils.

GEORGE WASHINGTON, 1781

Had it not been for the countless sacrifices of patriotic Americans both on the field of battle and off, the Revolutionary War would have ended with a different result. One American who literally pledged his life, his fortune, and his honor to the cause of independence was Fielding Lewis, the brother-in-law of General George Washington. Lewis (1725–81) died a sick, broken man at his plantation in Fredericksburg, Virginia, just two months after the British surrendered to his wife's brother at Yorktown. Since that time, Lewis's magnificent late-Georgian mansion, long known as Kenmore, has survived. So, too, has Lewis's brooding spirit.

Born into a wealthy family in Gloucester County, Fielding Lewis settled as a young man in Fredericksburg, where his good manners, so-phistication, and business acumen earned him a sterling reputation and high social standing. In Fredericksburg, he formed a lifelong friend-ship and business relationship with George Washington. In 1750, the two men became family when the twenty-four-year-old Lewis married Washington's only sister, Elizabeth, or "Betty."

Anxious to select a site on which to construct a home for his bride, Lewis turned to his brother-in-law, a surveyor by training. Washington suggested a spectacular eleven-hundred-acre tract on the outskirts of Fredericksburg not far from the Ferry Farm, where Washington had lived as a youth. Acting upon the advice, Lewis began construction of an imposing brick manor house in 1752.

Once completed, the Lewis mansion was regarded as one of the sturdiest and most beautiful in colonial America. Its outer walls, crafted of brick in the Flemish bond pattern, were two feet thick. From the estate, Lewis managed his extensive prewar enterprises, which included farming, a mercantile business, a shipyard on the Rappahannock River, and an import-export business.

From the outset of the American Revolution, the cause of indepen-dence had no greater champion than Fielding Lewis. Named commis-sary general of munitions with the rank of colonel, he took his charge very seriously. He used his personal wealth to construct and operate the Fredericksburg Arms Manufactory, which produced vital weapons for the Continental Army. In addition, Lewis personally funded three regi-ments of troops and built a ship for the war effort.

Because its coffers were almost always empty, the fledgling Ameri-can government was never able to recompense Lewis for his contribu-tions. As the war progressed, Lewis grew more and more somber as his fortune dwindled. He could often be found at Kenmore, then known as Millbank, brooding over his financial books. His fears that the struggle with Great Britain would bankrupt him were almost realized by war's end. Just before his death in December 1780, Lewis had debts total-ing seven thousand pounds. He took little consolation from the fact that his actions had played an instrumental role in securing America's independence.

Over the fifteen years following her husband's death, Betty Washington Lewis and the oldest of the couple's children prospered at the plantation and restored the family fortunes. Through good times and bad, the spirit of Fielding Lewis never left the place. It continues to haunt Kenmore today, exhibiting constant concern over the financial vitality of the estate.

Long after Kenmore left the ownership of the Lewis family, an overnight guest experienced the presence of Lewis's ghost. During each night of her stay, she and her mother heard footsteps in the hallway outside their bedroom. The guest got out of bed and closed the door. On each of the following mornings, the door was open. At length, in an attempt to ensure privacy, the guest placed a heavy table against the door. When she awoke the next day, the door was open and the table back in its original position.

In 1922, Kenmore and three surrounding acres were salvaged from destruction by the Kenmore Association, now known as the George Washington Foundation. Since that time, the home has been open to the public. Visitors can enjoy the charming elegance established by the financier of the Revolutionary War. On occasion, they may even come face to face with his ghostly presence.

On the first floor—which consists of the parlor, the dining room, Lewis's office, and his personal quarters—windows often mysteriously fly open. Doorknobs turn without the assistance of human hands. Unlocked doors cannot be opened for days at a time. But once a maintenance man arrives to determine the problem, the doors suddenly work perfectly. Heavy footsteps produced by no human feet pace the hallway. In the fireplace, ancient andirons crash to the floor. On hot summer days, visitors and staff members alike have reported a cold wind. Lights flicker on and off.

A renowned psychic investigator visited Kenmore in 1971 to study the supernatural aura about the place. In the master bedroom, she felt the spirit of a tired old man. She also saw a gray-haired figure dressed in clothes of the colonial period.

Upstairs are four bedrooms where the Lewis children slept. There, the investigator sensed sadness and confusion. In the light of day, a man in Revolutionary War–era dress often stands in one of the children's rooms with a worried look on his face. Sometimes, the same apparition sits at a desk poring over a mountain of paperwork. When the second story is empty of personnel and visitors, footsteps pound the old floorboards.

Down in the basement, the spirit of Colonel Lewis is often at work. Lights turn on and off when no one is about. The basement door is difficult to open even when unlocked. Employees report that it seems as if someone is pushing on the other side. A misty, cloudlike figure resembling a man floats from room to room. While monitoring the basement after business hours, security guards sometimes hear phantom footsteps on the floor above them.

Kenmore is open year-round to the public. During a tour of the lovely place, furnished with relics of the Lewis and Washington families, don't be surprised if you see or hear the ghost of General Washington's brother-in-law. After all, Fielding Lewis gave all he had, save his home and family, to the cause of independence. Now, his contemplative spirit seems determined to act as guardian of the place he built and called home.

The address for **Kenmore Plantation** is 1201 Washington Ave., Fredericksburg, Va. 22401; the telephone number is 540-373-3381.

Here, There, and Everywhere:
Mad Anthony, of Course
LOUDOUN COUNTY, VIRGINIA

If I am to die, I want to die at the head of the column.
GENERAL ANTHONY WAYNE

Apple trees were blossoming in May 1781 when an unlikely meeting took place between two Patriots near the Potomac River in northern Virginia. General Anthony Wayne was en route to aid the Marquis de Lafayette in his operations against Lord Cornwallis, who had recently arrived in Virginia from North Carolina. That beautiful spring day in Loudoun County, the general happened upon Philip Noland, the county sheriff and a local entrepreneur, who was hard at work on a beautiful Georgian house near the Carolina Road. Wayne stopped to introduce himself and admire the home, which was less than half complete. As the two men chatted about the fortunes of war, the general fancied the home under construction, dreaming that it, or one like it, might be his when the fighting finally came to an end.

As fate would have it, Noland never completed the house, and General Wayne spent the last fifteen years of his life in the military service of the United States. Today, only the foundation of the general's dream home remains. But on occasion, Mad Anthony's ghost makes return visits to the Noland ruins, which are also haunted by other ghosts of the American Revolution.

Noland (1718–84), a Virginia native, was elected high sheriff of Loudoun County in 1777. At the time, he was also a successful land speculator and the operator of Noland's Ferry, an important Potomac River passage near Leesburg. He lived in an impressive brick mansion within sight of the ferry landing. Noland's Ferry connected the Maryland route of the Carolina Road (now known as Rogues Road) with the Virginia portion of the byway.

During the Revolutionary War, Noland used a portion of his river estate as a military depot and a prison camp to hold captured Hessian soldiers. By the time General Wayne made his acquaintance, the sheriff, a staunch advocate for independence, had put together a cache of 920 muskets and 486 bayonets for Patriots in the serious fighting soon to follow in Virginia.

Why Noland decided to abandon construction of the house so admired by General Wayne is not known. Perhaps the war prevented its completion, or perhaps Noland made a conscious business decision. He died in 1784, and the partially completed structure was left to the elements.

When Wayne happened upon Noland's project that spring day in 1781, he and the one thousand elite American soldiers following him were desperately needed to reinforce Lafayette, who just days before had reported to George Washington, "I am determined to skirmish, but not to engage too far. I am not strong enough even to get beaten." About the same time, Lafayette's adversary, Lord Cornwallis, recently reinforced with six thousand troops from Sir Henry Clinton, had this to say about the youthful French commander: "The boy cannot escape me."

Mad Anthony had no sooner left Noland's construction site than he went to work proving the British general wrong. At one point, Wayne was ordered to launch an attack on what was assumed to be a detached element of the large army operating in Virginia. As it turned out, the enemy force was Cornwallis's entire army. Undaunted by the dangerous situation, the general, true to his nickname, led a headlong charge into an army that outnumbered his force by ten to one. His daring move so surprised the Redcoats that Mad Anthony was able to extricate his troops from an almost impossible predicament.

Over the next several months, Wayne returned to the site of his favorite house to monitor its progress. After personally witnessing the surrender of Cornwallis on the Tidewater peninsula on Friday, October 19, 1781, he departed Virginia without having another opportunity to visit Noland's construction project. Instead, he hurried south to aid General Nathanael Greene in his mopping-up operations in South Carolina and Georgia, which lasted well into 1782.

Not long after Philip Noland abandoned the house, strange occurrences began at the site. They continue to this day. Unearthly moans emanate from the old brick foundation. In the cellar, eerie scratching and pounding noises on the walls sound as if someone is attempting to escape. On some nights, two ghosts have been seen aimlessly roaming the basement. These spectres are said to be the revenants of two Hessian prisoners who escaped from Sheriff Noland's compound on the shores of the Potomac. They chose to hide in the wrong place. Noland and his men found the escapees in the cellar of his unfinished house and shot them on sight.

A far more pleasant spectre has also been observed on occasion. The ghost of the Revolutionary War officer encountered in more places than any other has been known to return to the site of the house he aspired to own. On spring days and nights, the apparitions of Mad Anthony and his beloved horse, Nab, sometimes appear at the ruins. General

Wayne's ghost is said to dismount and walk about the old construction site, as if trying to figure out when the house might be finished.

Located on private property off U.S. 15 near Leesburg, **Philip Noland's abandoned homesite** survives as a symbol of the unrealized personal goals of Patriots willing to sacrifice so the dream of an independent America could become reality.

The Haunted Twilight of Surrender
YORKTOWN, VIRGINIA

Humanity has won its battle. Liberty now has a country.

MARQUIS DE LAFAYETTE

At midmorning on Wednesday, October 17, 1781, a single British drummer stepped onto the earthworks at Yorktown, Virginia, to sound the beat of a parley. Though he could hardly be heard over the thunder of artillery, there was little doubt about the intent, once a dignified red-coated officer waving a white handkerchief began making his way to the front lines. Suddenly, the artillery fell silent. Stunned American, French, and British soldiers watched as Continental troops rushed forward to blindfold the enemy officer. He and his message intimating a possible British surrender were turned over to General Washington at his headquarters.

The following morning, representatives of the warring factions began negotiating the terms of surrender at the house of Augustine Moore. As the high-level meeting was called to order, two victims of the fighting at Yorktown were dying at the Moore residence. Ghosts associated with those mortally wounded men continue to haunt the house and grounds where the Revolutionary War effectively came to an end.

No one knows exactly why the two-story frame dwelling of Augustine Moore, a merchant and business partner of noted statesman Thomas Nelson, was selected for the surrender negotiations. A few reasons are possible: the house was outside the firing lines; its location was neutral with respect to the armies; and its setting along the York River made it accessible.

When the protracted negotiations got under way on the morning of October 18, four men selected as commissioners by their respective armies sat around a table to hammer out the details. Lieutenant Colonel Thomas Dundas and Major Alexander Ross represented the British. Lieutenant Colonel John Laurens, the South Carolinian who served as the personal translator for General Washington, represented the Americans. And the Viscount de Noailles, brother-in-law of the Marquis de Lafayette, represented the French.

Just before midnight, the weary Laurens returned to Washington's headquarters with a draft of the Articles of Capitulation. After a few changes were made, the general directed that a copy of the redrafted document be dispatched to Cornwallis for his approval and signature.

At two o'clock the following afternoon, the vanquished British army, its regimental flags cased, marched to the designated field of surrender, located a mile and a half from Yorktown. Along the route, Cornwallis's band played a fitting air, "The World Turned Upside Down."

Meanwhile, two men seriously wounded at Yorktown were dying or already dead at the Moore House.

One of them was Augustine Moore, Jr., the teenage son of the owner. Amid the combat during the second week of October, young Moore had been hit by a stray bullet. Somehow, he managed to make his way home, where he lost his fight for life in a matter of days.

But his spirit lingers. Though staff members of the National Park Service (which maintains and administers the house) are reluctant to discuss the supernatural presence, some employees have admitted they are unnerved by the eerie goings-on. In the early morning, custodians change the sheets and straighten the bed coverings before tour guides open the house to the public. Upon their arrival, the guides are often startled to find a large, noticeable impression on the bedding in the room where Augustine Moore, Jr., expired, as if the bed has been slept in.

Guides, custodians, and tourists often experience an uneasy feeling in that room. One psychic investigator captured the vision of a young man dressed in colonial clothing peering out the room's window.

While touring the house on a Sunday afternoon in the last decade of the twentieth century, one lady may have unwittingly recorded the voice of young Moore's ghost. At the outset of her tour, she decided to make an audio recording of the guide's commentary. The recorder continued operating while the visitors roamed freely about the house. While in the master bedroom, the lady noticed an unusual indentation on the bed covering. Later, when she replayed the recording, a slow-speaking voice was clearly audible on the portion of the tape that followed the guide's presentation. No rational explanation existed for the strange voice, since the recorder was in perfect working order and the tape was new.

Should you decide to tour the house to personally experience the ghost of Augustine Moore, Jr., pay particular attention to the red velvet chair in the room where the four commissioners met to reach an accord on the British surrender. Because of the chair's fragile, historic nature, sitting in it is prohibited. But upon close inspection, it is evident that some entity sits there on a regular basis.

The other man who died at the Moore House amid the turmoil surrounding the surrender was thirty-year-old John Turner, like Augustine Moore a Yorktown merchant. On Saturday, October 13, 1781, Turner was severely wounded as he watched the fierce assault by American and French artillerists on the besieged British army. His wound bleeding profusely, Turner was borne to the Moore House for attention. There, his wife, Clara, tried in vain to stabilize him until a physician could arrive.

After his body was buried on the grounds, his tombstone was etched with Clara's mournful words: "A cruel ball, so sudden to disarm, and tear my tender husband from my arms. How can I grieve too much, what time shall end, my mourning for so good, so kind, a friend."

At some point, Turner's grave marker was inexplicably removed from the burial plot and stored in the basement of the Moore House. After the National Park Service assumed ownership of the residence and grounds in 1934, the stone was returned to the grave. Clara's ghost, torn between the house where her husband died and the grave where his body was laid to rest, can be found in both places.

Inside the house, her apparition, bearing a sad countenance, has been observed floating about the hallways and staring forlornly from the window of the upstairs bedroom where John Turner died.

At night, Clara's ghost can be seen roaming the grounds near her husband's grave. One local resident observed the spectral figure of a lady dressed in a long, flowing white gown along the riverbank at the rear of the Moore House. Upon closer inspection, the apparition seemed to be crying and looked as if it were about to plunge into the water. The headlights of an automobile traveling on a nearby roadway passed directly through the wraith, which manifested itself for some fifteen minutes.

Other nighttime eyewitnesses have reported seeing the same white-clad ghost floating in the side yard of the house as phantom cannon fire rumbled in the distance. Still others have seen a shadowy figure standing at John Turner's grave.

The Moore House offers an opportunity for visitors to Yorktown to see the site where the world's most professional army conceded defeat to the Continentals, always short in materiel but mighty in spirit. Likewise, the house's ghosts survive as grim reminders of the great human costs incurred in the fight for American independence.

Historic Yorktown, of which the **Moore House** is a part, is open to the public. For visitor information, contact Colonial National Historical Park, P.O. Box 210, Yorktown, Va. 23690; the telephone number is 757-898-2410.

Other "Spirited" Revolutionary War Sites in Virginia, Briefly Noted

BOTETOURT COUNTY— SITE OF GREENFIELD MANSION

A state historical marker calls attention to Greenfield, the home built nearby by Colonel William Preston around 1760. Prior to the Revolutionary War, Preston served in the Virginia House of Burgesses. A fiercely independent frontiersman, he fought Indians and Tories in the wilds of western Virginia and British regulars at Guilford Courthouse and other battlefields. After a lifetime of public service, he returned to Greenfield, where he enjoyed his retirement until his death in 1783.

Almost immediately, his ghost made its presence known in the house by loudly stomping its boots and slamming doors. Colonel Preston's former servants were horrified when they witnessed his apparition. Greenfield was destroyed by fire in 1959, but the ghost of the old colonel is said to linger at the site.

The state historical marker for Greenfield is located on U.S. 220 near Fincastle, Virginia.

CHARLOTTESVILLE—CASTLE HILL

Located in the rolling countryside near Charlottesville, Castle Hill, a stately plantation house, was owned during the Revolutionary War by Dr. Thomas Walker, an outspoken Patriot. In the early-morning hours of Monday, June 4, 1781, Colonel Banastre Tarleton called at the plantation during his mission to capture Thomas Jefferson and other important personages at Charlottesville. Determined to delay the British and give another area Patriot, Jack Jouett, time to warn Jefferson and others, Dr. Walker prepared a bountiful breakfast for Tarleton and his officers. Then Walker's daughter, Mildred, and other young women about the plantation used their feminine wiles on the cavalry chieftain and his subordinates to prolong their sojourn.

Mildred's ghost is said to haunt her former room. Guests who have slept in the Pink Bedroom have smelled perfume from times past. Unusual noises and phantom footsteps have been heard in the room. Some people have even seen the ghost of a "charming-looking woman" attired in colonial fashions and carrying a fan. The spectre is said to have a playful nature. Objects in the chamber mysteriously move or disappear, and the rocking chair begins to rock when no visible presence is in it.

Castle Hill, located off Va. 231, is a private residence.

CHARLOTTESVILLE—THE FARM

By the time Banastre Tarleton rode into Charlottesville on the afternoon of June 4, 1781, Thomas Jefferson, warned of the British officer's intentions, had fled town. Tarleton called at The Farm, a beautiful estate in the heart of Charlottesville owned by Colonel Nicholas Lewis, the uncle of Meriwether Lewis. After the British colonel and his men rode through the rose garden to the house, Tarleton greeted Mrs. Lewis by observing, "What a paradise!" She responded curtly, "Then why do you disturb it?" Despite the cold welcome, Tarleton spent the night, enduring a troubled sleep because of worries about a possible Patriot attack on the home.

Psychic investigators have studied the unusually strong feelings of uneasiness experienced near the fireplace in the house, built in 1826 on the exact site of the original. Speculation is that the spirit of Colonel Tarleton haunts the place.

The address for The Farm is 1201 East Jefferson St., Charlottesville, Va. 22902.

CHARLOTTESVILLE—MONTICELLO

Construction on Thomas Jefferson's architectural masterpiece began in 1769. When Monticello is closed to the public, the spirit of the author of the Declaration of Independence and the nation's third president makes itself at home. Security staff frequently hear Jefferson's ghost cheerfully humming in his beloved house. In life, Jefferson was known to enjoy singing to himself and humming. Apparently, his is a contented ghost.

The address for Monticello is 931 Thomas Jefferson Pkwy., Charlottesville, Va. 22902; the telephone number is 434-984-9822.

FREDERICKSBURG—JAMES MONROE LAW OFFICE

In the postwar years, James Monroe practiced law in this brick building, which now houses a museum and library honoring his life and times. In the twentieth century, the apparitions of Monroe, the last Revolutionary War veteran elected president, and Thomas Jefferson were sighted walking through the door of Monroe's old office.

The address for the James Monroe Law Office and Museum is 908 Charles St., Fredericksburg, Va. 22401; the telephone number is 540-654-1043.

FREDERICKSBURG—MARY WASHINGTON HOUSE

George Washington is said to have purchased this handsome white clapboard house for his mother, Mary, in 1772. She lived here until her death from breast cancer seventeen years later. Apparently, Mrs. Washington enjoyed the place so much that her spirit has never left. Visitors have caught sight of Mary's apparition in the kitchen. Some have heard her skirts swish as she roamed from room to room. In the backyard, one of her favorite spots, the ghost of a lady in colonial dress has been observed walking a path of boxwoods.

The Mary Washington House is located at the corner of Charles and Lewis streets. The address is 1200 Charles St., Fredericksburg, Va. 22401; the telephone number is 540-373-1569.

JAMES CITY COUNTY—CARTER'S GROVE PLANTATION

This spectacular Georgian plantation house, constructed in the middle of the eighteenth century, is haunted as the result of two separate events involving a pair of Revolutionary War heroes subsequently elected president of the United States.

George Washington was little more than a teenager when Mary Cary, two years his junior, rejected his marriage proposal in the first-floor drawing room, better known as "the Refusal Room." He did not see her again until he made his way through Williamsburg on his triumphant departure from Yorktown in the autumn of 1781. Along the route, someone pointed out the house of Mary, who had long ago married another. Seeing her peering from the window, Washington recognized her with a broad smile and waved his sword as a salute. Mary promptly fainted.

In the 1760s, Thomas Jefferson encountered the same fate in the Refusal Room when he proposed to his first love, Rebecca Burwell, said to be a beautiful, flirtatious teenager.

To this day, when fresh carnations are placed in the Refusal Room, an invisible presence rips them to shreds during the night and throws them about the floor.

Carter's Grove, now in private ownership, is located along the James River in the Hampton Roads area.

STRATFORD—STRATFORD HALL

Robert E. Lee was born in this 1738 Colonial mansion on a high bluff overlooking the Potomac River. His great-uncle Richard Henry

Lee was one of the behind-the-scenes heroes of the American Revolution. In 1776, as a member of the Continental Congress, Richard Henry Lee was selected to introduce the bill seeking adoption of the Declaration of Independence. Then, as America fought for that independence, Robert E. Lee's father, Henry Lee III, better known as "Light Horse Harry," took to the field, where he served as one of George Washington's most trusted and capable cavalry leaders.

Today, the ghost of Light Horse Harry continues to haunt the grand house. His apparition is sometimes seen seated at a desk in the library.

For access to Stratford Hall, contact the Robert E. Lee Memorial Association, Inc., 483 Great House Rd., Stratford, Va. 22558; the telephone number is 804-493-8038.

WILLIAMSBURG—CAPITOL BUILDING

When the new state of Virginia moved its capital from Williamsburg to Richmond in 1780, the old Capitol Building was abandoned to the elements. A fire in 1832 left only its walls. Now, as one of the centerpieces of the Colonial Williamsburg restoration, the Capitol Building has been reconstructed to its past grandeur. A haunted portrait of Patrick Henry adorns its interior walls.

Henry's fiery oratory spurred his legislative comrades toward independence. In this hall on Wednesday, May 15, 1776, delegates voted for Virginia to join with the other colonies in declaring independence. Less than six weeks later, Henry was elected the first governor of the independent state of Virginia.

When Henry's portrait was first placed in the Capitol Building, the expression on his face was a most pleasant one. But after the building was reconstructed for Colonial Williamsburg, the British flag was placed atop it in deference to the British government formerly housed here. When the same portrait of Henry was returned to the restored building, the face bore the sullen expression it still exhibits today. It seems he does not approve of the Union Jack flying above the Capitol Building of his free, independent state.

Legend has it that when the clock strikes midnight ushering in July 4 in Colonial Williamsburg, a spectral procession of Patriots led by none other than Patrick Henry can be seen in the front of the old Capitol Building.

The address for the building is 900 Capitol Building Rd., Williamsburg, Va. 23815.

WILLIAMSBURG—COLLEGE OF WILLIAM AND MARY

Located in the heart of Williamsburg, this ancient school boasts an impressive list of superlatives and historic milestones: it is the only institution of higher learning in the United States to have a Royal charter; it is the second-oldest college in the United States, after Harvard; and it was the birthplace of Phi Beta Kappa, America's most prestigious academic honor society. Indeed, William and Mary is steeped in history. And a part of its great tradition is its ghostly lore from the Revolutionary War.

Erected on the campus more than seventy-five years before the Declaration of Independence was signed, the imposing Sir Christopher Wren Building was used as a military hospital for wounded French and American troops in the fall of 1781, during the events at nearby Yorktown. Once the three-and-a-half-story edifice was returned to academic use, professors and students began to hear disembodied footsteps on the upper floors. To this day, the same bizarre sounds are audible. Speculation is that the phantom footsteps belong to a French soldier who died here as a result of a wound at Yorktown.

Completed in 1733, the elegant three-story brick President's Home is also haunted by a French soldier brought to the makeshift hospital set up here during the Battle of Yorktown. For decades, the ghost has made itself known by descending the staircase from the third floor to the second.

The address for the College of William and Mary is 170 Wake Dr., Williamsburg, Va. 23185.

WILLIAMSBURG—GEORGE WYTHE HOUSE

A bittersweet romance that ended tragically in the dying days of the Revolutionary War is the source of the melancholy ghost at this mid-eighteenth-century brick mansion.

During the climactic fighting on Virginia's Tidewater peninsula in 1781, George Washington used the George Wythe House as his headquarters. Once Cornwallis surrendered, many wounded French soldiers were brought to the house for medical attention. One such soldier was Oscar LeBlanc. When his condition worsened, a local woman, Katherine Anderson, volunteered to care for him. Day and night, she ministered to LeBlanc until his recovery seemed a certainty. Nurse and patient fell in love and made plans to marry once the war ended. But as fate would have it, LeBlanc came down with malaria. Despite Katherine's loving care, he died within a week. His heartbroken fiancée perished of "natural causes" not long thereafter.

Today, Katherine's spirit haunts the site of her great misfortune. Phantom sounds and voices emanate from the second floor, where LeBlanc died, when all humans are downstairs. Visitors and residents alike have been mortified over the years to come face to face with the spectral figure of a female dressed in colonial clothing.

The George Wythe House is open to the public. The address is Palace St. and Prince George St., Williamsburg, Va. 23815; the telephone number is 757-220-7645.

WILLIAMSBURG—PEYTON RANDOLPH HOUSE

In 1775, on the eve of the Revolutionary War, the American colonies were robbed of one of the greatest champions of independence when Peyton Randolph, the first president of the Continental Congress and a cousin of Thomas Jefferson, died of a stroke. Upon his death, management of his expansive early-eighteenth-century house and plantation devolved to his wife, Elizabeth, or "Betty," a well-educated, forceful woman.

Once Lord Dunmore, the Royal governor, proclaimed freedom for all slaves who left their Patriot owners and joined the British army, Betty encountered difficulties with her personal attendant, Eva. Despite Betty's protestations, Eva fled the plantation. She was subsequently captured and returned to her owner, who subjected her to a whipping.

Eva was again carrying out her duties in 1781 when the likes of George Washington, the Marquis de Lafayette, and the Count de Rochambeau were entertained in the Randolph mansion. Meanwhile, tensions were intensifying between Betty and Eva.

A year later, when Mrs. Randolph died, her will provided that Eva be sold. Before she was led away to her new master, Eva cursed the house of her former owner.

For as long as anyone can remember, Eva's ghost has terrified those living in or visiting the home. Even the Marquis de Lafayette experienced the haunting. On his triumphant return to America in 1824, the French hero stayed overnight in the Peyton Randolph House. He subsequently noted, "Upon my arrival, as I entered the foyer, I felt a hand on my shoulder. I quickly turned, but found no one was there. The nights were not restful as the sound of voices kept me awake for most of my stay."

The famous red house, located on Market Square, is open to the public as part of Colonial Williamsburg; for information, call 757-229-1000.

YORKTOWN—CORNWALLIS CAVE

One of the most fascinating sites on a tour of Yorktown is the ancient man-made cave along the shore of the York River. Long known as Cornwallis Cave, it was used as a refuge by citizens as artillery roared and muskets blazed throughout Yorktown in October 1781. Unfounded legend has it that Cornwallis fled to the cave at the height of the hostilities.

After the war, townspeople began to hear strange noises and voices coming from the empty cave. The same phenomenon has been experienced in modern times.

Administered by the National Park Service, the haunted cave has been sealed off with metal bars at its entrance for safety reasons. For information, contact Colonial National Historical Park, P.O. Box 210, Yorktown, Va. 23690; the telephone number is 757-898-2410.

YORKTOWN—SURRENDER FIELD

American and French troops numbering in the thousands formed a mile-long human corridor for the defeated British army as it marched to its formal surrender at Yorktown that fateful autumn day in 1781. Tears flowed down the cheeks of the war-hardened Redcoats, while their victorious adversaries could hardly contain their celebration as Cornwallis's musicians played "The World Turned Upside Down."

Over the years, visitors to the well-preserved ground known as "the Surrender Field" have reported hearing phantom fifes and drums playing that same tune. Even the sounds of laughter and cheering can be heard on the empty field.

The Surrender Field is administered by the National Park Service. For information, contact Colonial National Historical Park, P.O. Box 210, Yorktown, Va. 23690; the telephone number is 757-898-2410.

YORKTOWN—SURROUNDING FORESTS

In the forests surrounding historic Yorktown, the ghost of a Patriot roams in an eternal effort to redeem himself in the eyes of his famous stepfather.

For most of his life, John Parke Custis, better known as "Jacky," was a ne'er-do-well. After his wealthy father died when Jacky was four years old, he inherited a king's ransom. His mother remarried. Her new husband, George Washington, loved his troubled stepson as if he were his own.

As a young man, Jacky failed in family and business matters. Anxious to turn his life around and make good with General Washington, he traveled in 1781 to Yorktown, where he volunteered to serve as an aide to his stepfather. Finally, it seemed Jacky had found his niche. He rendered effective service to the Continental Army until his frail body, unused to the rigors of military life, came down with camp fever. When Jacky could not shake the disease, General Washington insisted that he be transported to an area plantation to recuperate.

Jacky's stay there was short, for he was determined to please his stepfather. After setting out on foot to return to his post, he lost his way and died of exposure at the age of twenty-eight.

In the forests near where General George Washington gained his most important triumph, the ghost of Jacky Custis still walks in its endless quest to reunite with its loving stepfather. Pedestrians who have come upon the apparition describe it as a gaunt, bluish figure with blond hair, attired in a nightshirt. Its bare feet are bleeding.

For information, contact Colonial National Historical Park, P.O. Box 210, Yorktown, Va. 23690; the telephone number is 757-898-2410.

YORKTOWN—THOMAS NELSON HOUSE

Considered the most haunted house in Yorktown, this historic three-story masterpiece has graced the banks of the York River since 1711. During the Revolutionary War, it was owned by Thomas Nelson, Jr., a signer of the Declaration of Independence. But when the war came to Yorktown in 1781, Lord Cornwallis made the Nelson home his own.

On the morning of Tuesday, October 9, George Washington

positioned the allied forces for a grand attempt to dislodge the enemy from Yorktown. About three o'clock that afternoon, the American artillery commenced fire. Gunners asked Thomas Nelson, then serving as commander of the Virginia militia, "to point out a good target." Without emotion or delay, the Patriot selected his own house, in which he believed Cornwallis to be quartered.

The artillery made several direct hits on the target. One cannonball plowed into a secret stairway compartment, where a hiding Redcoat was hit and killed. His pathetic spectre has since been encountered near the place of his death.

In the field directly across the road from the house, ghost soldiers dressed in British uniforms are sometimes seen scurrying about, as if being attacked.

The Thomas Nelson House, administered by the National Park Service, is located at the corner of Main and Nelson streets in Yorktown. For information, contact Colonial National Historical Park, P.O. Box 210, Yorktown, Va. 23690; the telephone number is 757-898-2410.

North Carolina

ME
(WAS N. MA.)

VT
NH
NY
MA
CT RI
NJ
NORTH CAROLINA
PA
MD
DE
VA
NC
SC
GA

SHADED AREA SHOWS
COLONIAL AMERICA

Patrick, Benjamin, and Other Phantoms
RONDA, NORTH CAROLINA, AND KINGS MOUNTAIN, ON THE BORDER OF THE CAROLINAS

It was the joyful annunciation of that turn of tide of success which terminated the Revolutionary War with the seal of independence.

THOMAS JEFFERSON, REMARKING ON
THE IMPORTANCE OF THE AMERICAN
VICTORY AT KINGS MOUNTAIN

Patrick Ferguson and Benjamin Cleveland, two of the most famous officers of the Southern campaign in the Revolutionary War, were distinctly different men. Ferguson, the son of a Scottish judge and the nephew of a major general in the British army, was one of Lord Cornwallis's most trusted, most sophisticated, and most talented lieutenants. Cleveland, born in America, emerged as one of the crudest and fiercest of all Patriot officers in the back country of the Carolinas. Yet despite their disparate backgrounds, loyalties, and personalities, they had one commonality: each was hell-bent on doing all he could to swing the war in his favor. At Kings Mountain, Ferguson and Cleveland bravely led their charges into the battle widely acclaimed as the turning point of the American Revolution.

On the steep, rocky landscape along the border of the Carolinas, one of these officers died, while the other survived to fight until war's end. Today, the haunted imprints of Ferguson, Cleveland, and their comrades in arms are indelibly etched into the portion of the Carolinas where they fought so valiantly for diametrically opposed causes.

At the onset of the war, Benjamin Cleveland (1738–1806) served briefly as a junior officer in the Continental Army. But his skills as an intrepid hunter and scout in the remote areas of western North Carolina led to his appointment as colonel of the Wilkes County militia. By 1778, Cleveland had assumed additional responsibilities as a state legislator, justice of the county court, and chairman of the local Committee of Safety.

Clothed with military and judicial authority, the fiery-tempered frontiersman held the upper hand in the civil war that raged in the North Carolina mountains. Determined to avenge the criminal acts of Tories who ravaged the homes and farms of local Patriots, Cleveland and his warriors sought out the culprits and brought them to justice. Most often, that justice came in the form of hanging. According to noted North Carolina historian Marshall DeLancey Haywood, "Cleveland . . . probably had a hand in hanging more Tories than any other man in America. Though this may be an unenviable distinction, he had to deal with about as unscrupulous a set of ruffians as ever infested any land."

Although a few captured Tories avoided the noose, Cleveland never wasted an opportunity to exact revenge. In one instance, just after hanging a Tory who had stolen horses, he gave the victim's accomplice, who had witnessed the spectacle, a grim choice: "Either join your companion on a tree limb, or take this knife, cut off your ears and leave the country." Choosing to live, the Tory departed with blood pouring down his face.

One Tory was not so "lucky." Zacaria Wales participated in Cleveland's capture, only to have the tables turned when a posse led by Ben's brother, Robert, freed the Patriot colonel and took Wales prisoner.

Wales was promptly transported to Ben's plantation at Ronda, a small settlement along the Yadkin River in Wilkes County. There, he experienced justice Ben Cleveland–style. But the ever-defiant Wales placed a curse on the very ground where he was executed. In the moments before he was dropped at the end of a rope attached to a giant sycamore, the Tory said to the assembled crowd, "If I'm hanged here, grass will never grow on this spot."

Cleveland's home at Ronda vanished long ago. The cursed plantation grounds are an overgrown wilderness. Yet a barren spot remains at the site where Zacaria Wales was executed.

In comparison to Cleveland, Patrick Ferguson (1744–80) was a far more gentlemanly officer. Having aspired to a military career from an early age, he was a veteran soldier who had seen extensive action in Europe and the West Indies by the time he arrived in New York in 1777. A year later, Ferguson gained enduring fame with his invention of the breechloading rifle. It was said that the weapon could be fired up to six times a minute by a soldier lying on his back in a drizzling rain.

After the overwhelming British victory at Camden, South Carolina, on August 16, 1780, Lord Cornwallis began formulating plans to invade North Carolina, the one state that stood in the path of his conquest of the South. To pave the way, he dispatched Ferguson to northwestern South Carolina and the North Carolina Piedmont, where he was to punish insurgents, recruit Loyalists to assist in the invasion, and protect the left flank of the British army as it poured into North Carolina.

Ferguson was fearful of the North Carolina frontier Patriots, with whom he had skirmished throughout the summer of 1780 in the South Carolina Upcountry. He was also alarmed by the Overmountain Men, who had mustered near their homes in what is now Tennessee. In a vain attempt to dissuade the frontiersmen from tangling with him, Ferguson sent forth a courier with a threat. Referring to himself in the third person, he vowed to "march his army over the mountains, hang their leaders, and lay their country waste with fire and sword."

On the other side of the mountains, the fiercely independent Patriots of Scots-Irish descent did not wait for Ferguson to make good on his threat. Instead, they came after him, pouring over the mountains to join with Patriots from the foothills of the Carolinas and Virginia.

Ferguson positioned his eleven-hundred-man Loyalist army, Americans all, on Kings Mountain. This promontory—a rocky, forested spur of the Blue Ridge—featured a six-hundred-yard-long plateau rising sixty feet above the surrounding plain. There, Ferguson believed himself to be in a defensible position while awaiting reinforcements.

On October 5, Ferguson sent a letter to Cornwallis, who was camped forty miles away at Charlotte. His words exuded confidence: "I have taken a post where I don't think I can be forced by a stronger enemy than that against us." A day later, on the eve of the great battle at Kings Mountain, Ferguson restated his bold assuredness about his position: "God Almighty could not drive [us] from it."

By early afternoon on Saturday, October 7, Patriot leaders William Campbell, Isaac Shelby, John Sevier, and Ben Cleveland—all colonels—were poised to prove Ferguson wrong. When the first half of their eighteen-hundred-man army came within a mile of Ferguson's position, the soldiers tied their horses in the mist and proceeded to encircle the mountain. Gray skies suddenly began to give way to bright sunshine, perhaps a sign that the fortunes of the American war effort were about to turn.

So secretive was the Patriots' approach and so ineffective was Ferguson's intelligence that the Americans were within a quarter-mile of the enemy encampment before the first skirmishers opened fire in midafternoon. By the clock, the ensuing battle lasted exactly one hour. When it was over, the frontiersmen had achieved one of the most crucial victories in the fight for independence. Patrick Ferguson was dead. His Loyalist army had suffered staggering casualties: 157 killed, 164 wounded, and 698 captured. Patriot losses were but 38 killed and 64 wounded.

Much of the battleground has been preserved as Kings Mountain

National Military Park. Numerous well-marked trails, markers, and monuments interpret the site of the battle termed by Sir Henry Clinton, the longest-serving British commander in chief during the war, to have been "a fatal catastrophe." One of the site's most imposing features is the United States Monument, which bears the words of Thomas Jefferson quoted at the beginning of this story. Just east of it stands a marker at the spot where Ferguson fell.

Even as the Patriots began to close in on his position on the plateau, Ferguson, attired in a checkered vest, rode among his troops blowing his silver whistle, urging them to battle. As soon as his junior officers realized the futility of continuing the fight, they pleaded with Ferguson to surrender, rather than have his men annihilated. Their commander was unyielding. Replying that he would not submit "to such damned banditti," Ferguson galloped forward with sword in hand in a last desperate charge. His sword broke as he slashed his way through the oncoming Patriots, yet he rode on until he encountered the waiting rifles of John Sevier's men. Numerous shots rang out. Six or eight struck their target. One pierced Ferguson's head. The Loyalist commander's body and clothing were riddled by bullets. Both of his arms were broken. When he fell from his mount, one of his feet caught in a stirrup. Four of his soldiers stopped his fleeing animal, laid their commander on a blanket, and bore him out of harm's way.

There, Ferguson expired, his badly wounded body propped up by rocks and blankets. He was buried at the site in a grave now marked with a monument erected by the American people. It reads, "A soldier of military distinction and of honor." Beside the monument is a rocky cairn, a fitting tribute to the fighting Scot.

Ferguson's grave site is one of the most popular spots for park visitors. But in the stillness of the place, some patrons have unwittingly come face to face with his ghost.

On one occasion, two Revolutionary War enthusiasts well familiar with the battleground made their way to Ferguson's grave about twilight on a cold November day. They discussed the Scottish tradition associated with a cairn: rocks were tossed onto the pile not only to mark a grave and stop wild animals from disturbing it but to keep the spirit of the deceased from escaping.

During the course of their discussion, both men experienced intense feelings of unease. Sensing they were no longer alone, they turned around, fully expecting to see a park ranger. But instead they saw Major Patrick Ferguson standing no more than eighty feet away. They had no doubt about the identity of the phantom. It resembled the portraits of Ferguson they had seen many times. The ghost wore the gallant officer's famous checkered vest, and its right arm was twisted.

Astonished, the men were not prepared for what happened next. The phantom officer's eyes gazed at the rocks atop the grave, its mouth exhibiting a slight smile. Then came words from the ghost: "It doesn't always work, my lads." With that, the apparition threw its head back, laughed heartily, and moved backward into the forest, where it vanished.

Numerous other encounters with Ferguson's ghost have been reported in the vicinity of the cairn, but at a greater distance. Most say that the apparition appears as a blur of color flashing about the forest surrounding the grave.

The most common reports of supernatural experiences at the park concern a spirited Revolutionary War horseman who appears and vanishes on the battleground. Park rangers hear these stories often. Most likely, the phantom rider and horse are the ghosts of Ferguson and his prized mount, a splendid white Arabian.

After Ferguson was killed, the celebrated horse was captured by Patriots as a trophy of war. It was instantly bestowed on Benjamin Cleveland for three reasons: to honor him for his outstanding leadership in the battle; to replace his beloved horse, Roebuck, killed in the fight; and to provide a ride home for the portly colonel, who weighed in excess of three hundred pounds.

Cleveland rode Ferguson's horse back to Ronda, where the animal lived the rest of its life, remaining behind when its new master moved to South Carolina. Shortly after the horse died, reports circulated that it could be seen roaming Cleveland's former plantation. And atop the horse was Patrick Ferguson. To this day, folks in and around Ronda maintain that, on moonlit nights, Ferguson's ghost, attired in his vest and brandishing a sword, can be seen galloping a spectral horse along the banks of the Yadkin. Perhaps his spirit is bewildered in its quest to return to Kings Mountain to turn the tide of battle.

Ferguson's ghost is not the only supernatural entity confused by the events that took place on that fateful October day in 1780. Should you be traveling U.S. 74 between Kings Mountain and Charlotte, maintain a keen eye for two bewildered horsemen adorned in Revolutionary War clothing. These are the ghosts of James and Douglas Duncan, two couriers assigned to deliver news from Kings Mountain to Cornwallis in Charlotte. They never completed their assignment. For over two hundred years, their ghosts have been stopping travelers to seek directions. These green-skinned phantoms are sometimes seen along the roadside poring over an ancient map. Their quest continues to this day.

A single hour's battle in the Carolina back country in the fall of 1780 completely changed Euro-American history. And the personalities and events at Kings Mountain added an intriguing chapter to the haunted history of the republic born in large part from the Patriot victory earned there.

Ronda is located on N.C. 268 approximately seven miles southwest of Elkin. The former **Benjamin Cleveland plantation** is privately owned and is not open to the public. The address for **Kings Mountain National Military Park** is 2625 Park Rd., Blacksburg, S.C. 29702; the telephone number is 864-936-7921.

Shadows of a Shady Patriot
MOORE COUNTY, NORTH CAROLINA

A greater tyrant is not upon the face of the earth.
NORTH CAROLINA PATRIOT ROBERT ROWAN,
REFERRING TO PHILIP ALSTON

During much of the Revolutionary War, the fighting in the North Carolina Piedmont was little more than a civil war. Neighbor fought neighbor in bloody combat occasioned by divided political loyalties. Philip Alston and David Fanning, two rivals in central North Carolina, engaged in a spirited gun battle at Alston's plantation house on Sunday, August 5, 1781. Bullet holes from the deadly affair are yet evident in the house, which survives as the centerpiece of House in the Horseshoe State Historic Site. Also remaining is a supernatural reminder of the showdown—the ghost of Philip Alston, one of North Carolina's most controversial Patriots.

Known as "the House in the Horseshoe" because of its location atop a hill in a horseshoe bend of the Deep River, the magnificent frame home was constructed in 1772. At that time, it was one of the finest structures in the North Carolina back country. By all accounts, Philip Alston, the builder and first occupant, was a Patriot who did little to bring honor to the American cause. Labeled a "miscreant" and an "unprincipled scoundrel" by friend and foe alike, Alston (1745–91) was born into a wealthy family in Halifax, a prominent town in northeastern North Carolina. For reasons that may have had to do with Alston's character, his inheritance was limited to the slaves in his possession. Fortunately for him, his wife, the former Temperance Smith, the daughter of a wealthy Halifax County planter, received a sizable inheritance.

For unexplained reasons, Alston decided to relocate his family to a four-thousand-acre tract in central North Carolina, where he constructed the House in the Horseshoe at the very time political unrest was growing in the colonies. Contemporary rumors in Halifax hinted that Alston was involved in counterfeiting.

In 1775, Alston took up the cause of independence and was appointed a major of the militia. A year later, he was promoted to lieutenant colonel and appointed justice of the county court.

Power served only to corrupt him. His friends were few and his enemies many. Robert Rowan, a distinguished Patriot from southeastern North Carolina, wrote to Richard Caswell, elected the first governor of the independent state in 1776, that "two or three years ago no gentleman with the least regard for his character would have kept this hectoring, domineering person [Alston] company."

Alston's military career did little to improve his reputation. His promotion to colonel in 1778 was mired in controversy. A year later, he was captured during the fighting at Briar Creek, Georgia. After his release, Alston returned home. He stayed there for the duration of the war, matching wits with local Tories led by his archenemy, David Fanning.

Events during the summer of 1781 led to the showdown between

Alston and Fanning. In their quest to rescue some Patriot prisoners in Fanning's custody, Alston and his men happened upon Kenneth Black, one of Fanning's followers, near what is now Southern Pines. Black was leading Fanning's favorite bay horse, which was lame. He mounted the crippled animal in a desperate attempt to escape, but one of the Patriot band shot him. Once Alston reached the wounded man, he smashed Black's head with a gun butt and left him for dead.

After delivering his prisoners to Wilmington, Fanning learned of the savage attack on his soldier. In fact, Black spent his dying moments telling Fanning that Alston was responsible. Thus, the stage was set for the clash at the House in the Horseshoe.

At dawn on August 5, Fanning and his Loyalists rode to the Alston plantation, intent upon exacting revenge for Black's death. Alston was quartered inside the grand house, while twenty-five of his soldiers slept outside. As he approached, Fanning divided his army into three columns. His men captured a sleeping sentry, then dismounted to take cover.

The British officer accompanying Fanning promptly voiced his disapproval of the ground-hugging tactics, maintaining that he could take the house in a few minutes if he were in command. Fanning granted his wish. Sword drawn, the eager young officer implored the Tories to follow his lead. Just as he stepped forward to climb a fence, a musket ball fired from the house plowed into his heart.

Guns then blazed for several hours. Every window in the house was shattered, and the walls were pockmarked by bullets. Both sides suffered casualties, but neither could gain the upper hand.

As the bitter fight wore on, Fanning grew apprehensive that a Patriot force might come to Alston's aid. To end the stalemate, he ordered his men to load a cart with hay. Using the cart as a shield, the soldiers pushed it toward the house, where they were to set it afire.

From his tenuous position inside the house, Alston saw what was happening. Realizing he was about to be burned out, he hastily convened a council of war. Surrender seemed the only alternative, but Alston feared he and his men would be shot on sight if they walked out for that purpose.

During the protracted skirmish, Mrs. Alston and her two children had sought refuge in a bedroom, where the youngsters were placed in a chimney. Aware of the dilemma facing her husband, Mrs. Alston entered the room where he and the others were positioned. She offered to tender the surrender, reckoning that even the callous Fanning would not fire upon a woman. The Patriots, Colonel Alston in particular, were not so sure.

When Temperance Alston emerged from the house with a white cloth in her hand, all gunfire ceased. From his position behind the barn, Fanning ordered her to meet him halfway. As soon as the two came face to face, Mrs. Alston proclaimed, "We will surrender, Sir, on condition that no one shall be injured; otherwise, we will make the best defense we can, and if need be, sell our lives as dearly as possible."

Moved by her courage and sincerity, Fanning agreed. Colonel Alston and the surviving Patriots signed a parole penned by Fanning, whose men plundered the house but refrained from burning it, in deference to their leader's pledge to Mrs. Alston.

His military career over, Philip Alston turned to politics. Not long after his election to the state senate, he faced charges that he had intentionally killed a local man, Thomas Taylor, during the conflict. Governor Caswell, acting on Alston's assurance that the killing was a legitimate act of war, pardoned the senator. However, Dr. George Glascock, a local physician who had served the American cause at the Battle of Guilford Courthouse (see 268-72), successfully challenged Alston's right to keep his senate seat. Alston was removed from office in May 1787.

Three months later, Dr. Glascock, whose mother was George Washington's aunt, was murdered. Evidence indicated that Alston had ordered his slave, Dave, to commit the crime. At the time Glascock was gunned down, Alston was staging a lavish party at the House in the Horseshoe. Both owner and slave were implicated in the murder, but neither was ever tried.

Ruined politically, Alston sold his plantation in 1790 and moved to Georgia, where he was murdered in his sleep on October 28, 1791. Ironically, his killer was believed to be Dave, the same man Alston had supposedly used to murder Dr. Glascock.

Benjamin Williams, the governor of North Carolina, acquired the House in the Horseshoe in 1798 and thereafter enlarged it. The fully restored colonial masterpiece is now owned and operated by the state of North Carolina. In it and about its grounds, spirits thought to be those of the Alston family are heard and seen.

When the sun goes down in this isolated part of Moore County, the night masks the old plantation house and its grounds. Yet people passing by after dark have been astonished to see an eerie ball of light moving about the site where the factions led by Fanning and Alston squared off on that hot summer evening in 1781. According to eyewitnesses, the phantom light races erratically just above the ground until it suddenly ascends high into the sky. Some who have observed the phenomenon maintain that it is the spirit of Philip Alston, the rascally plantation master whose fortunes rose and fell here.

Inside the house, decorated with furniture from the Federal period, visitors and guides have been stunned to hear disembodied footsteps. Could they be sounds of the ghosts of the Alston family and the soldiers who defended the house?

Human whispers drift from the fireplace in the room where the Alston children were placed during the battle. Perhaps they are the ghostly voices of the terrified youngsters.

Awful squealing noises often unnerve humans inside the house. Maybe the shrieks are supernatural reminders of the sounds that reverberated throughout the dwelling on the day when a mini civil war was fought here.

Not all Patriots emerged from the fight for American independence as heroes. So it was with Philip Alston. His checkered military and political careers brought ignominy to him during his lifetime. Perhaps his ghost seeks atonement at the House in the Horseshoe. But given Alston's lifetime record, most likely not.

House in the Horseshoe State Historic Site is open to the public. Its address is 288 Alston House Rd., Sanford, N.C. 27330; the telephone number is 910-947-2051.

Ghosts of the Pyrrhic Victory
GREENSBORO, NORTH CAROLINA

Another such victory would ruin the British army.
CHARLES JAMES FOX,
MEMBER OF BRITISH PARLIAMENT

On March 15, 1781, the American army in the South, commanded by Major General Nathanael Greene, confronted the British army of Lord Cornwallis in the northern North Carolina Piedmont at Guilford Courthouse, a nondescript hamlet surrounded by Quaker settlements. For nearly two and a half hours, some sixty-five hundred cavalry, infantry, and artillery soldiers engaged in the largest battle of the Southern campaign. Cornwallis subsequently wrote, "I never saw such fighting since God made me. The Americans fought like Demons."

Although Cornwallis claimed a tactical triumph, the clash at Guilford Courthouse cost him one-fourth of his army and sent him on the road to ruin that ended at Yorktown, Virginia, less than seven months later. His Pyrrhic victory at what is now Greensboro troubled the British commander the rest of his days. Today, the well-preserved battleground and environs are haunted by the spirits of men in red and blue who fought, bled, and died in a battle that served as a significant milepost on the road to American independence.

On December 3, 1780, just three and a half months before Guilford Courthouse, Nathanael Greene assumed command of the beleaguered American army in the South from General Horatio Gates. Upon inheriting what he called "the shadow of an army," Greene lamented, "The appearance of the troops was wretched beyond description, and their distress, on account of provisions was little less than their suffering for want of clothing and other necessities."

By the end of January 1781, Cornwallis had his army on the march through the western Piedmont of North Carolina. His objective was clear: destroy the army of Nathanael Greene and effectively put an end to the rebellion.

A determined stand against Cornwallis by three hundred militiamen on the bitterly cold morning of February 1 at Cowan's Ford on the rain-gorged Catawba River bought Greene the time he needed to move the main body of his army east. Once across the Catawba, Cornwallis chased Greene halfway across North Carolina, into Virginia, and back into North Carolina over the ensuing six weeks. All the while, Greene reorganized, restored, and increased his army to the point that he was able to choose the time and place to stand and to do battle with the British.

Ironically, Greene, known as "the Fighting Quaker," decided that the killing field would be a Quaker settlement in Guilford County, named for the First Earl of Guilford, the father of Lord North, who served as British prime minister during the war. Buoyed by the arrival of reinforcements including the likes of Colonel William Campbell, a hero of Kings Mountain, Greene fielded an army of forty-four hundred regulars and militia. For once, he enjoyed a numerical superiority over Cornwallis. Though the British general commanded some of the finest battle-tested warriors in the world, the chase through North Carolina and Virginia had proven costly. Attrition reduced his fighting machine to approximately two thousand men.

Around one-thirty on the afternoon of March 15, 1781, the waiting came to an end. From the woods along Salisbury Road emerged the first wave of Cornwallis's troops, their once-resplendent red uniforms showing the wear and tear of the campaign. Having marched since daybreak without breakfast, the British and Hessian soldiers were greeted by American field pieces. Cornwallis's artillerists countered. Then the infantry took the field and engaged in a pitched battle. When the American artillery was captured and the British began a flanking movement, Greene commanded an orderly retreat.

Cornwallis's "victory" at Guilford Courthouse was purchased at a dear price. His losses were staggering: 93 killed, 423 wounded, and 26 missing. His 542 casualties depleted his army by 27 percent. Nearly 30 percent of his officer corps was down. In simple terms, the British army was no longer strong enough to fight Greene. The "defeated" American army suffered far fewer casualties: 79 killed and 185 wounded.

When Greene put his army on the retreat from the battlefield, he was forced to leave behind scores of severely wounded soldiers. He enlisted the aid of the Quaker community at New Garden, four miles south of the battleground, to minister to his fallen troops.

Some fifty-six years after the bloody clash at Guilford Courthouse, the Quakers at New Garden established a coeducational school now known as Guilford College. In the 1960s, Dana Auditorium, an imposing brick structure, was constructed on the campus at the site of a field hospital from the aftermath of the battle. Almost as soon as the building opened, eerie things began taking place there. The most plausible explanation for the strange occurrences is that they relate to the area's Revolutionary War history. By all accounts, the ghosts of soldiers ministered to in the building still dwell there.

Orbs thought to represent persons from the spirit world have been photographed floating about the otherwise empty edifice. At night after the auditorium is closed to the public, the lights are extinguished and the doors locked. Yet security guards often have to return to turn off lights that have mysteriously come on. Some nights, the exercise is repeated over and over. Watchmen have been unnerved by piano keys played by phantom hands. Others have found it virtually impossible to lock exit doors, noting that someone or something seemed to be pushing from the other side. Closet doors unlocked at the close of the day are often discovered to be locked from the inside the next morning.

One of the strangest supernatural occurrences at Dana took place in 1973 when two campus guards were on routine patrol. One of the men was walking on the stage and the other was standing in the front row when both felt a sudden rush of air and heard a whoosh. Above them, the four enormous crystal chandeliers hanging from the ceiling began swinging to and fro. No windows were open at the time, nor was any climate-control system producing gusts. At length, one of the chandeliers came crashing to the floor.

On several occasions, witnesses have seen ghosts in Dana.

While working on a theater production one evening, a coed was mystified to notice a transparent figure sitting alone in the balcony. Her eyes remained focused on the spectre until it vanished minutes later.

Another student witnessed a man dressed in an old military uniform sitting in the second row of the otherwise vacant auditorium. The apparition disappeared into thin air.

A sophomore in the company of a security officer was preparing to exit the building one night. Just as the light in the foyer was extinguished, a tall, thin spectral being briefly appeared before the two men. Similarly, another guard was securing the auditorium late one night when the apparition of a man wearing a weathered hat suddenly appeared around a corner. The guard demanded to know what the man was doing in the building. No answer was forthcoming. Another demand yielded the same result. With that, the strange entity looked at the guard and proceeded to walk through a nearby wall.

If on a visit to Guilford College you happen to see a uniformed figure resembling the Quaker Oats man, don't be alarmed. It's only Nathan, the school's mascot. But if you feel a phantom tap on your shoulder that leaves you with a cold, eerie feeling, it's more likely the spirit of one of "Nathan" Greene's men who died near where you are standing.

More than eleven hundred acres of the expansive Revolutionary War battlefield have been preserved at nearby Guilford Courthouse National Military Park. Numerous monuments throughout the park pay homage to the men who sacrificed here in 1781. Most of the soldiers from both armies who died on the battlefield were interred where they fell. Two mass graves have been identified within the park.

A more frightening reminder of the epic battle is the phantom horseman who gallops over the landscape sans head. In addition, the thunder of phantom cannon fire sometimes reverberates about the landscape. Visitors have reported the acrid smell of gunfire when no historical demonstrations are taking place in the park.

In recent years, a park patron returned to the visitor center after a trip to the eastern end of the battlefield. He reported that he had encountered a reenactor sitting on a bench near the restrooms. After an unsuccessful attempt to converse with the fellow dressed in Revolutionary War garb, the patron turned to walk away. He quickly looked back to bid farewell, but the bench was empty. When park staffers informed the patron that no reenactors were on the grounds, the man was visibly shaken.

Most likely, the landscape in and around the Guilford Courthouse battleground will forever remain haunted—haunted by what might have been for Cornwallis and the British, and by what was to be for Greene and the Americans.

The address for **Guilford College** is 5800 West Friendly Ave., Greensboro, N.C. 27410. The address for **Guilford Courthouse National Military Park** is 2322 New Garden Rd., Greensboro, N.C. 27410; the telephone number is 336-282-2296.

Haunted by Love and War
WILMINGTON, NORTH CAROLINA

I abhor war and view it as the greatest scourge of mankind.
THOMAS JEFFERSON

In the aftermath of its costly "victory" over Nathanael Greene at Guilford Courthouse, the battered, demoralized army of Lord Cornwallis limped into Wilmington in southeastern North Carolina during the second week of April 1781. For just over two weeks, Cornwallis made his headquarters in the stately Burgwin-Wright House at 224 Market Street in the heart of the old port city. More than two centuries later, haunting reminders of the British general linger in the colonial mansion sometimes referred to as "the Cornwallis House."

Now open to the public, the Burgwin-Wright House affords visitors an opportunity to appreciate the wealth and prestige of John Burgwin, who built the beautiful home in 1770. Constructed on the massive walls of an old jail, the two-story frame structure is the most opulent of the few remaining Georgian-style houses in the city.

Burgwin, an unrepentant Tory who served as colonial treasurer under Royal Governor Arthur Dobbs, found it necessary to flee to England at the outbreak of the Revolutionary War. He remained there until hostilities ended. In Burgwin's absence, Lord Cornwallis and his staff availed themselves of the sumptuous home during their stay in Wilmington. Original floorboards in the house reveal marks made by British muskets.

One of Cornwallis's junior officers who was quartered in an upstairs bedroom may still abide there. Before the young soldier arrived in Wilmington, he had fallen in love with a beautiful lady in South Carolina. While assigned to duty at the Burgwin-Wright House, he used his diamond ring to etch his true love's name in the windowpane in his tiny bedroom.

After the war, he returned to South Carolina, married the woman, and took her to England. Several years later, the young couple sailed to America and took up residence in New York. In 1836, the couple's son visited Wilmington as the guest of Dr. Thomas H. Wright, who had inherited the house. As fate would have it, the visitor spent the night in the bedroom once occupied by his father. He noticed the etched pane of glass and at once recognized the name as his mother's.

Forty years later, John W. Barrow, the grandson of the British officer, having been told the story of the windowpane by his father, came to Wilmington in search of it. After calling at the Burgwin-Wright House, he learned from the owner that the mansion had been remodeled. Barrow and the owner descended to the cellar, where Cornwallis had imprisoned local Patriots. There, they found the special pane, put in storage after the renovations. Barrow returned to his home with his prized possession.

Does his grandfather haunt the bedroom where he etched the windowpane? Very likely. When docents prepare to close the grand house each evening, they make sure the bedroom door is closed tight. Somehow, it mysteriously opens during the night and is found that way every morning. No rational explanation has been found. Perhaps the spirit of the Redcoat is desperately searching for the special window glass that vanished long ago.

The spirit has made its presence known to witnesses in other ways.

During one tour, a spinning wheel in an upstairs room suddenly began turning without a human near it. As startled as the tourists, the guide made haste to the wheel. When she approached, it stopped spinning. Prior to that time, the wheel had been stuck, and all attempts to make it work had been unsuccessful. An examination of the apparatus after the tour revealed that it was once again rigidly fixed in place. The spinning wheel was subsequently removed from the tour.

Every day, thousands of drivers and pedestrians travel the streets and sidewalks near the Burgwin-Wright House without realizing that a mysterious labyrinth of tunnels lies beneath them. During the twentieth century, workmen demolishing buildings and digging utility lines unearthed ancient tunnels in the vicinity of Cornwallis's old headquarters. At least four distinct passageways—one evidenced by a bricked-over opening in the cellar wall at the Burgwin-Wright House—were discovered. The brick tunnel at Cornwallis's headquarters led to a similar tunnel connected to Jacob's Run, which offered passage to the nearby Cape Fear River. During the Revolutionary War, the secret maze of passageways allowed American prisoners to escape from the British jail in the subbasement of the Burgwin-Wright House.

But during Cornwallis's brief occupation of the house, no Patriots had the good fortune to escape. Their ghosts are said to haunt the dark, dank former jail site. Horrifying sounds including rattling chains, anguished screams, and moans have been heard coming from the old prison. The shadowy figures observed in and under the cellar are most likely the restless spirits of Americans tortured by the Redcoats.

Cornwallis departed Wilmington for the long march up the North Carolina coastal plain for his rendezvous with destiny later in 1781. His swan song in the port city made one of Wilmington's most famous houses one of its most haunted.

The **Burgwin-Wright House** is open Tuesday through Saturday. Its address is 224 Market St., Wilmington, N.C. 28401; the telephone number is 910-762-0570.

Other "Spirited" Revolutionary War Sites in North Carolina, Briefly Noted

BURKE COUNTY—BROWN MOUNTAIN

Located in northern Burke County in western North Carolina, Brown Mountain is a sloping ridge of the Blue Ridge chain. Nearly a half-mile high, the mountain is the site of one of the most popular and enduring mysteries in American history. On certain nights, balls of colored lights appear from the forests covering Brown Mountain, split in two, and suddenly vanish into the darkness.

Numerous theories both scientific and supernatural have been espoused to explain the phenomenon. One of the more intriguing explanations comes from the Revolutionary War. As the legend goes, the patriarch of a family that settled on Brown Mountain prior to the war marched off to fight for American independence, leaving his wife and three children on their farm. Upon the soldier's return, he was shocked to find the place in ruins, the apparent work of either Tories or Indians. Even worse, his family was nowhere to be found. He immediately began a desperate but futile search of the mountain. Death soon came to the lonely, broken man atop the summit. His restless ghost, torch in hand, is said to roam Brown Mountain in a relentless search for a family claimed by the Revolutionary War.

The three primary viewing sites for the Brown Mountain Lights are a roadside pull-off on N.C. 181 seventeen miles north of Morganton, the Lost Cove overlook at Milepost 310 on the Blue Ridge Parkway, and Wiseman's View on Kistler Memorial Highway (Old N.C. 105) on the western side of Linville Gorge approximately four miles from Linville Falls.

CAMDEN COUNTY—GREAT DISMAL SWAMP

This massive wilderness of marshes, peat bogs, lakes, and cypress forests along the North Carolina–Virginia border in the Atlantic coastal plain encompasses a landmass the area of Rhode Island. One of the most intriguing supernatural legends of the swamp comes from the Revolutionary War. According to the story, a lost military payroll is the cause of eerie French voices often heard emanating from the North Carolina portion of the swamp.

A French warship laden with gold to pay troops for their service in America was forced to seek shelter at nearby Hampton Roads, Virginia, because of a severe storm. A British man-of-war sighted the ship and gave chase. Fearing capture, the French captain ordered his crew to load the gold into smaller boats. He then directed that his ship be burned. In order to avoid losing the gold, the French hid it in the Elizabeth River and on its banks. They then fled into the Great Dismal but were hunted down by the British. Furious hand-to-hand combat ensued. None of the French sailors survived. Thus, they carried the secret location of the gold with them. Still haunted by the debacle, the ghosts of the slaughtered sailors continue to roam the recesses of this great wilderness, their voices echoing through the dark nights.

The Dismal Swamp Canal Welcome Center is in Camden County. Its address is 2356 U.S. 17N, South Mills, N.C. 27976; the telephone number is 877-771-8333.

DAVIDSON COUNTY—ABBOTTS CREEK

As Lord Cornwallis chased General Nathanael Greene's army across North Carolina in the late winter of 1780–81, the British commander decided to intensify the pursuit by lightening his load during a brief sojourn along Abbotts Creek in the North Carolina Piedmont. To allow his warriors to move with all due speed toward a showdown with Greene, heavy barrels of gold and silver coins from the king's treasury were pulled from the British wagon train in the dark of night and rolled into the water.

As far as anyone knows, the treasure has never been recovered. Area residents can readily explain why: the ghosts of British soldiers roam the creek's banks as guardians of the cache of coins. From the time Cornwallis departed the area to the present day, these ghosts have been seen and heard by countless persons. They appear as strange lights that float along the still, shimmering water of the creek, up the banks, and into the adjacent forests at the point where the Redcoats crossed.

Mysterious noises are heard here, too. Generations of area residents have been disturbed by the unmistakable sound of barrels rolling down the banks and splashing into Abbotts Creek. The noises have been heard at all hours but are most often experienced at night.

Abbotts Creek can be viewed from the bridge on S.R. 1743 in Davidson County.

EDGECOMBE COUNTY—TAR RIVER

On a hot, muggy evening in August 1781, a small squadron of British troopers galloped up to a gristmill located on a curve in the Tar River in northeastern North Carolina. There, they beat and tortured mill operator Dave Warner, a staunch supporter of American independence. Just before the Redcoats drowned their defiant victim, he cried out that the river banshee would exact revenge for his death. No sooner had Warner, his body weighted with rocks, been thrown into the Tar than a misty cloud formed above the water and took the shape of a woman with flowing hair and a veil-covered face. Her terrible wails reverberated up and down the river. Within a short time, each of the terrified British soldiers drowned in the same river.

Since that night, August has remained a haunted month along the banks of the Tar. The agonizing cries and ghostly form of the Tar River banshee can still be heard and seen.

The Tar River can be viewed from Riverfront Park on Main Street (U.S. 64) in Tarboro, the county seat of Edgecombe County.

HUNTERSVILLE—HOPEWELL PRESBYTERIAN CHURCH

On the bitterly cold morning of February 1, 1781, General William Lee Davidson led several hundred area militiamen in a courageous but unsuccessful attempt to prevent Cornwallis's two-thousand-man army from crossing the Catawba River as the British chased General Nathanael Greene's beleaguered forces. In the bloody combat at Cowan's Ford, General Davidson was mortally wounded. By the time Americans recovered his body, it had been robbed and stripped of clothing. Davidson's wallet is now on display in a British museum.

Fearful that British raiders might yet be prowling the eastern side of the river, Davidson's friends and family buried his corpse under torchlight in the cemetery at Hopewell Presbyterian Church, south of Cowan's Ford. But the grave could not contain the indefatigable young general. Local residents maintain that on the anniversary of Davidson's death, his ghost rides atop his spectral steed through the ancient graveyard. Just before it vanishes into the night, the phantom general raises its saber high.

The address for Hopewell Presbyterian Church and Cemetery is 10500 Beatties Ford Rd., Huntersville, N.C. 28078.

MITCHELL COUNTY/YANCEY COUNTY—
NOLICHUCKY RIVER

John Sevier, one of the frontier commanders who masterminded the crucial Patriot victory at Kings Mountain in October 1780, emerged from the Revolutionary War a beloved hero. A leader in the effort to create Tennessee, Sevier was elected the first governor of the state. Known affectionately as "Nolichucky Jack," the fiercely competitive officer and statesman often walked or rode the banks of the Nolichucky River, a beautiful waterway flowing from its headwaters in western North Carolina into East Tennessee.

After Sevier's death in 1815, reports began to circulate that his ghost could be seen along the North Carolina portion of the Nolichucky. To this day, fishermen continue to witness his apparition, dressed in his buckskin uniform and carrying his trusted musket.

A bridge over the Nolichucky at Huntdale, located on S.R. 1304 in Mitchell County, affords a panoramic view of the river haunted by Sevier.

PLUMTREE—U.S. 19E

In 1780, Captain Robert Sevier, a giant of a man who stood nearly seven feet tall, followed his brother, John, over the mountains of what is now East Tennessee to fight at Kings Mountain on the border of the Carolinas. In the course of the battle, Robert sustained a serious gunshot wound to the kidney. Once the Patriot victory was assured, the wound was dressed by a captured surgeon, who suggested Robert would die unless he remained behind for rest and treatment. Despite his brother's pleas to follow the physician's advice, Robert mounted his horse with the aid of his nephew, James Sevier. The two set out for home. On the ninth day of their journey, Robert fell desperately ill and died near the Toe River some miles from its confluence with the Nolichucky. James buried the body under a towering oak.

Local folks familiar with the spot where Captain Sevier was buried swear that his spirit left the grave long ago and walks along U.S. 19E in southwestern Avery County near Plumtree, a small community less than four miles away. On numerous occasions over the years, unwitting pedestrians traversing the remote route have sensed someone following them. Upon turning around to look, they have found no human about. It is believed that the "following haunt" cannot rest because its earthly remains lie many miles from home and family, far across the Blue Ridge in the Nolichucky settlement.

ROBESON COUNTY—LUMBER RIVER SWAMP

During the fight for American independence, General Francis Marion's men camped on occasion in the swampy morass along the Lumber River in southeastern North Carolina. Walter Jenkins, one of the finest noncommissioned officers in Marion's command, fell in love with a local girl, Joan McDougald, whose family was loyal to the British Crown. On several occasions, the handsome Patriot gave Joan's father important information concerning the plans of Marion, the legendary "Swamp Fox." Finally, some of Jenkins's comrades surprised him as he was offering secrets to Joan one evening. General Marion ordered his once-trusted officer to be hanged. When Joan subsequently reached the site of the makeshift scaffold in the swamp, the horrifying sight of Jenkins's lifeless body swinging from a rope caused her to fashion a noose and join her lover in death.

Even now, when the moon beams down on the black water of the Lumber River, two ghostlike figures can be observed at the site of the Swamp Fox's former camp. One of the apparitions is thought to be Jenkins, a man yet torn between allegiances, and the other is Joan, pleading forgiveness.

The swamp can be seen at Lumber River State Park, located on S.R. 2246 in southern Robeson County.

ROUGHEDGE—N.C. 200

Ghostly sounds related to Revolutionary War hostilities in this Union County community north of Andrew Jackson's birthplace still reverberate up and down the highway. One of the most ardent Patriots in the area known then and now as "the Waxhaws" was Ned Richardson. He and his wife lived on a farm near Roughedge. One evening, Tory raiders descended on the Richardson homestead, captured Ned, and vowed to execute him on the morrow. His pregnant wife managed to escape from the back of the house and rode to the nearest Patriot camp, where she sounded the alarm. Before the morning sun rose, a small army of Patriots hastened to the Richardson farm, where they rescued Ned and executed his captors.

For as long as anyone can remember, the sounds of the galloping horses of the Patriot rescue party have been heard along the highway in this small settlement near the border of the Carolinas.

Roughedge is located at the junction of S.R. 1146 (Parkwood School Road) and N.C. 200.

STOKES COUNTY—
COLONEL JACK MARTIN'S ROCK HOUSE

As differences grew between the American colonies and Great Britain in the 1770s, John "Jack" Martin, an unabashed Patriot, began constructing a massive stone house in the shadow of Hanging Rock Mountain in north-central North Carolina. Throughout the ensuing war, the fortress served as a place of refuge for independence-minded neighbors seeking protection from marauding Indians and vindictive Tories. Constructed of native stone, the towering four-story structure resembled an English mansion. Its three-foot-thick outer walls were plastered with white stucco.

Because of Colonel Jack's dedicated military service to the cause of independence, he and his imposing residence were favorite targets for the bands of Tories operating out of caves at nearby Hanging Rock. Hoping to find Martin at home, raiders stormed the Rock House one day while the colonel's neighbors were holed up there. During the melee, an unarmed woman was shot to death by Tories as she stood on the doorstep.

Devastating fires in the late nineteenth and early twentieth centuries claimed the roof and one of the exterior walls, thus rendering the house uninhabitable—by humans, at least. But the ghost of the murdered lady continues to roam the premises. Mysterious lights shine about the place on dark nights. Even more disconcerting are the strange sounds coming from the shell of the structure. Persons hearing the eerie commotion have likened it to two bony hands being clapped together.

By the time the nation was preparing for its bicentennial celebration, the remnants of the Rock House were covered in vines and on the road to ruin. In 1975, the Stokes County Historical Society acquired the site. Since that time, the grounds have been cleared and the walls of the once-grand house stabilized.

The Rock House is located west of Hanging Rock State Park on S.R. 1186 in western Stokes County.

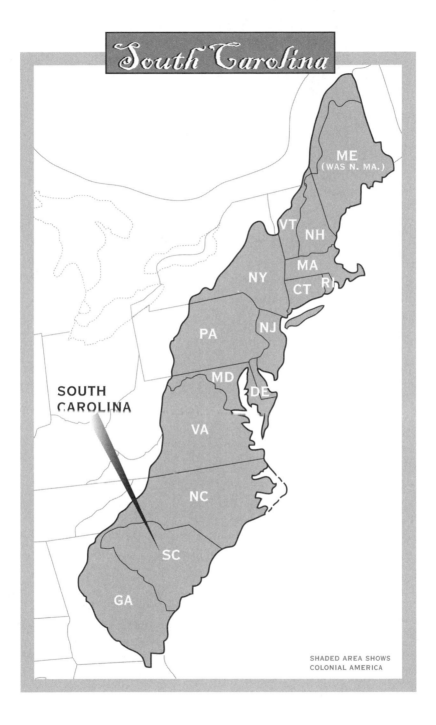

South Carolina

ME
(WAS N. MA.)

VT

NH

MA

NY

CT

RI

PA

NJ

MD

DE

SOUTH
CAROLINA

VA

NC

SC

GA

SHADED AREA SHOWS
COLONIAL AMERICA

The Black Menace at Blackstock's
CROSS ANCHOR, SOUTH CAROLINA

The enemy in this event cried victory and the whole country
came in fast to [General] Sumter.

LORD CORNWALLIS, IN RESPONSE TO
GENERAL THOMAS SUMTER'S VICTORY
AT FISH FORD DAM, SOUTH CAROLINA,
NOVEMBER 9, 1780

During America's bicentennial, South Carolinians coined the slo-
gan "Battleground of Freedom" for their state because of its longstanding claim that more Revolutionary War combat took place there than
anywhere else. Indeed, over two hundred battles and skirmishes were
fought on South Carolina soil. In each of the state's three distinct geographic regions, a great partisan military leader rose to lead Patriots
against the British army and local Tories. In the mountains, that leader
was General Andrew Pickens, nicknamed "the Fighting Presbyterian
Elder"; along the coast and in the surrounding lowlands was General
Francis Marion, "the Swamp Fox"; and in the Piedmont was General
Thomas Sumter, "the Fighting Gamecock."

On Monday, November 20, 1780, General Sumter led his army into battle against British forces at Blackstock's Plantation in the Upstate region of South Carolina. Located in an isolated setting in Union County, the ancient battlefield is little disturbed from the days of the Revolutionary War. Other than a state historical marker and a D.A.R. monument, no other tangible reminders of the battle remain—unless you include the terrifying black demon dog that has chased away many visitors.

In the wake of his impressive victory over British forces at Fish Ford Dam on November 9, 1780, Sumter was anxious to turn the fortunes of war in South Carolina in favor of the Americans. But the Gamecock was a marked man. British military operatives had been instructed to take him dead or alive.

To lead the hunt for Sumter, Lord Cornwallis summoned his cavalry chieftain, Banastre Tarleton, from the South Carolina sand hills. Tarleton, more hated by Americans than any other man in the British army, was described by eminent Revolutionary War historian Christopher Ward thusly: "As a leader of cavalry, he was unmatched on either side for alertness and rapidity of movement, dash, daring, and vigor of attack. As a man, he was cold-hearted, vindictive, and utterly ruthless. He wrote his name in letters of blood all across the history of the war in the South."

"Bloody Ban," as Tarleton was known to American fighters, promptly took up the chase of General Sumter. Fortunately for the Gamecock, a British deserter alerted the Americans of Tarleton's mission. Consequently, Sumter put his thousand-man army on the move in hopes of avoiding a showdown with Tarleton's Legion.

As darkness descended on November 20, the American army arrived at Blackstock's Plantation, cognizant that Tarleton's van was not far behind. Then a local woman, Mary Pollard, rode into Sumter's camp bearing tidings that the main body of Tarleton's army, including his artillery, was still some miles away. Sumter reckoned that Tarleton was anxious to prevent him from crossing the nearby Tyger River. But rather than attempt a perilous night crossing, the Gamecock decided to use his troop superiority to destroy the scattered elements of the approaching army.

Four hundred Patriots rushed forward to attack the first wave of Tarleton's soldiers, a company of eighty dismounted regulars. To Sumter's chagrin, the Patriot force was thoroughly routed despite its five-to-one numerical superiority. A subsequent charge by the American mounted infantry brought temporary success until it, too, had to fall back.

At that juncture in the battle, Sumter was severely wounded as he rode back to the center of his line. A musket ball plowed through his right shoulder, tearing the shoulder blade and chipping his backbone.

When Sumter went down, Colonel John Twiggs of Georgia assumed command of the Americans. Rallying behind Georgia sharpshooters and Wade Hampton's marksmen, the Patriots took charge about the time of Tarleton's arrival. By then, the battle had been raging for four hours. Tarleton rode with abandon to a dangerous position on the front line, where he skillfully extricated his troops and withdrew into the night.

In the aftermath of the battle, both sides claimed victory. Tarleton prevented Sumter's army from crossing the river, at least temporarily. But the British success came at a heavy price. Of the 270 British soldiers engaged, 50 were killed. By contrast, American losses were extremely low—three killed and five wounded. Without question, the greatest loss was Sumter, who was incapacitated for more than two months.

At Blackstock's, Bloody Ban badly bloodied but failed to capture or destroy his nemesis, the Gamecock. Sumter lived to fight another day. In fact, at the time of his death in 1832 at the age of ninety-eight, he was the oldest surviving general of the Revolutionary War.

Today, the remote fighting ground is preserved by the state of South Carolina as Blackstock's Battlefield Historic Site, accessible via a mile and a half of unpaved roads. The granite D.A.R. marker stands on a prominent ridge overlooking the hilly, wooded, desolate landscape where Sumter and Tarleton had their showdown.

A visit to the site during the day offers a panoramic view, while a nighttime sojourn provides a setting similar to that faced by the troops in November 1780. But be forewarned that the place is spooky after dark. Supernatural forces are at work here once the sun drops. Phantom troops have been heard as they march to form a line of battle. The shouts of weary soldiers echo about the valley. The cries of wounded and dying warriors and horses fill the air. Smoke from blazing weapons and the smell of gunpowder permeate the air. Shadowy spectres float about the darkness.

No one disputes that the most terrifying supernatural force at Blackstock's is a strange black dog. The huge canine emerges out of the Stygian darkness as a grim reminder of the pain and death sustained here by the British army.

One of the most terrifying of all creatures in British folklore is the spectral black dog with glowing red eyes. Over the centuries, this animal has been regarded as a portent of death. One dark night at Blackstock's, a visitor to the historic site was driving along the lonely unpaved road leading from the battleground to the highway when a huge black dog with burning red eyes pounced from the wilderness. Startled, the driver pressed his accelerator as he looked into his rearview mirror. Much to his relief, the strange dog had vanished. He drove at a speed of thirty miles per hour for the remaining mile to the stop sign. There, waiting for him, was the same demonic animal.

Some speculate that the black dog is the ghost of a pet that followed Tarleton's army on its travels throughout the Carolinas. If so, it likely remains here to stand watch over the graves of its friends who gave their lives for the British Crown.

On the other hand, the eerie ghost animal at Blackstock's could be the black dog long feared by the British as a symbol of death. Sumter's marksmen killed two and a half score of Tarleton's soldiers at this site. Does the black dog represent the greatest fears of the British soldiers who fought here?

Visitors to Blackstock's should take any and all precautions to avoid this ominous creature of the night. It is definitely not a tail-wagger they will want to pet.

To reach **Blackstock's Battlefield Historic Site**, proceed west on S.C. 49 from its junction with I-26 near Cross Anchor. Turn right onto S.R. 44-51 and drive 3 miles north to the first unpaved road on the right. Follow the unpaved road northeast for 0.3 mile to an unpaved road leading to the left. Follow the second unpaved road for 1.3 miles to the granite monument on the battlefield. Blackstock's is administered by another nearby site. For information, contact Musgrove Mill State Historic Site, 398 State Park Rd., Clinton, S.C. 29325; the telephone number is 864-938-0100.

The Eternal Martyr
CHARLESTON, SOUTH CAROLINA

I earnestly entreat that my execution may be deferred, that I may at least take a last farewell of my children, and prepare for the dreadful charge.

ISAAC HAYNE TO
LORD FRANCIS RAWDON, JULY 29, 1781

Isaac Hayne (1745–81), one of the most popular young Patriot leaders in South Carolina, was publicly hanged by British officials without trial in the heart of Charleston on August 4, 1781, just months before Yorktown. As news of his execution spread throughout the colonies, Americans were outraged over the injustice and the tragic loss of one of their heroes. British authorities intended for the execution to serve as an example to South Carolina Patriots. To the contrary, Hayne was seen as a martyr. "The Hayne Affair," as the incident became known, served as a rallying cry during the waning days of the Revolutionary War.

At Hayne's grave site, a monument erected in his honor reads in part, "In life a soldier of his Country, In death a martyr to her sacred cause. His memory an undying inspiration to his fellow countrymen, His monument the freedom of his Native Land." But the grave could not hold the restless spirit of Isaac Hayne. Ever since his burial, his ghostly presence has been experienced at several places associated with the last days of his life.

In the months following Hayne's death, cries for vengeance came from many South Carolinians. Shortly after the British surrender at Yorktown in October 1781, the state's delegation to the Continental Congress demanded that General George Washington execute Lord Cornwallis in retaliation for Hayne's murder. Congress defeated the proposal only after being informed that such action would violate the terms of the surrender agreement.

Another target for retribution was Lord Rawdon, Cornwallis's skillful subordinate. But before the Americans could make any such attempt, Rawdon, then a prisoner of war, was transported to Brest, France, where he was released on parole. Upon his return to England, he was subjected to scorn on the floor of the House of Lords.

Why such an uproar over the death of one man in a conflict that stretched for eight years?

Isaac Hayne was thirty years old when the war came to South Carolina. Despite his relative youth, he was already an affluent planter, a developer of iron mines, a horse breeder, and a statesman. Hayne was among the Patriot officers captured when General Benjamin Lincoln surrendered Charleston on May 12, 1780. Paroled to his plantation fifteen miles southeast of the city, he arrived to find his family in distress. One of his children had died of smallpox. His wife and two of their other children were desperately ill with the disease.

As Hayne attempted to minister to his family, he received an urgent summons to report to the British high command in Charleston. He hurried to the port city, where a document was placed before him for signature. Under its terms, Hayne would declare himself to be a British subject.

Torn between the dire situation back home and his ardent patriotism,

Hayne signed the paperwork under duress. As he prepared to return to his family, he penned a letter to a friend, Dr. David Ramsey, a noted local physician and a strong advocate for independence. Noting that his decision "had been forced upon by hard necessity," Hayne wrote, "I will never bear arms against my countrymen. My master can require no service of me but what is enjoined by the old militia law of the Province, which substitutes a fine in lieu of military service. This I will pay for my protection. If my conduct should be censured by my countrymen, I beg that you will remember this conversation and bear witness for me that I do not mean to desert the cause of America."

Hayne's homecoming was filled with agony, grief, and trouble. His wife soon succumbed to her illness. As he dealt with the loss, British authorities descended upon him with a new demand: he was to immediately take up arms against the Americans. Deeming his parole invalidated by the demand, Hayne accepted the invitation of Charleston-area Patriots to serve as colonel of a newly raised militia company. His brief return to military service came to an end in July 1781. After playing a significant role in the capture of turncoat general Andrew Williamson, Hayne was caught by pursuing British troopers when his horse broke a leg while leaping a ditch.

Returned to Charleston under heavy guard, he was incarcerated in the infamous dungeon of the Old Exchange in the heart of the city. Charged with treason and espionage, Hayne was brought before a British tribunal, which sentenced him to death without affording him an opportunity to present a defense.

Once news of Hayne's pending execution circulated, Charlestonians were outraged. From all quarters came protests. Although Lieutenant Governor William Bull was seriously ill, he directed servants to carry him on a stretcher to Lord Rawdon, to whom he made an impassioned plea for Hayne's life. But the twenty-seven-year-old British commander only grew more determined to make an example of Hayne.

On the eve of the execution, Mrs. Mary Peronneau, Hayne's sister, brought the colonel's two surviving boys to Rawdon's headquarters at the Miles Brewton House. In the drawing room, the lads knelt before Rawdon, who was not far in age from their father. Tears streamed down their cheeks as they begged the general to save their "papa." Rawdon was unmoved. He snorted, turned away, and directed an aide to provide the children an opportunity to bid farewell to their father at his cell in the Old Exchange.

The morning of Saturday, August 4, 1781, dawned fair and bright in Charleston. Under heavy guard, Colonel Hayne emerged from the dungeon to begin his death walk. A multitude of friends and sympathizers lined the streets along the route. Some even joined the procession to offer their support.

Finally, the somber parade reached the Peronneau House at the junction of Meeting and Atlantic streets. Hayne glanced up to see three pairs of tear-filled eyes as his sister and his two young sons watched from the windows while British drums pounded the call to death. Unable to control her emotions, Mary Peronneau called down to her brother, "Return! Return to us!" From the noisy street below, Hayne's voice rang out, "I will, if I can!"

At the gates of King Street, the death detail came to a halt. Colonel Hayne was aghast at what he saw. There before his eyes was a gibbet, the prescribed method of execution for treason under military law. Hayne had expected to die before a firing squad as a prisoner of war.

Head erect, the Patriot climbed aboard a cart. When someone in the crowd exhorted him to die like a man, he responded, "I will try." For a brief time, he joined in prayer with the minister at his side. Then the noose was placed around his neck and the death cap upon his head. Hayne took a deep breath and nodded his readiness to the executioner.

The colonel kept the promise he made to his sister. For eighty years after Isaac Hayne passed the Peronneau House on his death walk, his spirit lingered in the dwelling. At twilight each day, his distinct voice could be heard calling out from the street alongside the home. Then, as the sky faded, his phantom footsteps were audible on the entrance steps, always going up. But once a later generation of South Carolinians rose to fight another war in 1861, Hayne's spirited presence rarely manifested itself at the Peronneau House.

Over at the Old Exchange and Provost Dungeon, located on East Bay Street, Hayne's spirit is alive and well. One of the jewels in Charleston's treasure chest of historical architecture, this magnificent building was completed around 1771 and is open to the public today. The monumental structure rises two stories above a massive arcaded basement.

A tour of the restored basement is a must on a visit to Charleston, for history abounds here. And so does the ghost of Isaac Hayne. During the British occupation of Charleston, this dungeon area was used for political and military prisoners, one of the most prominent of whom was Colonel Hayne.

Cells have been restored in the dungeon and mannequins placed behind the bars. Guides leading nighttime tours are sometimes overcome with fear as a result of the supernatural activities in the otherwise empty dungeon. Phantom footsteps attributed to Hayne's ghost are commonly heard in the area where he was incarcerated. Orbs thought to represent his spirit have been seen and photographed. Guides and tourists have experienced eerie hot and cold spots in the same area.

On one tour, ancient prison chains out of the reach of visitors suddenly began to swing and shake. As the commotion continued, the entire group, leader included, witnessed an even more frightening spectacle. One of the fixed, immobile prisoner mannequins—said by some to represent the doleful Hayne—began to move without human assistance.

One day, Hayne's ghost may be able to escape the miserable confines of the dungeon onto the streets of Charleston, where it might finally rest, satisfied that liberty reigns supreme in its beloved South Carolina.

The address for the **Old Exchange (Custom House) and Provost Dungeon** is 122 East Bay St., Charleston, S.C. 29401; the telephone numbers are 888-763-0448 and 843-727-2165.

The Endless Summer Siege
NINETY SIX, SOUTH CAROLINA

The General presents his thanks to both Officers and soldiers,
and hopes to give them an early opportunity of reaping fruits
of their superior spirit by an attack, in the open Field, upon the
Troops now led by Lord Rawdon.

GENERAL NATHANAEL GREENE,
FOLLOWING THE SIEGE AT NINETY SIX

After badly damaging the British army in the South at Guilford
Courthouse on March 15, 1781 (see 268-72), General Nathanael
Greene left the task of finishing Cornwallis to George Washington.
Greene instead moved into South Carolina, intent upon eliminating
the remaining British strength within its borders. His first order of
business was the Tory stronghold at Ninety Six in the northwestern
part of the state. Considered impregnable, the well-fortified compound
was manned by a contingent of 550 well-trained Tories from New York,
New Jersey, and South Carolina.

Greene and his 1,100-man army laid siege to the installation a day or so after his arrival on May 22. For twenty-eight long days, the impasse depleted both armies. A pitched battle to take the Tory works failed, and Greene ultimately retreated. Within weeks, the British abandoned the post upon the arrival of Lord Rawdon, who chose to chase Greene. Yet the spirits of the 275 soldiers who died during the hot days in the late spring of 1781 abide as ghosts at the site, now preserved as Ninety Six National Historic Site.

Visitors can walk about the American entrenchments and the grassed-over star fort where the Tories made their remarkable stand and endured the siege. The National Park Service notes of the zigzagging earthworks, "There are few better examples on this continent of 18th century siegecraft or of the close personal nature of battle in that day."

When touring the old fort and the American positions surrounding it, visitors shouldn't expect to come face to face with apparitions of soldiers. But chances are great that they might hear sounds and voices from beyond the Revolutionary War graves here. Phantom footsteps have been heard about the forested area near the rear of the park. Many visitors have reported the eerie sensation that they were being followed in the dense woods, even to the point that they heard footsteps on the forest floor. But upon close inspection, no human pursuer has ever been found. These mysterious sounds have been attributed to the ghosts of Nathanael Greene's soldiers and to the spirits of the slaves forced by the British army to construct the compound at Ninety Six.

Reenactors have been frightened by the ghostly sounds at Ninety Six. On one occasion, a veteran reenactor departed the park in the middle of a special weekend event because of the spooky noises he heard. During the night he spent on the historic grounds, he camped a great distance from his comrades. Alone at his campsite, he became unnerved when ghostly voices speaking in accents from past centuries began to emanate from a nearby well. The incessant chatter continued throughout the night, even though no other humans were anywhere about. Early the next morning, the reenactor reported the mysterious phenomenon to park rangers just before he beat a hasty retreat home.

On another occasion, a longtime park volunteer reported hearing the voice of a soldier from the past. One rainy evening, the man walked with his dog to the old siege site to look for bullets and other pieces of Revolutionary War metal often found after a downpour. As the volunteer made his way from the star fort in the direction of the reconstructed stockade, his dog suddenly stopped in its tracks, frightened. Its tail went between its legs, its head dropped, its hair bristled, and it whimpered. As its master, a retired military officer, looked about to ascertain the reason for the dog's fear, not a person was to be seen. But then came two loud, distinct words: "Company, halt!" A subsequent search of the entire complex revealed that the volunteer was the only living human about the site.

Those who traverse the grounds of the old fort and the siege works at Ninety Six can imagine the gunfire and screams that filled the air during the dreadful action played out here so many years ago. And if they listen carefully, they just might catch the very words and sounds of the spirits who have remained since 1781.

The address for **Ninety Six National Historic Site** is 1103 S.C. 248, Ninety Six, S.C. 29666; the telephone number is 864-543-4068.

When Bloody Bill Called
ROEBUCK, SOUTH CAROLINA

*I often heard it said Cunningham was a coward, but who-
ever said so, did not know him, he was as brave a man as ever
walked the earth.*

WILLIAM CALDWELL, A CONTEMPORARY
OF WILLIAM "BLOODY BILL"
CUNNINGHAM

Walnut Grove Plantation, located five miles southwest of Spartanburg, South Carolina, survives on a portion of the three thousand acres granted to Charles and Mary Moore by King George III. The centerpiece of the colonial plantation is the beautifully restored two-story frame house constructed by the Moores in 1765. In the waning days of the Revolutionary War, Major William "Bloody Bill" Cunningham, one of the most ruthless and bloodthirsty Loyalist officers in the struggle for American independence, called at Walnut Grove, where he continued his reign of terror against Patriots. Today, no evidence exists that Bloody Bill lingers in spirit form at Walnut Grove. But the ghostly presence of one of his victims has been experienced in the house and on the grounds. In addition, the spectre of Kate Moore Barry, a Patriot heroine and a nemesis of Cunningham, yet walks the plantation where she grew to womanhood.

Cunningham, a native South Carolinian, did not begin the war as the callous barbarian who plagued Patriot fighters for much of the conflict. Described as a man of extraordinary physical strength and outstanding personal appearance, he volunteered in 1775 for service as a private in a South Carolina company commanded by Captain John Caldwell. Cunningham's early service as a Patriot soldier was so meritorious that Caldwell promoted him. A trivial disciplinary matter intervened, however, and Cunningham found himself before a court-martial. He was sentenced to a whipping. After the degrading and painful punishment was carried out, Cunningham deserted the Patriot army and spirited away to Florida.

While in St. Augustine, he received news from South Carolina that Patriots led by William Ritchie had raided the home of his father, turning the aged man out of doors. His rifle on his shoulder, Cunningham set out on foot for the Palmetto State. Once he made it back home, he called at the Ritchie homestead. There, in front of the entire family, Cunningham emptied his rifle into the hapless William Ritchie.

Then it was on to the home of his former commander, Captain Caldwell. Finding the elderly Caldwell, retired from military life, sitting in his home barefoot, Cunningham proceeded to gleefully dance and stomp on Caldwell's toes and kick his shins. At length, he announced to Caldwell that he had gained ample satisfaction for his earlier humiliation.

A month after the British surrender at Yorktown in October 1781, Bloody Bill and his ruthless band of mounted Loyalists returned to the home of the old captain, where two of Cunningham's soldiers executed Caldwell without permission. Upon learning of the murder, Bloody Bill directed that Caldwell's killer be burned out of his house.

In the following months, Cunningham and his raiders continued to terrorize Patriots and their families in Upstate South Carolina. By sword, by gun, by noose, and by torch, Bloody Bill etched his name in infamy. As word of Cunningham's intended attack on Walnut Grove Plantation leaked from his camp, a young heroine sprang into action. Catherine "Kate" Moore Barry, one of ten children of Charles and Mary Moore, mounted her horse and galloped off to sound the alarm that Bloody Bill was on the prowl.

From the early days of the war, Kate, the wife of Patriot officer Andrew Barry, had rendered magnificent service as a scout in northern South Carolina. Her expert horsemanship, her keen knowledge of local geography, and her gender enabled her to travel freely in and out of military encampments, including that of her husband and her brother, Thomas. Kate's observations of the enemy and her other intelligence proved invaluable to the American cause.

Her brightest moment came in January 1781, when she acted as a special scout and aide for General Daniel Morgan in advance of his clash with Banastre Tarleton. Her tireless efforts to rally local Patriots, including her husband, to join Morgan at Cowpens helped the Americans win the victory there.

Kate Moore Barry's remarkable military exploits were fraught with peril. One day, Tories looking for her were observed approaching Walnut Grove. Realizing she had not a second to spare, Kate secured Katherine, her two-year-old, in a bed and rode off to summon her husband and his charges to chase the marauders away. On another occasion, she suffered the wrath of the Tories when they suddenly showed up at her home. Refusing their demands to provide information concerning her husband's whereabouts, Kate was tied up by the raiders and whipped mercilessly with a leash.

During Bloody Bill's raid at Walnut Grove in the fall of 1781, Kate mounted her speedy steed to warn others in the neighborhood. But three Patriots at the plantation could not escape. One of the unfortunate soldiers was Captain Ben (also referred to as John) Steadman, who tradition maintains was engaged to Kate's sister. Considered an officer of great promise, he was confined to a sickbed in the manor house when Bloody Bill made his call. In short order, he was shot to death. Two of Steadman's comrades heard the commotion and attempted to flee. Cunningham's marauders gunned them down as they ran toward the Moore family cemetery.

Strange dark spots still visible on the floor of the upstairs bedroom where Steadman died were long said to be his bloodstains. But after modern investigators concluded that the stains were not the result of human blood, tour guides at the plantation were instructed not to repeat the legend. Whatever the case, the ghost of a Patriot officer thought to be Steadman has been sighted about the venerable house.

On the plantation grounds, employees and visitors sometimes witness the apparition of a young lady adorned in a cape making her way from the graveyard to the house. Tradition has it that this is the ghost of Kate Moore Barry. Her grave and those of her husband, her parents, Captain Steadman, and his two compatriots are in the family cemetery. It seems that in death as in life, Kate Barry remains devoted to two causes—her family and her country.

Bloody Bill Cunningham's campaign of violence against Patriots in the Upcountry and the foothills of South Carolina finally came to an end almost a year after Yorktown. Despite being pursued by relatives of his victims, he lived to an old age in the West Indies, dying peacefully in his bed. Cunningham's supernatural presence has never been encountered anywhere in his native state. But at Walnut Grove Plantation, two ever-vigilant Patriot ghosts are on patrol just in case Bloody Bill should make a "spirited" raid.

Walnut Grove Plantation is open to the public. Its address is 1200 Otts Shoals Rd., Roebuck, S.C. 29736; the telephone number is 864-576-6546.

Other "Spirited" Revolutionary War Sites in South Carolina, Briefly Noted

BRATTONSVILLE—HISTORIC BRATTONSVILLE

On July 11, 1780, Captain Christian Huck and his band of lawless Tories settled down for the night at Williamson's Plantation in northern South Carolina in anticipation of a raid on the farms of local Patriots, including that of Colonel William Bratton, less than a half-mile distant. Instead, Colonel Bratton and his men attacked Huck at daybreak. During the ensuing battle, known as "Huck's Defeat," the Tories lost almost 90 percent of their 115-man force.

Colonel Bratton's restored wooden farmhouse stands at Historic Brattonsville, a 775-acre site dedicated to the preservation of Revolutionary War history. The Bratton homestead is haunted by a ghost wearing a tricorn hat. Some believe the apparition is that of Colonel Bratton. A spectre attired in a Revolutionary War uniform also patrols the grounds.

The address for Historic Brattonsville is 1444 Brattonsville Rd., McConnells, S.C. 29726; the telephone number is 803-684-2327.

BUSH RIVER—NEAR BOBO'S MILLS

Many engaged couples were robbed of a lifetime of happiness as a result of the Revolutionary War. So it was with two South Carolinians, Henry Galbreath and Charity Miles. Their love was so strong that Henry's ghost, adorned in his Continental Army uniform, yet rides along the Bush River in the South Carolina Upcountry to honor his promise to his fiancée.

Charity was the nineteen-year-old daughter of David and Esther Miles, a modest Quaker couple who lived on a simple farm along the Bush River, which runs a thirty-mile course in the South Carolina Piedmont. Henry Galbreath, a scout for Patriot forces in the area, was the love of Charity's life. The couple pledged to marry as soon as the war was over.

On a cold night in January 1780, Henry and Charity were spending blissful moments by the fireplace in the Miles cabin when Henry announced that he had enlisted as a regular in the Continental Army. Bidding his tearful betrothed adieu, he promised, "One year from this day, my dear, I shall be back, whether alive or dead. My horse and I will come galloping up the river road. So look for me, my lovely lass."

In the weeks that followed, news from the front was sparse. Charity could learn nothing about her Henry. Patriot soldiers fleeing north from the fall of Charleston in the spring of 1780 brought no word. In their wake, Redcoats invaded the Upstate.

Then came the battle at Cowpens in mid-January 1781, when General Daniel Morgan used a combined force of Continentals and militiamen to whip Banastre Tarleton. Henry did not come home from that battle, nor did Charity receive any news of his whereabouts.

On April 25, 1860, as South Carolinians prepared to engage in another fight for independence, the *Rising Sun* of Columbia publicized the existence of a spectral rider and an account of a haunted love story. On the first anniversary of the American victory at Cowpens, Charity had gone to bed but found herself unable to sleep. Around two o'clock in the morning, she heard the distinct sound of galloping hooves. As she listened, the horse seemed to draw closer and closer. Unable to contain her excitement that Henry had returned, she hurried to the cabin door and peered into the darkness. She saw a handsome Continental soldier proudly riding atop a magnificent white horse. Covering the soldier's blue uniform was a black cape riddled with a dozen bullet holes. Without stopping, the horseman rode on until fading into the blackness.

Early the next day, Charity and her father made a thorough inspection outside the cabin but found no hoofprints. Sadly, the heartbroken girl came to the realization that Henry had kept his promise in the only way he could.

Charity never married. Though the Miles family's cabin succumbed to the elements many years ago, the phantom rider with its black cape flying in the night still gallops along the banks of the Bush River.

S.C. 395 crosses the Bush River south of Newberry.

CAMDEN—GRAVE OF AGNES OF GLASGOW

Camden, located in north-central South Carolina, was a hotbed of military activity throughout the Revolutionary War. On August 16, 1780, on a site just north of town, Continental soldiers and militiamen commanded by General Horatio Gates sustained the worst field defeat in any battle in which an American army has participated.

In the heart of the town known for its historic preservation efforts, a grave marks the burial spot of Agnes of Glasgow. While living in her native Scotland, Agnes faced an interminable wait for the return of her fellow, Lieutenant Angus McPherson. She finally prevailed upon a sea captain to allow her to sail for coastal South Carolina on his ship. Upon her arrival at Charleston, Agnes learned that Angus had been wounded in battle and was being treated in Camden. Accompanied by Indians, she made the long trip to the British compound there. In a hospital tent, she came face to face with Angus, who was lying on a cot in serious condition. Their reunion was ever so brief. Within minutes, the soldier was dead. Emotionally overwrought and greatly fatigued from her journey, Agnes flung her body over that of her lover and died of a broken heart.

After a British officer directed that Agnes's body be buried, Angus's bayonet was used to etch the letters on her tombstone. But she could not rest in the grave. Her ghost floats about the historic streets of old Camden to this day, maintaining a constant vigil for Lieutenant McPherson.

Agnes of Glasgow's grave is located near the gate of the Quaker Cemetery close to the intersection of Campbell and Meeting streets. The address for the cemetery is 713 Meeting Street, Camden, S.C. 29020.

CAMDEN—HOBKIRK'S HILL

Hobkirk's Hill, a ridge now integrated into residential Camden, was the site of a hard-fought battle between the British, led by Lord Francis Rawdon, and the Americans, commanded by Major General Nathanael Greene, on April 25, 1781. Casualties were heavy on both sides in the Redcoat victory. Among the American fatalities was a Continental horseman whose head was severed by a cannonball. His comrades watched in horror as the terrified horse, still bearing the headless body, raced off into the swamp bordering Black River Road.

A long-held legend in these parts maintains that on warm spring nights when the moon is full and fog envelops Hobkirk's Hill, the ghost rides once again in search of its head. By daybreak, it is gone.

Hobkirk's Hill is located in the 200 block of Broad Street in Camden.

GAFFNEY—COWPENS NATIONAL BATTLEFIELD

In northwestern South Carolina on the bitterly cold morning of January 17, 1781, General Daniel Morgan inspired a combined army of militia and regulars to best a wing of Cornwallis's army commanded by Banastre Tarleton. By the time the British cavalry chieftain retreated from the field, he had lost nearly a thousand men. Cornwallis never recovered from the loss of manpower at the Battle of Cowpens. In contrast,

Morgan's losses were less than seventy-five.

The well-preserved battlefield is now a national park. As they traverse the site, visitors often sense the presence of an unseen entity. Some have even seen the ghost of a Revolutionary War cavalryman galloping about the battlefield.

The address for Cowpens National Battlefield is 4001 Chesnee Hwy., Gaffney, S.C. 29341; the telephone number is 864-461-2828.

GEORGETOWN—HENNING HOUSE

Georgetown, the historic port city located halfway between Myrtle Beach and Charleston, was the first town in America to welcome the Marquis de Lafayette after he arrived on the South Carolina shore on June 13, 1777, to join the war effort. Today, the port boasts a treasure trove of architectural gems dating from the Revolutionary War. Among the surviving homes is the Henning House, built around 1760. While the town was under British control, this dwelling was used to quarter Redcoat troops. One of their number was relaxing in an upstairs bedroom when the cry was heard that General Francis Marion had been sighted in Georgetown. Scrambling to his feet, the soldier hastened toward the staircase, stumbled on a loose floorboard near the top of the steps, and tumbled to the first floor. His neck broken by the fall, he died instantly.

Over the years, many persons in the house have avoided a similar fate thanks to a phantom hand that has steadied them at the top of the staircase. Tradition says the ghostly touch is that of the Redcoat who was not so lucky himself.

The address for the Henning House is 331 Screven St., Georgetown, S.C. 29440.

GEORGETOWN—WEDGEFIELD PLANTATION MANOR

Located in a residential resort community five miles from Georgetown, the extant manor house at Wedgefield Plantation replaced its predecessor (built around 1764) in the 1930s. A British soldier is said to roam the grounds where high drama played out during the Revolutionary War.

As area Patriots skirmished on a frequent basis with the British occupation forces at Georgetown, a number were taken prisoner. Some were incarcerated at Wedgefield. Determined to help the Patriots escape, the daughter of the plantation owner, a young woman of spectacular beauty, devised a scheme. Pretending to be a Redcoat sympathizer, she held a fete for the British soldiers quartered at the manor house and area dwellings. Patriot forces were alerted to make their rescue attempt during the party.

Once the festivities commenced, the Redcoats were so engrossed that only one of their men remained on guard. When he attempted to notify the reveling soldiers of the approach of the American rescue party, a Patriot sword slashed his head from his body. For the briefest moment, the bloody corpse staggered before falling to the ground. Anxious to hide the evidence, a detachment of Patriots hurriedly dug a makeshift grave in the plantation garden and threw the headless corpse in. No one knows what happened to the severed head.

Less than two months after the garish spectacle, Redcoats began to see the headless spectre of their former comrade roaming the plantation, sidearm in hand. Many such sightings were recorded over the years. Some people even heard the galloping of the phantom American rescue force. Since the original manor house was replaced, the ghost has been observed less frequently.

The address for Wedgefield Plantation is 129 Clubhouse Ln., Georgetown, S.C. 29440; the telephone number is 843-448-2124.

HEATH SPRINGS—HANGING ROCK

On August 6, 1780, General Thomas Sumter, his forces outnumbered more than two to one, launched a surprise attack on the army of British regulars and Tories under the command of Major John Carden in northern South Carolina near what is now Heath Springs. Sumter earned a badly needed victory for Americans at the Battle of Hanging Rock, named for the prominent outcropping at the site. About twenty-five feet in diameter, the huge spherical boulder does not hang. Rather, it is firmly affixed. In 1849, noted Revolutionary War historian Benjamin Lossing described the unusual geologic formation as a "concavity . . . in the form of the quarter of an orange paring, and capacious enough to shelter fifty men from rain."

Little changed from the day of the clash, Hanging Rock and the surrounding landscape have a spooky, haunted aura about them. For as long as anyone can remember, visitors have experienced uneasy feelings, as if they are being watched by an invisible force. Dogs are wary of walking about the area; their fur bristles upon approaching the place where Sumter bested Carden. Children begin to cry without reason. Adults are often overcome with a sense of foreboding and woe. The unseen spirits of the troops who suffered here in the summer of 1780 are said to be the cause.

To reach Hanging Rock, proceed south on S.R. 29-15 for 1.7 miles from the battle's historical marker in Heath Springs to the junction with S.R. 29-467. Turn left on S.R. 29-467 and drive 0.7 mile east across a creek to where a dirt road leads to the right. The rock and a D.A.R. monument are an 0.25-mile walk from the dirt road.

LANCASTER COUNTY—GREEN HAND BRIDGE

Green Hand Bridge, named for the Revolutionary War legend associated with it, is an old, abandoned one-lane trestle that crosses Cane Creek in the Waxhaws area of northern South Carolina. Generations of local residents have maintained that the creek is haunted by the ghost of a British soldier killed in one of the many skirmishes fought against General Thomas Sumter and his Piedmont partisans. In the course of the bloody encounter, the unfortunate Redcoat lost his hand when an American soldier slashed it from the arm and sent it into the dark water near the bridge. Countless witnesses contend that they have seen a green hand rise out of the water on clear, cloudless nights. Some have even witnessed the spectre of a Revolutionary War soldier in a British uniform floating about the creek in an apparent search for its hand and the saber it was holding.

Remnants of the bridge are located along the abandoned, overgrown Old Landsford Road near S.C. 9 Business.

MONCKS CORNER—EXETER PLANTATION SITE

Captain Archie Campbell was a quirky and controversial British officer headquartered in Charleston after General Benjamin Lincoln surrendered the city to General Henry Clinton in May 1780. Captain Campbell became infatuated with Margaret Pauline Philips, one of the most beautiful ladies of Charleston. In short order, "Mad Archie" wagered with some of his fellow officers that "Miss Polly" would be his wife within three days.

The cocky Campbell wasted little time making good on his bet. He cajoled his intended into taking a carriage ride into the country. When the buggy reached Goose Creek and St. James Anglican Church (which survives today as the oldest church building in South Carolina), Mad Archie brandished a pistol and put it to the head of the minister. Upon being ordered to marry the couple, the rector calmly proclaimed he would not do so without the consent of Miss Polly and her mother. When the gun was placed against the young lady's temple, she promptly "consented" to the nuptials.

Over the next year or so, the newlyweds lived at nearby Exeter

Plantation. Mrs. Campbell gave birth to a child. Meanwhile, Captain Campbell battled Americans, including the likes of General Francis Marion.

On January 2, 1782, Mad Archie was captured by Patriot forces at the Battle of Videau's Bridge. He died from wounds in a subsequent attempt to escape. Miss Polly soon followed him to the grave. Ever since her death, her ghost has haunted the grounds of Exeter Plantation, established in 1726. Her apparition wanders the historic landscape in an eternal search for the infant child she left behind so many years ago.

The ancient home at Exeter Plantation was destroyed by fire in December 1967. Berkeley Country Club, located on Exeter Plantation Road (old S.C. 52) in Moncks Corner, now owns the site.

SOCIETY HILL—TOMB OF COLONEL ABEL KOLB

Widely recognized as one of General Francis Marion's most able senior officers, Lieutenant Colonel Abel Kolb had a plantation on the banks of the Great Pee Dee River in the sand hills of north-central South Carolina. In 1781, vengeful Tories, approximately fifty in number, approached Kolb's home under cover of darkness in an effort to surprise the colonel, who was known to be in residence with his wife and eight-year-old daughter.

As the Tories neared the house, they came upon two of Kolb's officers and summarily executed them. What happened next was subsequently related by Kolb's daughter, Ann, an eyewitness to the grim events. Captain Joseph Jones, the Tory commander, demanded that Mrs. Kolb produce her husband, saying that no harm would come to the colonel but that the house would be torched if she refused. She complied and came walking down the steps with her arms around her spouse. No sooner had their feet touched the porch than a Tory soldier fired a bullet that plowed into Abel Kolb's heart. The Tories then set fire to the house.

Abel Kolb's tomb overlooks the river near the site of his former

dwelling. And his spirit has been encountered nearby. Persons witnessing the apparition have noted that its appearance is preceded by the
sound of footsteps in the adjacent forest.

To see the well-marked grave of Colonel Abel Kolb, follow U.S.
15/U.S. 401 north from Society Hill to its junction with S.R. 35-167,
where a historical marker honoring Kolb stands. Follow S.R. 35-67 to
the grave site.

Georgia

ME
(WAS N. MA.)

VT
NH
NY
MA
CT RI
NJ
PA
MD
DE
GEORGIA
VA

NC

SC

GA

SHADED AREA SHOWS
COLONIAL AMERICA

A Patriot Still at Home
SAVANNAH, GEORGIA

The gentleman of the family, he is a youth of strict honor and of uncommon sweetness of temper, perhaps too much so.
JAMES HABERSHAM, SR.,
WRITING OF HIS SON JAMES JR.

Having survived the wars, storms, and fires that significantly altered the architectural landscape of old Savannah through American history, the Olde Pink House stands in the heart of the port city as one of Georgia's most outstanding eighteenth-century buildings. Construction of the imposing structure was commenced in 1771 by James Habersham, Jr., one of three brothers who played prominent roles in the movement toward independence in the southernmost of America's thirteen colonies. Important strategic meetings of the Sons of Liberty were held in Habersham's house during the early stages of the Revolutionary War. Though postwar financial difficulties forced Habersham to part with his mansion, his ghost has been in residence for as long as anyone can remember.

James Habersham, Jr. (1745–99), and his brothers, Joseph and John, were born in Georgia and educated at Princeton. Their father had immigrated to the newly established colony of Georgia from England in 1737. By the time the fervor for independence spread about the colonies, the patriarch of the Habersham family was one of the wealthiest planters and merchants in Georgia. A strong supporter of the British government, James Sr. played an integral role in suppressing protest against the Stamp Act in Savannah. When his close friend James Wright, the Royal governor of Georgia, was in England from 1771 to 1773, the elder Habersham served as acting governor. During a trip to New Jersey to restore his health, James Sr. died on August 28, 1775.

James Jr., Joseph, and John all held political beliefs in stark contrast to those of their late father. His death allowed them to take more active roles in the movement toward independence. Although their father had made Savannah a city loyal to British rule, the brothers arranged secret meetings with like-minded individuals to plan strategies to aid the cause of liberty.

Many clandestine gatherings of the so-called Liberty Boys took place in a second-floor room of the Pink House. Fearful of reprisals, the attendees parked their carriages blocks away and pretended to be on nighttime strolls, only to sneak into the back entrance of James Jr.'s mansion. Inside, they ascended the grand Georgian staircase to the room where they devised ways to disrupt the Royal government.

Joining the Habersham brothers at the meetings were famed Georgians Edward Telfair and John Houston, as well as Button Gwinnett and George Walton, both future signers of the Declaration of Independence. Among the successful operations designed at the Habersham home were the kidnapping of Royal Governor Wright, a raid on a provincial powder magazine, and the erection of the first "Liberty Pole" in Georgia.

When the fight began, each of the Habersham brothers sacrificed mightily for the American cause. From January 1, 1776, until war's end, John served as an officer in the Continental Army, seeing heavy action in his native state. He also represented Georgia in the Continental Congress. Likewise, Joseph became an officer in the Continental Army early in 1776. After the fighting, he helped build the new republic by serving in a number of positions: speaker of the Georgia legislature, member of the convention that ratified the United States Constitution, and postmaster of the United States. While James Jr. held the military title of major during the war, his greatest service came through his generous financial contributions. Unfortunately, the postwar years were not kind to him economically. Strapped for cash, he found it necessary to sell his beloved home in the years preceding his death in 1799 at age fifty-four. He was interred in a plot beside his parents at Savannah's famed Colonial Cemetery.

Over the ensuing years, the mansion served as a private residence, a bank, a headquarters for Union generals during the Civil War, a law office, and a bookstore. Today, it graces Savannah's historic Reynolds Square as one of the few structures surviving from the Revolutionary War. Its pink hue is legendary. The house was constructed of red bricks covered with white plaster. Soon after it was completed, the red of the bricks bled through the plaster, resulting in a pink exterior. Dismayed by the unwanted color change, James Jr. had the house painted over and over, but the result was always the same: the pink returned. In the twenty-first century, the Olde Pink House remains aptly named.

Since the 1970s, the grand structure has housed one of the finest restaurants in the city. Diners admire the stunning architectural features, including the heart-of-pine floors, the finest Georgian staircase in the state, and the spectacular Palladian window above the Greek portico. While feasting in the dining rooms or enjoying a cold beverage in the basement bar, many have seen or experienced the ghost of the home's original master. Restaurant owners and employees readily admit that the spirit of James Habersham, Jr., lingers in the Olde Pink House.

One of the ghost's favorite spots is the special area where the owners have restored a dining room behind a locked wrought-iron gate. Through the bars, diners can view furniture from Habersham's time, arranged just as it was in 1775. After the restaurant closes for the night, it seems that James Jr. uses his private, gated dining area. On the street, people walking past the window that looks into the special room have reported seeing a shadowy figure. When employees report for work the next day, they sometimes find candles ablaze in the otherwise dark room. Moreover, the antique furniture is sometimes mysteriously rearranged.

James Jr. annoys staffers by playing tricks on them. An invisible force locks and unlocks one of the doors to the ladies' room. Attempts to remove tablecloths are thwarted by tugs on the opposite side by unseen hands. Table lights blown out by wait staff are once again burning when employees reenter the room.

Because he often makes himself visible to patrons and staffers, James Jr. enjoys a reputation as the most frequently seen ghost in Savannah. Quiet Sunday afternoons are his favorite time to show, but he has no regular schedule.

During a banquet one evening, a diner was overwhelmed with the feeling that someone was standing behind him. He turned around to find a man in clothing and a wig from colonial times. Impressed by the authenticity of the costume, the patron was about to compliment the man when a waiter stopped to pour coffee. When asked about the identity of the fellow in special dress, the waiter responded that no such person had been in the room the entire night.

On another occasion, a patron asked to see other portions of the building after completing his meal. An employee escorted him through the second floor before being summoned downstairs. All alone, the visitor continued his tour. As he walked down a corridor, he came upon a man in eighteenth-century clothing and a powdered wig. Assuming the unidentified man was an employee in period clothes, he greeted the man and offered praise for his costume. No response was forthcoming. Concerned by the strange encounter, the patron hurried downstairs to look for his guide. In the process, he was startled to come upon a portrait of James Habersham, Jr. It was an exact likeness of the stranger he had just left upstairs.

One evening shortly after closing, some twenty-six members of the restaurant staff were assembled in the first-floor lounge when the door to the second floor suddenly opened. Well aware that no one was allowed in that portion of the building after hours, they all looked up the stairway. The temperature in the lounge rose dramatically as a white, misty vapor floated down the stairs. Without waiting to see who or what the strange cloud was, everyone bolted from the building.

Down in the basement tavern, James Jr. exhibits a jovial spirit. When a city resident stopped by after work one afternoon, he took notice of a man dressed in Revolutionary War clothing seated at the end of the bar and holding a drink. Assuming the strange dress was meant to lend ambiance to the place, the local fellow smiled and raised his beer in a toast. His smile and toast were returned by the man "in costume." Turning to the bartender, the local fellow commented on the eighteenth-century clothing of the man at the end of the bar. With a perplexed look, the bartender asked, "What man?" The mysterious figure had disappeared without walking out of the room.

James Jr.'s ghost has also been observed walking to the Habersham plot at Colonial Cemetery. But somehow, some way, his spirit always returns to the Olde Pink House, his former home and the birthplace of Georgia's independence.

The address for the **Olde Pink House Restaurant** is 23 Abercorn St., Savannah, Ga. 31401; the telephone number is 912-232-4286.

A Vengeful Haunting
AUGUSTA, GEORGIA

We shall hang thirteen of the prisoners, one for each of the
rebellious colonies.

COLONEL THOMAS BROWN

Augusta's second-oldest home, the Ezekiel Harris House, is considered one of the most haunted places in the United States. It stands
within sight of the long-vanished Mackay Trading Post (also known as
the White House), where a bloody clash took place between American
troops under Colonel Elijah Clarke and Loyalist forces under Colonel
Thomas Brown in September 1780. In the deadly encounter, Brown
exacted a heavy measure of revenge for his personal mistreatment by
Patriots five years earlier. The spirits of the victims of Brown's retribution dwell in the Ezekiel Harris House as a reminder of those dark days
in Augusta's Revolutionary War history.

Thomas Brown (1750–1825), born into an affluent family on the
northeastern coast of England, came to Georgia at age twenty-four to

develop business interests for his father. At the time of his arrival, revolutionary sentiment was growing in Georgia and the other colonies. Brown settled in the Augusta area, where his loyalty to King George III did not play well with the local Liberty Boys. When Brown publicly denounced the group and its cause, he became its target.

Intent upon making an example of the loyal British subject, the rebels captured Brown on the morning of October 5, 1775, tied him to a tree, poured hot tar over his body, and emptied feather pillows upon him. He was then bound, loaded on a mule-drawn wagon, and paraded along the heaviest-traveled thoroughfare in Augusta. Affixed to the wagon were derisive placards proclaiming his name, as he was otherwise unidentifiable. Some of the Liberty Boys walked alongside the wagon, exclaiming to the highly amused bystanders, "Behold! We present Thomas Brown, the mightiest rooster in King Georgie Porgie's service!"

To add injury to insult, Brown's tormenters severely beat and nearly killed him. His skull was fractured, causing him to suffer excruciating headaches the remainder of his life. He also lost two toes in the incident.

Before Brown's captors freed him, they issued a harsh ultimatum: he was to leave Georgia within twenty-four hours or face even more severe treatment. With the aid of one of his many slaves, he promptly scrubbed away the tar and feathers and made haste to South Carolina. Just prior to his departure, Brown was heard to say, "You citizens of Augusta will pay dearly for the indignity and suffering you inflicted upon me!"

Threatened with arrest in South Carolina, Brown subsequently made his way to Florida, where he recuperated and then volunteered his services to the Crown. By 1776, he was appointed a lieutenant colonel in command of a regiment of the king's rangers. An additional appointment as superintendent of Indian affairs in the Georgia-Florida area enabled Brown to recruit numerous Indian allies.

Over the next four years, Colonel Brown showed exceptional

talent as a Tory leader, overseeing numerous successful operations on the Georgia frontier. In June 1780, he felt a sense of vindication when his army ran the Patriots out of Augusta and captured the city for the British. Charleston had been wrested from the Patriots just a month earlier. Thus, the British strongholds at Augusta and Ninety Six became vital western outposts in the grand strategy to bring an end to the rebellion in the South.

As the military commander of Augusta, Colonel Brown no longer heard the jeers to which he had been subjected five years earlier. Yet he still sought revenge. An opportunity presented itself on September 14, when his forces were attacked at the Mackay Trading Post by the 430-man army of Colonel Elijah Clarke.

In the fierce gun battle that day, Clarke's soldiers were unable to overwhelm the heavily outnumbered Loyalists and Cherokees commanded by Brown. Clarke decided to lay siege to the three-story frame building and the surrounding land where the enemy was entrenched. Although Brown and his men were completely encircled by American troops, several Indians managed to escape and make their way to Ninety Six to sound the alarm.

Twenty-four hours passed, then forty-eight. The shooting, wounding, and killing continued on both sides, the Tories picking off Patriots from the high windows of the house. At the outset of the siege, Clarke had managed to cut off the water supply to the Tory position. The searing temperatures forced Brown's men to drink their own urine. Their only food was rotting pumpkins. Medicinal supplies were nonexistent.

Thirty-six more hours passed. Desperation began to prevail among the suffering Tories. Their impassioned cries for water and mercy had no effect on their commander, who would not suffer the disgrace of surrendering to the vile Patriots. When gunshots wounded the Tory colonel in both thighs, he resolutely continued the fight. After the bleeding was stopped, Brown was placed in a chair by his men. From a window on the third floor, he rained deadly fire down upon Clarke's men.

On the morning of September 18, the Americans called off the siege when Clarke received intelligence that Colonel John Cruger and a sizable army from Ninety Six were fast approaching. In ordering his army to retreat, he was forced to leave twenty-eight badly wounded Patriots on the battleground. He reasoned that they would be taken as prisoners of war and would receive medical attention. He was wrong. Soon, the unfortunate men became Colonel Thomas Brown's ultimate revenge.

According to Brown's orders, the Patriots were dragged to the house. Meanwhile, two Tory soldiers labored to carry the seriously wounded colonel down the stairs to the first floor. A rifle rested in Brown's lap as he sat in a chair, his body propped up with pillows. His weary eyes surveyed the twenty-nine men and boys before him. All but one bore the wounds of the furious fighting. Tom Glass, a fifteen-year-old local soldier unharmed in the combat, had remained behind to minister to his older brother, Will, who was badly injured. When Tom asked for water for his emaciated brother, two years his elder, Colonel Brown reminded the young American that the Tories had been intentionally denied fresh water for four days.

Brown studied the pathetic assemblage to ascertain whether or not he had been lucky enough to capture one of the Liberty Boys. Unable to recognize a face from the past, he demanded to know who had wounded him in the thighs. No answer was forthcoming.

Then Brown's voice rose above the moans of the suffering soldiers: "These men are not prisoners of war. They are traitors. And they will be dealt with accordingly."

After directing Tory soldiers to fashion a gibbet in the open-air stairway of the Mackay Trading Post, Colonel Brown proceeded to handpick thirteen captives, one for each of the rebellious colonies. Among those selected were the Glass teenagers. The thirteen were soon executed at the end of a rope. From a bed, the Tory colonel watched every execution, his eyes transfixed on the face of each victim as death came.

The remaining sixteen Americans were spared, albeit for a brief time. Brown had them delivered to his Cherokee warriors to do with as they pleased. On the grounds surrounding the house, the Indians tortured the ailing soldiers before killing them.

Colonel Brown was captured in Augusta nearly a year later by the combined forces of Andrew Pickens, Elijah Clarke, and Light Horse Harry Lee. So hated was he that a special guard was assigned to protect him while he was a prisoner of war.

Because the Ezekiel Harris House has always been considered haunted by ghosts of the Revolutionary War, Augustans long believed it to be the former Mackay Trading Post. Research during the American bicentennial, however, revealed that the Ezekiel Harris House was constructed in 1797 across the road from the old trading post, which apparently was a victim of the war.

Open to the public, the three-story Ezekiel Harris House is the finest eighteenth-century frame house in all of Georgia. Standing on the ground of the killings in September 1780, it manifests supernatural reminders of that grim incident in the Revolutionary War. Visitors often take away a sense of dread. Some have actually heard the creaking of a phantom rope that seems to be hanging from a rail on the stairway. Some reports indicate that the invisible rope sounds as if it bears the weight of a body.

Upon stepping onto the thirteenth step of the stairway, various individuals have been horrified to hear unearthly screams and moans. The eerie noises are said to represent the thirteen Patriots hanged by Colonel Brown.

A matronly ghost dressed in a shimmering white gown and bearing a white handkerchief is often encountered floating about the house. Most often, the spectre is observed on the second or third floor, gliding from room to room as if looking for someone. Over the generations, the story has been told that this is the ghost of the heartbroken mother of the Glass brothers, maintaining an eternal vigil for the teenage boys. On one occasion, the melancholy apparition made its way down the steps to a first-floor bedroom. There, its outstretched arms seemed to make a supernatural appeal to Thomas Brown for mercy for its sons.

Few incidents in Revolutionary War history can compare to the garish spectacle played out on the landscape surrounding the Ezekiel Harris House for several days in September 1780. It left a deep wound that continues to fester, as evidenced by the restless souls lingering on the old battleground in Augusta.

The **Ezekiel Harris House** is open to the public as a museum. Its address is 1822 Broad St., Augusta, Ga. 30904; the telephone number is 706-724-0436.

Other "Spirited" Revolutionary War Sites in Georgia, Briefly Noted

MIDWAY—ST. CATHERINES ISLAND

In 1765, ten years after his arrival in America, English-born Button Gwinnett acquired a plantation on St. Catherines Island, one of Georgia's famous Sea Islands. Gwinnett prospered as a planter and enmeshed himself in colonial politics as the war with England grew inevitable. Elected to the Continental Congress, he was one of Georgia's three signers of the Declaration of Independence. In fact, he was the second man to affix his name to the document, following only John Hancock. Gwinnett's signature is the first on the left side of the Declaration. Thanks in part to its rarity, his autograph is considered among the most valuable in the world, ranking just behind those of William Shakespeare and Julius Caesar. Today, Gwinnett's ghost haunts coastal Georgia as the result of a dispute and a subsequent duel during the Revolutionary War.

After signing the Declaration in Philadelphia, the fiery Georgian, anxious to take up arms against his native country, hurried south, where he assumed he would become brigadier general of the First Georgia. To the contrary, a political rival, Lachlan McIntosh, was selected.

Not to be outdone, Gwinnett served as speaker of the Georgia legislature before being elevated to president (governor) of Georgia in 1777 upon the death of the first president. During a subsequent campaign for governor, Gwinnett decided to invade the portion of eastern Florida then held by British forces. General McIntosh led the expedition, which was a calamity for the Georgians. Voters punished Gwinnett by sending him to defeat at the ballot box.

The hot blood between McIntosh and Gwinnett ended in a formal duel on Friday, May 16, 1777, near Savannah, fifty miles up the coast from St. Catherines Island. Although neither man died in the showdown, both were hurt. So serious was Gwinnett's leg wound that he succumbed three days later.

For many years, the location of his grave was unknown. It was subsequently found in Savannah's historic Colonial Cemetery. But Gwinnett's spirit left his burial spot long ago. When storm clouds cover the sky on hot summer evenings, the steady gallop of his trusted steed, Chickasaw, can be heard on the old road leading from the mainland town of Midway toward St. Catherines Island. Sometimes, a phantom horseman dressed as a colonial gentleman comes into view near the mainland shore where Gwinnett often moored his boats. Other times, a ghost ship resembling Gwinnett's schooner, *Beggar's Benison*, can be seen sailing St. Catherines Sound in the direction of his old plantation.

Midway is located at the intersection of Ga. 38 and Ga. 25. Though St. Catherines Island is privately owned by a foundation, its beaches, accessible only by boat, are open to the public.

SAVANNAH—BONAVENTURE CEMETERY

Graveyards are usually seen as spooky places. But Bonaventure Cemetery in old Savannah is a quiet, peaceful site. The ghosts lingering there from America's early history seem a happy lot.

Moss-draped trees shade the expansive graveyard, the site of the plantation house and grounds of Colonel John Mulryne. The affluent Mulryne built his great manor house in the 1750s of brick imported from Great Britain. There, his daughter married Josiah Tattnall, another wealthy resident of Savannah. Two sons, John and Josiah Jr., were born to the marriage. When war with Great Britain grew inevitable, members of the Mulryne and Tattnall families loyal to King George III sailed to England. Only Josiah Jr. stayed in Georgia to fight for American independence.

A leader in the government of the new state of Georgia, he was ultimately elected its governor. In the aftermath of the war, he threw a lavish dinner party at Bonaventure Plantation, which he then owned. Savannah's high society attended the grand soiree. During the course of the evening, a massive fire erupted in the plantation house. Governor Tattnall remained calm, directing his servants to carry the tables and food onto the grounds, where his guests dined as the conflagration consumed the house.

Cemetery visitors strolling near the site of the plantation house insist that they hear laughter and the clanging of silverware against dishes. The spirit of Josiah Tattnall, Jr., thus continues the dinner party with fellow Patriots that began so many years ago.

Bonaventure Cemetery is open to the public. Its address is 330 Bonaventure Rd., Savannah, Ga. 31402; the telephone number is 912-233-6651.

Index

Abbotts Creek, 278
Abington Social Library, 62
Adams House, 48, 49
Adams, John, 106. 110, 164, 184, 222
Adams, Samuel, 41, 48
Adirondack Mountains, 100
Admiral Farragut Inn, 81
Admiral Vernon Inne, 186
Agnes of Glasgow, 306–7
Agnew, James, 191, 192
Albany, N.Y., 95, 96
Alice Austen House Museum, 113
Allen, Catherine, 154
Allen, Ethan, 13–15, 16, 17, 74, 85, 86
Allen, Zachariah, 154
Allens Lane, 189
Alliance, 215
Alloway Creek, 152
Alston, Philip, 262–67
Alston, Temperance Smith, 263, 265
Altoona, Pa., 182
American Philosophical Society, 166, 167
Anderson, John, 90
Anderson, Katherine, 248
André, John: arrested as spy, 121; at Battle of Bran-
   dywine, 170; biographical information, 89–92;
   at Cooch's Bridge, 204; as a ghost, xii, 92, 188;
   quoted, 73, 74, 170; relationship with Peggy Ship-
   pen Arnold, 164
Annapolis, Md., 211–19
Antiquarian and Landmarks Society, 58
Apthorp House, 48–49
Aquidneck Island, 73, 74, 76
Armstrong, John, 169
Arnold, Benedict: as an American traitor, 89–91, 92,
   118; biographical information, 67; at Fort Stan-
   wix, 119; at Fort Ticonderoga, 14, 17; as a ghost,
   xii, 67, 163, 164, 165; rumored to be grandfather
   of Edgar Allan Poe, 187; in Virginia, 213
Arnold, Hannah Waterman King, 67
Arnold, Peggy Shippen, 90, 163, 164
Articles of Capitulation, 238
Articles of Confederation, 199
Asgill, Charles, 136
Ashland, Va., 225, 226, 228
Atlantic City, N.J., 151
Attucks, Crispus, 48
Augusta, Ga., 322–27
Austen, Alice, 113
Avery County, N.C., 281
Ayers-Allen House, 154–55

Bacon, John, 154
Baltimore, Md., 219
Bancroft Hall, 216
Bannister, John, 74

Barker's Bloody Brook, 77
Barnegat Shoals, 154
Barrow, John W., 274
Barrows, Jemina, 69
Barry, Andrew, 302
Barry, Catherine "Kate" Moore, 301, 302, 303
Barton, William, 74, 75
Basking Ridge, N.J., 133
Batsto, N.J., 152, 156
Battle Road, 41
Bear Mountain, 111
Bear Mountain State Park, 111
Beaverdam, Va., 228
Bedford County, Pa., 184
Beggar's Benison, 329
Belleville Dutch Reformed Church, 148
Belleville, N.J., 148
Belmont, N.C., xii
Belmont Hall, 206–7
Bemis Heights, 96
Bennington, Vt., 19, 20, 33, 221
Bennington Monument, 19
Bensalem, Pa., 183–84
Bentley Manor, 105
Benton, Daniel, 69
Benton, Elisha, 69
Bergen County, N.J., 139
Berkeley Country Club, 312
Berkshires, 49
Bernardsville, N.J., 148–49
Bernardsville Public Library, 148–49
Betsy Ross House, 166–67
Bickley, Robert, 183
Billop, Christopher, 105, 106–9
Billop House, 105, 106
Biltmore Hotel Building, 115
Birmingham Meeting House, 169–70
Black, Kenneth, 264
Black Snake, 135
Blackledge-Kearney House, 153
Blacksburg, S.C., 261
Blackstock's Battlefield Historic Site, 289, 291
Blackstock's Plantation, 288, 290
Bloody Pond, 111
Blue Ridge Mountains, 281
Blue Ridge Parkway, 277
Bobo's Mills, S.C., 304
Bonaventure Cemetery, 329–30
Bonaventure Plantation, 330
Bonhomme Richard, 215
Boston Common, 47
Boston Freedom Trail, 47, 48
Boston Gazette, 198
Boston Harbor, 4
Boston, Mass., 4, 41, 42, 47–48, 61
Boston Massacre, 47–48
Boston Tea Party, 8
Botetourt County, Va., 242

Boudinet, Elisha, 105
Boy Scouts, 138, 139, 142
Boyer, Hans, 191
Braddock, Edward, xx–xxi
Bradshaw, Wesley, xxiii
Brandywine, Battle of, xiii, 168–72, 199, 205
Brandywine Battlefield Historic Site, 172
Brandywine River, 168–72
Brandywine Valley, 171
Bratton, William, 304
Brattonsville, S.C., 304
Breeds Hill, 49, 59
Brest, France, 293
Briar Creek, Ga., 263
Bronx, N.Y., 117
Brooklyn, Conn., 59, 62–63
Brooklyn Navy Yard, 112
Brooklyn, N.Y., 112
Brown Mountain, 276–77
Brown Mountain Lights, 276–77
Brown, Thomas, 322–27
Bryan, Alexander, 94–99
Bryan, John, 97
Buck, Jonathan, 10
Buckeystown, Md., 219, 220
Bucks County, Pa., 188
Bucksport Cemetery, 10
Bucksport, Maine, 10
Buffin, Esther, 27
Bull, William, 294
Bunker Hill, Battle of, 49–50, 61
Bunker Hill Monument, 47, 49–50
Burgoyne, John "Gentleman Johnny": at Battles of
    Saratoga, 31, 95, 96, 102, 119; at Fort Ticond-
    eroga, 86; as a ghost, xii, 49, 50; headquartered at
    Fort Edward, 112; headquartered at Skenesbor-
    ough, 102; operations at Lake Champlain, 102;
    operations in Vermont, 19; quoted, 100; troops
    imprisoned at Camp Security, 193
Burgwin, John, 273–74
Burgwin-Wright House, 273–75
Burke County, N.C., 276
Burlington, N.J., 157
Burlington, Vt., 13, 15, 16
Burr, Aaron, 114–15, 116, 188
Burwell, Rebecca, 245
Bush River, 304, 305, 306
Butterick, John, 44
Buttermilk Hill, 118
Byram, Phyllis Parker, 148–49

Caesar, Julius, 328
Caldwell, Hannah, 149–50
Caldwell, James, 149
Caldwell, John, 301
Caldwell, William, 300
Cambridge, Mass., 48–49, 61
Camden, Battle of, 306

Camden County, N.C., 277
Camden, S.C., 257, 306, 307
Camp Glen Gray, 138, 141–43
Camp Security, 193
Campbell, Archie, 311–12
Campbell, Duncan, 86, 87
Campbell, Margaret Pauline "Miss Polly" Philips,
    311–12
Campbell, William, 268–69
Canada, 3, 14, 17, 18, 38–39, 85, 86, 92, 96, 114, 178
Cane Creek, 310
Cannonball Trail, 139, 140
Canton, Conn., 64–65
Cape Fear River, 275
Capitol Building (former Virginia), 246–47
Capitol Building (national), 6
Carden, John, 310
Carnegie Abbey Golf Club, 77
Carolina Road, 233, 234
Carpenter, Lydia, 57
Carroll, Charles, 219, 220
Carrollton Manor, 219, 220
Carter's Grove Plantation, 245
Cary, Mary, 245
Castine, Battle of, 3–5
Castine, Maine, 3–5
Castle Hill, 242, 243
Caswell, Richard, 263, 265
Catawba River, xii, 269, 279
Catherine II, 215
Chadds Ford, Pa., 168–72, 205
Chamberlain, Joshua, xxv–xxvi
Champlain, Lake, 13, 14, 20, 85, 86, 100, 102
Charlemont Inn, 49
Charlemont, Mass., 49
Charleston, S.C., 292, 293, 294, 295, 296, 305, 306,
    308, 311
Charlestown, Mass., 42, 49–50
Charlestown, N.H., 33
Charlotte, N.C., xii, 261
Charlottesville, Va., 242, 243, 244
Cherbourg, France, 216
Cherokee Indians, 324, 326
Chesapeake Bay, 169, 211
Chew, Benjamin, 190
Christ Church Burial Ground, 166, 167
Chronicle, William, xii
Church of St. Andrew Cemetery, 114
Clark, William, 221
Clarke, Elijah, 322, 324, 325, 326
Cleveland, Benjamin, 255–57, 258, 260, 261
Cleveland, Robert, 256
Clinton, Henry, 80, 91, 111, 128, 129, 131, 136, 152,
    234, 259, 311
Clinton, S.C., 291
Cliveden Manor, 190
Closter Landing, 153
Coates, Nancy, 88

Cole, Julia Weeks, 92

College of William and Mary, 247–48

Collins, Thomas, 207

Colonel Jack Martin's Rock House, 282–83

Colonial Cemetery, 319, 321, 329

Colonial Inn, 44–46

Colonial National Historical Park, 241, 250, 251, 252

Colonial Williamsburg, 246, 247, 249

Columbia, S.C., 305

Common Man Restaurant, 33–34

Conanicut Island, 80

Concord, Battle of, 44

Concord Common, 50

Concord, Mass., 38, 41, 42, 43, 44–46

Concord River, 44

Concord Town Hall, 44

Conference House, 105–6, 107–10

Conference House Park, 107, 109

Connecticut: as birthplace of Alexander Bryan, 94; haunted sites in, 55–69; Philip Skene incarcerated in, 102

Connecticut Farms, 149

Continental Army: aided by Anthony Wayne, 179; aided by Benedict Arnold, 67, 90, 164; aided by Benjamin Cleveland, 256; aided by Betty Wert, 145; aided by Daniel Benton's grandsons, 69; aided by Henry Galbreath, 305; aided by Israel Putnam, 61; aided by Jacky Custis, 251; aided by James Caldwell, 8; aided by John Habersham, 318; aided by Joseph Habersham, 319; aided by Nathan Hale's brothers, 57; aided by William Barton, 12, aided by Fielding Lewis, 230; Batsto as a supply center for, 18; at the Battle of Monmouth, 128, 131; at the Battle of Rhode Island, 78; crosses Delaware River, 135; defeated at Brandywine, 168, 170; fights as a national unit, 203; at Fort Mifflin, 191; George Washington appointed as commander of, 165; iron products produced for, 126; Nathan Hale enlists in, 56; retreats into Pennsylvania, 134; uniforms of, 88; uses Cannonball Trail 138; at Valley Forge, 173, 174, 176

Continental Congress: actions of regarding Charles Lee, 132, 133; appoints delegates to Peace Conference, 106; authorizes construction of Camp Security, 183; confiscates private property, 33; controversies among members of, 197; delegates to, 182, 198, 199, 218, 225, 226, 246, 293, 319, 328; demands to for execution of Cornwallis, 293; Ethan Allen acts on behalf of, 14; Massachusetts fails to consult with, 9; reluctance to accept Vermont as a state, 15

Continental Navy, 25, 26

Cooch House, 204

Cooch's Bridge, 202, 204, 205

Cook, Benjamin, 75

Cook, Kittymouse, 75

Corbin, Mary, 130

Cornwallis Cave, 249–50

Cornwallis, Lord: at Abbotts Creek, 278; aided by Banastre Tarleton, 288; association with James Agnew, 191; at Battle of Brandywine, 169, 170, 171; at Battle of Guilford Courthouse, 268, 269; at Battle of Monmouth, 129; chases George Washington, 153; at Cooch's Bridge, 204; at Cowan's Ford, 279; as a ghost, xii, 153; plans invasion of North Carolina, 257; quoted, 235, 268, 287; relationship with Patrick Ferguson, 255, 258; retreats into Virginia from North Carolina, 15; threatened with execution, 293; troops of imprisoned at Camp Security, 193; at Wilmington, N.C., 273, 273, 275; at Yorktown, 212, 248, 250, 251, 252

Cornwall, England, 15

Country House Restaurant, 120

Coventry, Conn., 55, 57, 58

Coventry, R.I., 79

Cowan's Ford, 269, 279

Cowan's Ford, Battle of, xii, 269

Cowpens, Battle of, 213, 302, 305, 307, 308

Cowpens National Battlefield, 307–8

Cowperwaithe, Nathaniel, 152

Craven Hall, 192–93

Crooked Billet, Battle of, 192

Cross Anchor, S.C., 287, 291

Crown Point, 101, 102

Cruger, John, 325

Cumberland Island, 79

Cunningham, William "Bloody Bill," 300–303

Custis, Eleanor Parke, xx

Custis, John "Jacky" Parke, 250–51

D'Agostino Residence Hall, 114

Dana Auditorium, 270–71

Danbury, Conn., 68

Daniel Benton Homestead, 69

Davidson County, N.C., 278

Davidson, William Lee, 279

Dawes, William, 42

Dayton, Elias, 118

Declaration of Independence: John Dickinson refuses to sign, 197, 199; Richard Henry seeks adoption of, 246; signed in Philadelphia, 56, 163, 165, 166, 219, 247; signers of, 33, 48, 145, 188, 218, 219, 251, 318, 328; Thomas Jefferson as author of, 244

Deep River, 263

Delaplace, William, 14

Delaware, 197–207

Delaware River, 135, 144, 152, 155, 183, 187, 191

Destouches, Charles René Dominique, 213

Detroit, 179

Dey Mansion, 159–60

Dey, Theunis, 159

Dickinson, John, 197–98, 207

Dismal Swamp Canal Welcome Center, 277

Dobbs, Arthur, 273

Dogue Run, xx
Donop, Emil von, 155
Dover, Del., 197, 198, 201, 206
Duck Creek, 207
Dudley Case's Tavern, 64
Dumpling Rock, 80
Dunbar, Moses, 68
Duncan, Douglas, 261
Duncan, James, 261
Dundas, Thomas, 238
Dunmore, Lord, 249
Dzhones, Pavel, 215

East Amwell Township, N.J., 144
East Granby, Conn., 65
Eden, Robert, 219
Edgecombe County, N.C., 278–79
Elizabeth, N.J., 149, 150
Elizabeth River, 277
Elizabethtown, N.J., 199
Elk Forge Bed and Breakfast, 220
Elk River, 202, 220
Elkton, Md., 203, 220
Emerson, Ralph Waldo, 41
Englishtown, N.J., 150
Erie County History Center, 181
Erie, Pa., 179, 180–81
Erskine, Robert, 125–27
Estaing, Charles, 77
Ethan Allen Homestead, 16
Exeter, N.H., 30
Exeter Plantation, 311–12
Ezekiel Harris House, 322, 326, 327

Fabius, 199
Fagen Gang, 150
Fallen Timbers, Battle of, 179
Fanning, David, 262, 263, 264–65
Farm, The, 243
Farmingdale, N.J., 150–51
Fenton, Lewis, 150, 151
Ferguson, Patrick, xxii, 255, 257, 261
Fergusson, Elizabeth "Maggie" Graeme, 185–86
Fergusson, Henry Hugh, 185–86
Ferry Farm, 230
First National Bank of the United States, 190–91
First Presbyterian Church (Huntington, N.Y.), 113
First Presbyterian Church Cemetery (Elizabeth, N.J.), 149, 150
Fish Dam Ford, 287, 288
Flamborough Head, Battle of, 214
Florida, 301, 323, 329
Fort Andrew, 38
Fort Black Rock, 66
Fort Carillon, 86, 87
Fort Defiance, 88
Fort Duquesne, xxi
Fort Edward, 87, 95, 112

Fort George, 3–5
Fort George State Memorial, 3, 5
Fort Golgotha, 113
Fort Lafayette, 180
Fort Mercer, 155
Fort Mifflin, 141
Fort Nathan Hale, 66
Fort Number Four Reconstruction, 33
Fort Ontario, 117
Fort Ontario State Historic Site, 117
Fort Presque Isle, 179
Fort Roberdeau, 182
Fort Roberdeau Historic Site, 182
Fort Stanwix, 116, 118–19
Fort Stanwix National Monument, 118–19
Fort Ticonderoga, 14, 17, 20, 85–88, 101
Fort Ticonderoga National Historic Landmark, 86, 88
Fort Washington, 57, 130
Fort Wetherill, 80
Fort Wetherill State Park, 80
Fox, Charles James, 268
Franklin, Benjamin: at Annapolis, Md., 212; as delegate to the Peace Conference, 106, 110; as father of William Franklin, 136, 185; as a ghost, xii, 163, 165–66, 184; at Merion, Pa., 87; Philadelphia as his home, 89, 164, 165; prewar association with Anthony Wayne, 178; quoted, 125, 163
Franklin, Deborah, 166
Franklin, William, 136, 185
Frederick County, Md., 219
Frederick, Md., 220, 221
Fredericksburg Arms Manufactory, 230
Fredericksburg, Va., 229, 230, 232, 244, 245
Freeman, Douglas Southall, 62
Freeman, John, 119
Freeman's Farm, 96, 119
Freeman's Farm, Battle of, 119
French and Indian War, 14, 28, 38, 60, 134
French, William, 21–22

Gabriel Davies Tavern, 151
Gaffney, S.C., 307, 308
Gage, Thomas, 42
Galbreath, Henry, 305
Garret Mountain Reservation, 156
Gates, Horatio, 49, 94, 95, 96, 133, 268, 306
General Arnold, 39
General Warren Inn, 186–87
General Wayne Inn, 187
Georgia, xi, 289, 317–30
George, Lake, 85, 86
George School, 188
George II, 158
George III, 153, 215, 300, 323, 330
George Washington Association, 231
George Wythe House, 248
Georgetown, S.C., 308, 309

Germantown, Battle of, 190, 191
Gettysburg, Pa., xxv–xxvi
Glascock, George, 265, 266
Glass, Tom, 325, 326
Glass, Will, 325, 326
Glendora, N.J., 151
Glocester County, Va., 229
Goose Creek, S.C., 311
Goose River, 6–9
Goose River Bridge, 7, 8, 9
Graeme Park, 185, 186
Graeme, Thomas, 185
Granary Burying Ground, 47–48
Graves, Stephen, 68
Great Bay, 151, 152, 156
Great Dismal Swamp, 277
Great Falls of the Passaic, 156
Great Pee Dee River, 312
Green Hand Bridge, 310–11
Green Mount Cemetery, 15
Green Mountain Boys, 14
Green Mountains, 13
Greene, Christopher, 155
Greene, Nathanael: at Battle of Brandywine, 169, 170; at Battle of Guilford Courthouse, 268, 269, 270, 272; at Battle of Rhode Island, 77; at Charlotte, xii; commands final stages of war in the South, 182, 235; as a ghost, xii, 79; at Hobkirk's Hill, 307; at Hunt House, 145; at Ninety Six, 287, 298; pursued by Cornwallis in North Carolina, 278; at Valley Forge, 174
Greenfield Mansion, 242
Greensboro, N.C., 268, 272
Grey, Charles, 186
Growden, Joseph, 183–84
Growden Manor. See Trevose Manor
Grumblethorpe, 191–92
Guilford College, 270–72
Guilford County, N.C., 269
Guilford Courthouse, 268, 269, 270, 272
Guilford Courthouse, Battle of, 213, 265, 268–70, 272
Guilford Courthouse National Military Park, 272
Gurnet Point Lighthouse, 37–40
Gurnet Point, Mass., 37–40
Gwinnett, Button, 318, 328–29

Habersham, James, Jr., 317–21
Habersham, James, Sr., 317, 318
Habersham, John, 318, 319
Habersham, Joseph, 318, 319
Haldimand, Frederick, 102
Hale Homestead, 55, 57, 58
Hale, John, 58
Hale, Joseph, 57, 58
Hale, Nathan, 55–58, 89, 115
Hale, Richard, 55, 57, 58
Hale, Sarah, 58

Halifax County, N.C., 263
Halifax, N.C., 263
Hamilton, Alexander, 39, 114, 116, 138, 139–40, 156, 160, 190, 191
Hammonton, N.J., 157
Hampton, N.H., 28–32
Hampton Roads, Va., 245
Hampton, Wade, 289
Hancock, John, 6, 41, 42, 48, 328
Hancock, William, 153
Hancock's Bridge, N.J., 152, 153
Handy, Hannah, 21
Hanging Rock, 310
Hanging Rock, Battle of, 310
Hanging Rock Mountain, 282, 283
Hanging Rock State Park, 283
Hanover County, Va., 226
Harpswell, Maine, 7
Hart, John, 145
Harvard University, 49, 247
Haverstraw, N.Y., 90
Hayne Affair, 292
Hayne, Isaac, 292–96
Hays, John, 129
Hays, Mary Ludwig, 129
Haywood, Marshall DeLancey, 256
Heath Springs, S.C., 310
Henning House, 308
Henry Overing House, 74
Henry, Patrick, xi, xii, 3, 225–28, 246, 247
Henry, Sarah Shelton, 226–28
Herkimer, Nicholas, 116, 117
Hesse-Kassel, Germany, 77
Hessian Barracks, 220–21
Hessian Hole, 77
Hessian Lake, 111
Hessians: in American folklore, 202; at Battle of Bennington, 19, 20; at Battle of Brandywine, 168, 172; at Battle of Guilford Courthouse, 270; at Battle of Monmouth, 129; at Battle of Red Bank, 155; at Cooch's Bridge, 204; ghosts of, xii, 51, 69, 77, 111, 131, 155, 188, 221; imprisoned at Camp Security, 193; imprisoned at Frederick, Md., 220; at Trenton, 134–35
Hesston, Pa., 184–85
High Rock Spring, 97
Highfields, 144
Hillman Hospital House, 151
Hillyard, Charles, 206
His Royal Highness' Black Watch Brigade, 87
Historic Brattonsville, 304
HMS Niger, 38
Hobkirk's Hill, 307
Honeyman, John, 134–35, 137
Hopewell Presbyterian Church, 279
Horsham, Pa., 185, 186
Horton, John, 21
Hosford Tavern, 64–65

Hosmer, Joseph, 44
House in the Horseshoe, 262, 263, 264, 265, 266, 267
House in the Horseshoe State Historic Site, 262, 267
Houston, John, 318
Howe, Ezekial, 50
Howe, Richard, 106
Howe, William, 56, 77, 112, 118, 133, 168, 169, 202–3
Howe's Tavern, 50
Huck, Christian 304
Huck's Defeat, 304
Huddy, Joshua, 135–37
Hudson Highlands, 61
Hudson Palisades, 153
Hudson River, 90, 91, 95, 96, 111, 112, 153
Hudson Valley, 96
Hunt House, 145
Hunt, Jonathan, 50
Huntdale, N.C., 280
Huntersville, N.C., 279
Huntington, N.Y., 113
Hutchins, William, 5

Independence Hall, xxiii, 165, 166
Independence, Mount, 20–21, 86, 87
Irving, Washington, 202
Island Beach State Park, 154
Israel Putnam Monument, 63

Jackson, Andrew, 282
Jacob Whittemore House, 43
Jacob's Run, 275
James City County, Va., 245
James Monroe Law Office and Museum, 244
James River, 245
Jamestown, R.I., 80
Jefferson, Thomas: at Annapolis, 212; at Charlottesville, 242, 243, 244; as a ghost, xii, 222; kinship with Peyton Randolph, 249; proposes marriage to Rebecca Burwell, 245; quoted, 28, 37, 211, 255, 259, 273
Jeffries Ford, 169
Jenkins, Walter, 281
Jerome, Chauncey, 68
Jersey Devil, 156–57
John Dickinson House, 200
John Hancock's Bridge, 152–53
John Paul Jones House Museum, 26–27
John Roberts House, 188, 189
John Yorke House, 66–67
Johnson, Ebenezer, 68
Jones, David, 112
Jones, John Paul, 25–26, 27, 214, 215–16, 217
Jones, Joseph, 312
Joseph Ambler Inn, 188, 189
Jouett, Jack, 243

Judge William Hancock House, 153
Jumel, Elisha, 115
Jumel, Stephen, 115

Katherine, 102
Keith House, 185–86
Keith, William, 185
Kenmore, 230–32
Kenmore Association. See George Washington Association
King George's War, 28
Kings Mountain, 255, 258, 261
Kings Mountain, Battle of, 255, 258–59, 269, 280
Kings Mountain National Military Park, 258–59, 261
Knitting Betty's Rock, 145, 146, 147
Knyphausen, Wilhelm, 149, 169, 170
Kolb, Abel, 312–13

Lafayette, Marquis de: at Annapolis, 212; arrives in America, 308; at Battle of Brandywine, 169; at Dey Mansion, 160; ghost of, 163, 213; at Great Falls of the Passaic, 156; at Hunt House, 145; kinship with Viscount de Noailles, 238; lays cornerstone at Bunker Hill Monument, 49; at Merion, Pa., 187; at Newport, R.I., 81; at Philadelphia, 164; pursued by Cornwallis, 234; quoted, 234, 237, 249; quotes Washington, 129; selected as member of John André tribunal, 90; at Wilmington, Del., 203
Lancaster County, S.C., 310
Langdon, John, 26
Langdon, Woodbury, 26
Laurel, Md., 221–22
Laurens, John, 238
LeBlanc, Oscar, 248
Lee, Charles, 74, 129, 132–33, 134, 137, 145, 150
Lee, Henry III, 246, 326
Lee, Richard Henry "Light Horse Harry," 245–46
Lee, Robert E., 245–46
Leed's Point, N.J., 156
Leesburg, Va., 234, 236
"Legend of Sleepy Hollow, The," 202
Legion of the United States, 179
"Letters from a Farmer," 198
Lewis, Elizabeth "Betty" Washington, 230, 231
Lewis, Fielding, 229–32
Lewis, Meriwether, 221, 243
Lewis, Nicolas, 243
Lexington and Concord, Battles of, 38, 41–46, 145
Lexington, Mass., 38, 41, 42–43, 44, 60
Liberty, 102
Liberty Boys, 318, 323, 325
"Liberty Song, The," 197, 198
Lincoln, Benjamin, xii, 39, 293, 311
Lincoln County, N.C., xii
Lindbergh, Charles, 144, 145
Linville Falls, 277

Linville Gorge, 277
Lippincott, Richard, 136
Little Egg Harbor, 154
Little Round Top, xxv–xxvi
Logan Inn, 187, 188
Long Beach Massacre, 154
Long Island, Battle of, 112
Long Island, N.Y., 56, 89–93, 106, 120
Long Island Sound, 117
Longfellow, Henry Wadsworth, 4
Longfellow's Wayside Inn, 50
Lossing, Benjamin, 310
Loudoun County, Va., 233, 234
Louis XVI, 215
Lumber River, 281
Lumber River State Park, 281
Lumber River Swamp, 281
Lutwyche, Edward Goldstone, 33

Mackay Trading Post, 322, 324, 325, 326
Magog, Quebec, 18
Mahwah, N.J., 138, 143
Maine, xii, xxvi, 3–10
Malvern, Pa., 186, 187
Marriner's Tavern, 150
Marion, Francis, 281, 287, 308, 312
Martin, John "Jack," 282–83
Mary Post Inn, 139, 140
Mary Post Maple, 141–42
Mary Post Road, 139
Mary Washington House, 244–45
Maryland, 202, 211–22, 234
Maryland School of the Deaf, 220–21
Mashamoquet Brook State Park, 62–63
Massachusetts, 3, 4, 37–52, 133, 145
Master of Ballantrae, The, 86
Maxwell, William, 169, 203, 204
McConnells, S.C., 304
McCrea, Jane, 112
McDonnell, Carlton, 139–40
McDougald, Joan, 281
McIntosh, Lachlan, 329
McKean, Thomas, 199, 207
McLane, Allan, 207
McLean, Francis, 4
McNeil, Sarah, 112
McPherson, Angus, 306–7
Meadville, Pa., 178
Memphremagog, Lake, 17–18
Merion, Pa., 187
Merrimack, N.H., 33–34
Metuchen, N.J., 154–55
Middleton Tavern, 211, 212, 213
Middletown, R.I., 76
"Midnight Ride of Paul Revere, The," 4
Midway, Ga., 328, 329
Miles Brewton House, 295
Miles, Charity, 305–6

Miles, David, 305
Miles, Esther, 305
Millbank, 230
Miller, Charles, Sr., 203
Miller, Charlie, Jr., 203, 204, 205
Minot, Timothy, 44–46
Minuteman National Historical Park, 43, 46
Mitchell County, N.C., 280
"Molly Pitcher." See Hays, Mary Ludwig
Moncks Corner, S.C., 311–12
Monmouth, Battle of, 128–31, 132, 133, 145, 146
Monmouth Battlefield State Park, 129, 130, 131
Monmouth, N.J., 128–31
Monroe, James, 212, 244
Monticello, 244
Montpelier Mansion, 221–22
Moore, Augustine, 238
Moore, Augustine, Jr., 238–39
Moore, Charles, 300, 302
Moore County, N.C., 262, 266
Moore, Edwin Coutant, 164
Moore House, 238–41
Moore, Mary, 300, 302
Morgan, Daniel, 119, 302, 305, 307, 308
Morganton, N.C., 277
Morris Jumel Mansion, 114–15
Morris, Roger, 114
Morristown, N.J., 126, 139
Mortlake Commons, 63
Mortlake District, 60
Mortlake Manor, 62
Moulton, Abigail, 29–32
Moulton House, 32
Moulton, Jonathan, 28–31
Moulton, Sarah Henry, 29–31
Mount Hope Bay, 74
Mount Independence State Historic Site, 20–21
Mount Vernon, xx
Mud Island Fort, 191
Muhlenberg, Peter, 175
Mullica River, 151–52, 157
Mulliner, Joe, 157
Mulryne, John, 330
Musgrove Mill State Historic Site, 291
Myrtle Beach, S.C., 308

Narragansett Bay, 76
Nassau Hall, 158, 159
Nathan Hale Homestead, 55, 58
Nathanael Greene Homestead, 80
National Park, N.J., 155
National Park Service, 165, 239, 240, 252, 298
National Trust for Historic Preservation, 193
National Tribune, xxiii
Navesink Highlands, 132, 133, 134, 135, 136, 137
Nelson House, 251–52
Nelson, Thomas, Jr. 238, 251–52
New Brunswick, Canada, 107

New England, 15, 38, 90
New Garden, 270
New Hampshire, xi, 13, 15, 23–34
New Haven, Conn., 66, 80
New Hope, Pa., 187, 188
New Jersey: border with New York, 91; Christopher Billop imprisoned in, 107; Continental troops from, 297; haunted sites in, 125–60; James Habersham, Jr., dies in, 318; troops from fight in South Carolina, 297; wartime prisons in, 105; William Franklin as governor of, 136, 185
New London, Conn., 56
New London Inn, 34
"New Wife and the Old, The," 31–32
New York: border with Massachusetts, 51, 52; border with New Jersey, 125; governed by William Tryon, 61, 68; haunted sites in, 85–121; Patrick Ferguson arrives in, 257; as site of Battles of Saratoga, 31; troops in South Carolina, 297
New York City, N.Y.: Ethan Allen paroled at, 15; haunted sites in, 105–10, 112, 113, 114, 115, 116; Joshua Huddy imprisoned at, 136; Mary Post visits, 139; Nathan Hale executed at, 56; occupied by British forces, 89, 139
New York Supreme Court, 103
New York University, 114
Newark, Del., 202, 204, 205
Newberry, S.C., 306
Newport, R.I., 74, 75, 76, 80, 81, 82
Newport, Vt., 18
Newtown, Pa., 188
Ninety Six National Historic Site, 298, 299
Ninety Six, S.C., 297, 299, 324
Noailles, Louis Marie de, 238
Noland, Philip, 233–35
Noland's Ferry, 234
Nolichucky River, 280
Nolichucky Settlement, 281
North Carolina, 203, 255–83
North Egremont, Mass., 51
North, Lord Frederick, 101, 269
North Stonington, Conn., 66–67
North Wales, Pa., 188–89
Northampton, Mass., 50
Northwest Indian War, 179
Norwich, Conn., 67
Nova Scotia, Canada, 4

Oganquit, 10
Oganquit Playhouse, 10
Ohio, 179, 180
Old Albany Turnpike, 64, 65
Old Burial Hill Cemetery, 113
Old Burying Ground, 20
Old City Hall, 221
Old Exchange and Provost Dungeon, 294, 296
Old New-Gate Prison, 65–66
Old North Bridge, 44

Old North Church, 42
Old Norwichtown Cemetery, 67
Old State House, 48
Old Taft Tavern, 51
Old Tennent Church, 130, 136
Olde Bryan Inn, 94, 97–99
Olde Pink House, 317–21
Oneida Indians, 116
Ordre du Mérite Militaire, 215
Oriskany, 116–17
Oriskany Battlefield State Historic Site, 117
Oriskany Creek, 116
Orwell, Vt., 21
Oswego, N.Y., 117
Oswego River, 117
Our House Restaurant, 150–51
Overmountain Men, 257
Oyster Bay, N.Y., 89, 92, 93

Paca House, 218
Paca, William, 218
Paine, Robert Treat, 48
Paine, Thomas, 132, 144
Palisades Parks Conservancy, 153
Palmer, Nathan, 61
Paoli Massacre, 186
Papillault, Capitan, 216
Papillault, Georges, 216
Paris, France, 214, 215, 216
Parker, John, 42
Passaic River, 156
Paterson, N.J., 156
Patriot's Park, 120–21
Paul Revere House, 47
Paulding, John, 90, 121
Pawtuxet River, 80
Peace Conference, 106
Peale, Charles Willson, 218
Pearl Harbor, 5
Pelham Dale, 117–18
Pelham Manor, N.Y., 117–18
Pell, David J., 118
Pell's Point, Battle of, 118
Pen Ryn, 183
Pendennis Castle, 15
Penn Common, 193–94
Pennsylvania: as birthplace of Anthony Wayne, 17; border with New Jersey, 144; Continental troops deployed in Delaware, 203; haunted sites in, 163–94; as home of John Honeyman, 134; legislature of, 198; ratifies U.S. Constitution, 200
Pennsylvania Supreme Court, 190
Penn, William, 192
Penobscot Bay, 3, 4
Penobscot Mountains, 8
Peronneau House, 295
Peronneau, Mary Hayne, 294, 295
Perth Amboy, N.J., 106, 107

Peyton Randolph House, 248–49
Phi Beta Kappa, 247
Philadelphia, Pa.: as American capital, 106; captured by British forces, 168, 185; haunted sites in, 163–67, 189–92; as home of Continental Congress, 198, 212, 225; as home of John Honeyman, 134; Howe's movements on, 169, 203; as important port, 101, 151, 155; John Dickinson practices law in, 198; occupied by British forces, 89, 128, 189; proximity to Merion, Pa., 187; proximity to Radnor, Pa., 178; proximity to Valley Forge, 174
Philadelphia Press, 175
Phillips' Rangers Monument, 184, 185
Phillips, William, 184–85
Pickens, Andrew, 287, 326
Pigot, Robert, 77
Pine Barrens, 152, 156–57
Piper, John, 185
Pitcairn, John, 42
Pittsburgh, Pa., 179, 180
Pleasantville, N.Y., 118
Plumtree, N.C., 280–81
Plymouth Bay, 37, 38
Poe, Edgar Allan, 187
Police Plaza, 116
Pollard, Mary, 288
Pomfret, Conn., 62
Poplar Hall, 200
Port Monmouth, N.J., 158
Porter, Horace, 216
Portsmouth Naval Yard, 25
Portsmouth, N.H., 25–27
Portsmouth, R.I., 73, 74, 76–78
Post, Mary, 138–42
Potomac River, xx, 233, 245
Potter, Joseph, 103
Potts, Isaac, 176
Powel House, 164–65
Powel, Samuel, 164
Preakness Valley, 159
Prescott Farm, 73
Prescott Farm Restoration, 74–75
Prescott, Richard, 73–75
Prescott, Samuel, 42
Preservation of Virginia Antiquities, 227
President's Home, 247
Preston, William, 242
Prince, Ebenezer, 113
Princeton, Battle of, 159–59
Princeton, N.J., 147, 158–59, 318
Princeton University, 158–59
Purcell, Gregory, 26
Purcell, Sarah Wentworth, 26, 27
Putnam, Daniel, 60
Putnam, Israel, 49, 59–63
Putnam, Joseph, 59

Quaker Cemetery, 307

Quebec City, Canada, 134
Queen's Rangers, 91–92, 152

Radnor, Pa., 178, 181
Rall, Johann, 134
Ramapo Mountains, 138, 139, 141
Ramseur's Mill, Battle of, xxii
Ramsey, David, 294
Randolph, Elizabeth, 249
Randolph, Peyton, 248
Ranger, 26
Rappahannock River, 230
Raritan Bay, 132, 146
"Raven, The," 187
Rawdon, Francis, 292, 293, 294, 295, 298, 307
Raynham Hall, 89, 91–93
Reason: The Only Oracle of Man, 15
Red Bank, Battle of, 155
Red Bank Battlefield, 155
Red Hawk, xxii, xxvi
Redding Ridge, Conn., 68
"Refusal Room," 245
Revere, Paul, 4, 42, 48, 152
Rhode Island, 73–82, 277
Rhode Island, Battle of, 77
Richardson, Ned, 282
Richardson, William, 6–9
Richmond, Va., 225, 246
Ringwood Manor, 125–27
Ringwood Manor State Park, 126
Ringwood, N.J., 125, 127
Rising Sun, 305
Ritchie, William, 301
River Edge, N.J., 159
Riverfront Park, 279
Roberdeau, Daniel, 182
Robert E. Lee Memorial Association, Inc., 246
Roberts, John, 189
Robeson County, N.C., 281
Robin Hood, 157
Rochambeau, Comte de, 81, 127, 249
Rockingham Hotel, 27
Rockport, Maine, 6–9
Rodney, Caesar, 207
Roebuck, 260
Roebuck, S.C., 300, 303
Rogues Road, 234
Rome, N.Y., 116, 118, 119
Ronda, N.C., 255, 257, 260, 261
Ross, Alexander, 238
Ross, Betsy, xii, 163, 166, 167
Roughedge, N.C., 282
Rowan, Robert, 262, 263
Royal Navy, 4, 38, 77
Royalton Raid, 21
Royalton, Vt., 21
Russian navy, 215
Rutledge, Edward, 106, 110

Saddle River, 125
Saint John, Canada, 107
Saint Louis Cemetery, 216
Salem, Mass., 59
Salisbury Road, 270
Saltonstall, Dudley, 4
Sandy Hook Bay, 132, 136, 169
Sanford, N.C., 267
Saratoga, Battles of, 49, 51, 86, 94, 95–96, 102, 221
Saratoga National Historic Park, 119
Saratoga Springs, N.Y., 94, 97, 99
Savannah, Ga., 317–21, 329–30
Schuylkill River, 124
Scotchtown, 226–28
Scott, Charles, 128
Scott, Upton, 219
Sears Weatherbeater paint, 26
Serapis, 215
Serle, Ambrose, 77
Sessions House, 50
Seventy-Fourth Regiment of Foot (Argyle Highlanders), 4
Severn River, 211
Sevier, James, 280
Sevier, John, 258, 259, 280
Sevier, Robert, 280–81
Seymour, George, 57, 58
Shelby, Isaac, 258
Shelton, Sarah. See Henry, Sarah Shelton
Sherman, Anthony, xxiii
Shippen, Peggy. See Arnold, Peggy Shippen
Shipwright Street, 219
Simcoe, John Graves, 91, 92, 152
Simmoneau, Pierre François, 215
Sinnipink Lake, 111
Sir Christopher Wren Building, 247
Skene, Katherine, 100, 101, 102, 103–4
Skene Manor, 104
Skene Mountain, 104
Skene, Philip, 100–102
Skenesborough, N.Y., 100–103
Sleepy Hollow, N.Y., 120–21
Smith College, 50
Smith, Francis, 42
Smyrna, Del., 206, 207
Snowden, Thomas, 221
Society Hill, S.C., 312, 313
Sons of Liberty, 38, 60, 317
Sourland Mountains, 144, 145, 146, 147
South Carolina, 257, 274, 287–313, 323
South Mills, N.C., 277
Southern Pines, N.C., 264
Spa Creek, 219
Spartanburg, S.C., 300
Spinning Wheel Inn, 68
Spy House, 158
Spy House Museum, 158
St. Anne's Episcopal Church, 219

St. Augustine, Fla., 301
St. Catherines Island, 328, 329
St. Catherines Sound, 329
St. Clair, Arthur, 86, 88
St. David's Church, 180, 181
St. James Anglican Church, 311
St. Leger, Barry, 119
St. Margaret's Cemetery, 219
St. Peter's Church, 19
Stamp Act Congress, 198
Stamp Act of 1765, 198, 221, 318
Stark, John, 19
Stark, Molly, 19
Stars and Stripes, 119
"Stars and Stripes, The," xxiii
Staten Island, N.Y., 105, 107, 110, 113
State of Rhode Island and Providence Plantations, 73
Steadman, Ben, 302, 303
Steuben, Baron von, 159, 174
Steuben House, 159
Stevenson, Robert Louis, 86
Stillwater, N.Y., 95, 119
Stokes County Historical Society, 283
Stokes County, N.C., 282–83
Stony Brook, N.Y., 120
Stony Point, Battle of, 120
Stony Point, N.Y., 17, 111, 120, 179
Stratford Hall, 245–46
Stratford, Va., 245, 246
Sudbury, Mass., 50
Sugar House, 115
Sugar House window, 115–16
Sullivan, John, 77, 169
Sumter, Thomas, 287, 288–89, 310, 311
Surrender Field, 250
Sutphin, Charles, 144

Taft, Samuel, 51
Talbot County, Md., 198–99
Tales of a Wayside Inn, 50
Tappan, N.Y., 91
Tarleton, Banastre, 242, 243, 288–89, 302, 305, 307
Tarleton's Legion, 288
Tar River, 278–79
Tarboro, N.C., 279
Tarrytown, N.Y., 90, 120–21
Tate House, 188
Tate, James, 188
Tattnall, John, 330
Tattnall, Josiah, 330
Tattnall, Josiah, Jr., 330
Taylor, Thomas, 265
Telfair, Edward, 318
Tennessee, 257, 280
Terryville, Conn., 68
Thacher, James, 126
Thomas, Hannah, 37–40

Thomas, John, 37–39, 40
Thomas, John, Jr., 39
Thompson, Benjamin, 113
Thornton, Matthew, 33
Tilghman, Tench, 212
Tiverton, R.I., 74
Toe River, 280
Tolland, Conn., 69
Tolland Historical Society, 69
Tom Ball Mountain, 51–52
Tomb of Colonel Abel Kolb, 312
Tomb of the Unknown Revolutionary Soldier, 192
Toms River, 135
Tory Den, 68
Townsend, Joseph, 170
Townsend, Sally, 91–92
Townsend, Samuel, 91
Treaty of Paris, 8
Trenton, N.J., 128, 134
Trevelyan, George Otto, 135
Trevose Manor, 183–84
Trinity Church, 116
Trotter, John, 180
Trotter's Curse, 180
Tryon, William, 61, 68
Tucker, Samuel, 7
Tuckerton, N.J., 152
Turnbridge, Vt., 21
Turner, Clara, 240
Turner, John, 239–40
Tuttle, Joel, 68
Twain, Mark, xiii
Twiggs, John, 289
Twin Lights of Navesink Lighthouse Historic Site, 137
Tyger River, 288

Union County Courthouse, 149, 150
Union County, N.C., 282
United States Constitution, 200, 319
United States Monument, 259
United States Naval Academy, 214, 216, 217
United States Naval Academy Chapel, 216–18
United States Navy, 102
United States Veterans Administration, 175
University of Delaware, 205
USS *America*, 26
USS *Brooklyn*, 216
Uxbridge, Mass., 51

Valley Forge National Historical Park, 175, 177
Valley Forge, Pa., xxiii–xxv, 15, 128, 129, 133, 173–77, 191
Van Wart, Isaac, 90, 121
Vaughan, John, 111
Vealtown Tavern, 148
Veitch, Karen, 97–98
Vermont, xii, 13–22, 86

Vernon House, 81, 82
Vernon, William, 82
Versailles, France, 215
Videau's Bridge, Battle of, 312
Village Inn, 150
Virginia, 133, 203, 212, 225–52, 258, 269, 277
Virginia House of Burgesses, 242
Vreeland, Lake, 142

Wadsworth, Peleg, 4
Wagner, Franz, 51–52
Wales, Zacaria, 256, 257
Walker, Mildred, 243
Walker, Thomas, 242, 243
Wallabout, 112
Wallace, John, 181
Wallace, Richard, 20
Walnut Grove Plantation, 301–3
Walton, George, 318
Ward, Artemas, 133
Ward, Christopher, 288
Warminster, Pa., 192–93
Warner, Dave, 278
Warner Library, 121
Warren, Joseph, 42
Washington, George: admiration for Anthony Wayne, 179; aided by John Laurens, 239; aided by Light Horse Harry Lee, 246; aided by Nathan Hale, 56; aided by Nathanael Greene, 287; aided by Robert Erskine, 125, 126; alerted to treason by Benedict Arnold, 92; at Annapolis, 212; association with Alexander Hamilton, 114, 139–40, 190; association with Betsy Ross, 167; association with John Honeyman, 136; attempts prisoner exchange for Benedict Arnold, 81; attempts to buy High Rock Spring, 97; avoids execution of Cornwallis, 293; chased by Cornwallis, 153; correspondence from Lafayette, 234; at Dey Mansion, 159; at Dogue Run, xx; at Englishtown, 150; enlists Betty Wert as spy, 146; establishes military hospital, 151; at Fort Duquesne, xxi, xxii; as a ghost, xii, xix, xx, xxv–xxvi, 222; at Great Falls of the Passaic, 156; at Hunt House, 145; incarcerates prisoners of war, 65; kinship with George Glascock, 265; at Monmouth, 128, 129, 132; at Morristown, 139; at Mount Vernon, xx; at Newport, 81; outrage over execution of Joshua Huddy, 136; pays homage to Nathanael Greene, 79; at Philadelphia, 164; at Princeton, 158; proposes marriage to Mary Cary, 245; purchases home for his mother, 245; quoted, xix, 15, 173, 202, 229; recognition of John Thomas, 38; relationship with Jacky Custis, 251; at Ringwood Manor, 126; selects members of John André tribunal, 90; supernatural experiences of, xiii, xxii, xxiii–xxvi, 205; at Trevose Manor, 183; at Valley Forge, xxiii–xxv, 15, 128, 173–77; visits Samuel Taft, 51; visits Sarah Moulton, 31; at Williamsburg, xx, 248, 249; at Wilmington, Del., 203;

at Yorktown, 237–38, 251
Washington, Mary, xxi, 244
Washington Square, 192
Waxhaws, 282, 310
Wayne, Isaac, Jr., 180–81
Wayne, Isaac "Mad Anthony": at Battle of Brandy-
    wine, 169, 170, 171, 172; at Battle of Monmouth,
    129; biographical information, 178–79; captures
    spy, 149; at Dey Mansion, 159; at Fort Lafay-
    ette, 180; at Fort Ticonderoga, 85; as a ghost, xii,
    17–18, 87–88, 172, 176, 178, 179, 234, 235–36; at
    Hunt House, 145; at Malvern, Pa., 186; at Me-
    rion, Pa., 187; at Valley Forge, 176; in Vermont,
    17–18; in Virginia, 233; at York, Pa., 194
Wayne, N.J., 159, 160
Webster, Ephraim, 20
Wedgefield Plantation Manor, 309
Wert, Betty, 145–47
West Creek, N.J., 154
West Indies, 257, 303
West Paterson, N.J., 156
West Point on the Hudson, 90, 91, 126, 139
West Stockbridge, Mass. 51–52
Westminster Abbey, 89, 91
Westminster Massacre, 21–22
Westminster, Vt., 21–22
Wharton State Forest, 156
Whitall, Ann, 155
Whitall House, 155
Whitall, James, 155
White, Philip, 135–36
Whitehall, N.Y., 100, 104
Whitehall Skene Manor Preservation, Inc., 104
Whitemarsh, Pa., 173
"White Lady of Rockingham, The," 27
Whitney, Joseph, 62
Whittier, John Greenleaf, 31–32
Wilkes County, N.C., 256

Wilkinson, James, 184
Williams, Benjamin, 266
Williams, David, 90, 121
Williamsburg, Va., 226, 245, 246–50
Williamson, Andrew, 294
Williamson, Annette, 120
Williamson's Plantation, 304
Wilmington, Del., 203
Wilmington, N.C., 264, 273–75
Winooski River, 13, 15, 16
Wiseman's View, 277
Wister, John, 191
Wolfe, James, 134
Wood Creek, 100
Woodburn, 206
Woodcock Valley, 184
Woodlawn Plantation, xx
World Trade Center, 105
"World Turned Upside Down, The," xiii, 238, 250
World War I, 80
World War II, 80, 103
Wright, James, 318
Wright, Thomas H., 274

Yadkin River, 261
Yale University, 55
Yancey County, N.C., 280
York, John, 66
York, Pa., 193–94
York River, 249, 251
York Square, 194
Yorktown, Va.: British prisoners taken at, 221; Brit-
    ish surrender at, xiii, 92, 154, 212, 229, 237–38,
    268, 292, 293, 301; haunted sites, 238–41, 249–
    52; Washington departs, 245

Zabriski, John, 159